FIVE GUYS IN A BEETLE

The Grandest Grand Tour—Europe, 1963

FIVE GUYS IN A BEETLE

The Grandest Grand Tour—Europe, 1963

Thomas Tierney
with
Maureen Tierney

Sunstone Press
Santa Fe

© 2021 by Thomas Tierney
All Rights Reserved
No part of this book may be reproduced in any form or by any electronic or mechanical means including information storage and retrieval systems without permission in writing from the publisher, except by a reviewer who may quote brief passages in a review.

Sunstone books may be purchased for educational, business, or sales promotional use. For information please write: Special Markets Department, Sunstone Press, P.O. Box 2321, Santa Fe, New Mexico 87504-2321.

Design › R. Ahl
Printed on acid-free paper
∞

Library of Congress Cataloging-in-Publication Data

Names: Tierney, Thomas, 1942- author. | Tierney, Maureen, 1941- author.
Title: Five guys in a Beetle : the grandest grand tour--Europe, 1963 / by Thomas Tierney with Maureen Tierney.
Description: Santa Fe, New Mexico : Sunstone Press, [2021] | Summary: "This travel memoir, about a group of college buddies exploring 1963 Europe, provides the backdrop for a journey of self-discovery that ignites the bonds of friendship that will last a lifetime"-- Provided by publisher.
Identifiers: LCCN 2021032106 | ISBN 9781632933485 (paperback)
Subjects: LCSH: Tierney, Thomas, 1942---Travel--Europe. | Tierney, Thomas, 1942---Friends and associates. | Europe--Description and travel.
Classification: LCC ML410.T4555 A3 2021 | DDC 782.14092--dc23
LC record available at https://lccn.loc.gov/2021032106

WWW.SUNSTONEPRESS.COM
SUNSTONE PRESS / POST OFFICE BOX 2321 / SANTA FE, NM 87504-2321 /USA
(505) 988-4418 / FAX (505) 988-1025

To my Mother, Jane Rollo Tierney
who faithfully read and preserved these letters.

CONTENTS

Author's Note // 8

Map of this 1963 Grand Tour // 9

Prologue // 10

1 / Paris—"Like an Authentic New Orleans" // 11

2 / Germany—Castles, Dungeons and Festivals Along the Rhine // 34

3 / Window Shopping in Hamburg—"Hope you're not offended!" // 51

4 / Scandinavia—Celebrations, Conflicts and a Welcoming Swedish Family // 55

5 / Berlin—Trouble at Checkpoint Charlie // 74

6 / Southern Germany—From Storybook Bavaria to the Horrors of Dachau // 100

7 / Austria—Minnesota Girls and Magnificent Music // 119

8 / Italy—Getting Lost in Venice, Finding Art in Florence // 129

9 / Rome—The Forum, the Fountains, and a Surprise on the Appian Way // 144

10 / The Rivieras—Monaco Sightings and No Room at the Inn // 164

11 / France—Chateau Country and a Dressmaker's Tale // 172

12 / England—Sherwood Forest, Very English Hospitality and a Wise Fortune Teller // 195

13 / Scotland—The Moors, Bagpipes and Family History // 216

14 / London—"Kings, Queens, Saints and Worthies" // 233

Epilogue // 251

Notes // 252

Acknowledgments // 256

About the Authors // 257

AUTHOR'S NOTE

Here are my daily recollections about this particular European Grand Tour of 1963. The letters were transcribed as written. The opinions and observations mentioned in my letters and reproduced in this book are as I felt them at the time. For purposes of authenticity, most of the numbers, grammatical errors and misspellings are left as originally written (spelling corrections in brackets). Where there are errors in names of cities, streets and monuments, the fault lies with my twenty-one-year-old self. The names of my friends and fellow Beetle travelers have been changed. The photos were taken and shared by all of us.

—T. Tierney, September 1, 2020

Map of this 1963 Grand Tour

PROLOGUE

A young, vibrant president had just been elected. The world was captivated by his charisma, wit and the wholesome image he projected. Even his wife oozed charm and sophistication. Americans were welcomed abroad. And Europe, newly recovered from the trials of a devastating World War, was eager to introduce the Yanks to the sights, culture and food of the old world.

So it was that five fraternity friends at the University of Illinois in the summer of 1963 decided it would be a perfect time to travel to Europe. The trip had been pretty much arranged when the author was asked to replace a classmate who withdrew. The guys chose to order a new Volkswagen Beetle for pickup upon arrival in Paris. They then proceeded to travel by car through twelve countries in two-and-a half months.

At the end of the trip the car was shipped from London to the States. The Beetle cost $1200, shipping totaled $200 and they sold the car for $1400, thereby breaking even. The author's share of the auto expenses (gas and oil) for the entire trip was $90.00—thus giving the guys (two lawyers, one professor, a businessman and a songwriter) something to look back on with understandable pride for the rest of their lives.

The secret was to travel light. Luggage had to fit in the small VW trunk or the luggage rack on top of the car. The real challenge, however, was how to accommodate all five guys in the Beetle. Fear not. The number five had been predetermined as the optimum number of twenty-something, fully grown men that could squeeze into a Volkswagen. How this was accomplished is aptly described in Chapter 3, complete with a diagram. It stands as a true testament to American ingenuity and the restlessness of youth.

From the beginning the author had decided to write daily to his mother—outlining for posterity in minute detail his experiences. Staying up into the wee hours, after a long day of sightseeing, he was determined to complete this epic. We will leave it to you to decide if it reveals more about the participants in this adventure, than it does of the sights and sounds of Europe.

PARIS
1

"Like an Authentic New Orleans."

Only eighteen years had passed since the end of World War II. Paris had survived intact. The city was alive with night life, proudly showing off its elegant and imposing monuments and cultural icons. The superb cuisine, served even in modest bistros, was still the *piece de resistance*.

President Charles de Gaulle had recently signed the Elysée Treaty with West Germany's Konrad Adenauer. The fiftieth edition of the Tour de France, the biggest international sporting event in all of Europe, took place between June 23rd and July 14th. The five guys were there for the start of the race. It was eventually won, to the immense joy of the entire land, by the Frenchman Jacques Anquetil.

All this and more to take in. But first they had to get there...

§ § §

Paris—Wednesday, June 19, 1963

Hi–

Well, you probably received my cablegram—without qualm, I hope! Paris is everything you hear and imagine about it, only better. Let me first tell about the plane trip.

We left Chicago at about 1:00 PM—Dad, Mary and Mary L.[1] saw me off. Since I had miscalculated the departure by about 3 hours, they decided not to wait, which was probably just as well, since I was so busy running around telling everyone hello, introducing, etc., that they were getting bored with all of the confusion. We had a stroke of luck with the plane. It was a DC-7 instead of a DC-6, so our trip was non-stop from Chicago to Paris. The flight itself was fairly smooth, and we were in the air about 14 hours, which was much too much time to be cramped in a 1 x 1 seat. However, the trip was real interesting. We flew over Lake Michigan up the St. Lawrence Seaway to Newfoundland, which was deserted looking and picturesque with white caps on the mountaintops. We then were over the Atlantic for about 5 hours, and I never did see the ocean itself. Between night and the 3 or 4 cloud layers, it was difficult to see anything. One strange phenomenon: we were only in darkness for about 4 hours—and I could always see some kind of light on the horizon. The sunset lasted for a very long time and seemed to spread from one side of the world to another. It was very beautiful.

The plane seemed to occupy our time with eating more than anything else. We had a lunch, steak dinner and breakfast before we landed in Paris. We arrived in Paris about 3:00 AM Chicago time, and about 9:00 AM Paris time, and we still haven't quite adjusted to those six hours.

After going through customs, getting our baggage and using a Paris special corrugated toilet paper john, we were off. A gal in the airport found a room for us. We are at the Rue de St. Michael [Michel] at the Cluny Hotel. Of course we had to argue with the landlady, and that took some time which we really didn't have to spare. The taxi ride to the hotel was really an experience since the driver didn't speak a word of English. So I sat up front and translated. Since my French wasn't exactly the best, it wasn't easy, and paying was even harder. But it was great fun!

After arrival at the hotel, getting settled, etc., we went on a short excursion doing such things as having a beer in an outdoor café, touring in Notre Dame, which is fantastic. Everything is so old and so beautiful. We bought some French bread, cheese and wine and brought it back to the hotel to eat for lunch—very cheap and very good!

Paris is like an authentic New Orleans—especially the section where we are staying—trees on the boulevards, ancient looking shutters, rot [wrought] iron in the windows. We are near the left bank of the Seine, and even the view from our windows is worth the price of the room—about $2/day. The traffic in Paris is maddening—no one looks or cares—they just go.

We slept for 5 hours this afternoon and had dinner in a Self Service Café (cafeteria)—good & very cheap—only $1. Then we walked up la Rue de Tuileries toward de L'Arc de Triomphe and le Tour Eiffel (Eiffel Tower)—had another beer and came back to the hotel. We're in a great location—beautiful shops, and all kinds of interesting people. It is great fun using my French—and it really helps. I could kick myself for not learning more. Will write again tomorrow.

Love, Tom

P.S. Weather—cold and rainy

Paris—Thursday, June 20, 1963

Hi,

Well, my 2nd day in Paris has just come to an end, and what a wonderful day it was. So many interesting things have happened—I just hope I remember them all and do them justice.

Since yesterday was so confusing sleep-wise, we had decided to sleep late this morning so as not to get sick (we must have walked for 4 hours in the rain last night and I had a headache as well as sore feet and eyes.) I took 3 Coriciden [Coricidin] before going to bed.

But alas! At exactly 9:00 this morning, we awoke to loud banging and a shrill French voice. *"Bonjour, bonjour, il est matin."* (Good day, good day, it is morning.) And then this little old French concierge comes bounding in the room (me half-naked at that) carrying a tray with 2 enormous cups of black coffee and about 6 patisseries (rolls). So after gulping our surprise and readjusting our eyelids, we sat down dazed and had breakfast. The little lady had long gone by the time we actually knew what had happened. After breakfast, we laid in bed for an hour or so, and then decided it was about time to go (since we had to pick up the car and do a little more shopping around (American Express, etc.)

We then took a walk and the morning was beautiful, not anything like last night. I decided that an umbrella would be a good investment, so four of us (obviously, I wasn't the only one with that idea) bought umbrellas. It cost 29 francs which is about $5.80.

We then took the metro (a fantastic underground subway system unparalleled in the U.S.) to Rue le Franklin D. Roosevelt, the street where the Volkswagen dealer was. The area was Fifth Avenue-ish, with many trees lining the streets and wide spacious parks where the Parisians sit on ice-cream parlor like chairs to rest or talk—very picturesque. The bldg.

of the Volkswagen was gray stone, and rather foreboding. I assume it was the VW center rather than the typical dealer. The lovely creature behind the desk spoke English with a combination British-French accent (very becoming, I might add), and she informed us that the car wouldn't be ready until about 2:30 or 3:00 (they had to check papers and Karl's passport.) So we went to a nearby restaurant for lunch. I had a club sandwich and a soda, and it was delicious. French mayonnaise is far superior to ours. After lunch, we split up. Karl and Rick were picking up the car—Bill and I struck off for American Express. The district of American Express is out of this world. Very beautiful and expensive shops lined the streets. It was very much like North Michigan Avenue in Chicago. We stopped at Église de la Madeleine on the way—a beautiful church surrounded by two rows of immense columns. By the way, the churches here are fantastic. The Am. Express is on the Rue de la Scribe between Boulevard Haussmann and Blvd Madeleine des Capucines. It is also right across the street from the French opera. We got tickets to see *La Bohème* this Monday Night (*Opéra Comédie*). American Express is very big, modern and efficient. There are all sorts of attractions—money changers, cable senders, stationery and perfume counters, mail takers, etc. I ran into 2 girls I met on the plane and we had a brief visit. We then crossed the street to the post office where it took us ages to purchase 10 air mail post cards and 2 stamps. However, my French is getting much better and I can do most anything essential—it's really fun trying, anyhow.

The new arrivals strolling the Champs-Élysées.

We then came back to the hotel and slept for a couple of hours. Before that, Bill and I (Freddy went back) stopped for a beer. My feet were killing me. After last night, my feet had had it—one especially. I literally was hobbling along (must be those damned shoes!) Bill then went with Karl (who later joined us) to see the car, and I, being too tired, came back to the hotel to rest. Bill and I slept till 9:30 this evening and then decided to go out for the evening. The others went on earlier without us—it's kind of nice being away from the group. We'll see enough of each other anyway.

So then Bill and I went to the Self-Service Café for dinner—had chicken and French fries, wine, bananas and French bread for about $1.11—cheap, but good.

We then went walking. Paris on a balmy summer night—and especially in the Latin Quarter on the Left Bank—is very exciting and beautiful. I wore tennis shoes to conserve the flesh on my aching feet—and we walked for quite a while investigating. We saw the Pantheon—a tomb for great men of the Renaissance. Rousseau, Voltaire, Victor Hugo and others are entombed there. It's a very ominous building—and at night the area surrounding it is very quiet. It is said that the left bank is much quieter than the right. There was a tiny French restaurant across the street—it was very interesting—a few people sitting around talking, drinking wine. All of the restaurants seem to have the sidewalk eating areas, and the chairs are always wicker, the drink always wine or beer. We then decided to investigate some of the areas where many University students congregate at night—which is in and around the Place de la St. Michael [Michel]—a large square surrounded by small restaurants, night clubs and shops. There was much activity in this area. There were small crowds of students or young people singing and shouting. There were many lovers arm in arm looking very much like you would expect. In one small (very small) alley-like street which branched off of this square were several small clubs that seemed to be very popular. One called the "La Caveau" ("The Cave") was closing just as we arrived, but as the couples and people poured out, we could hear the echoes of jazz from the basement. Through the window the stairs to the basement looked like the descending staircase to some Medieval wine cellar. Right across the street from La Caveau was another place where Chet Baker was playing (an American jazz trumpeter). It was called *"Le Chat qui Peche."* (I believe this means "The Cat that (who) Fishes.") Since everything was closing up, we decided to come back another time when things were more lively (if that is possible.) There were many different kinds of people there from all over the world (obviously). One girl with no makeup, hair stringy, with a knap sack was being loud with some fellows of like garb. She was from Scotland and had a very strong brogue. They (the boys) were from England and Northern Ireland—very beat types. The air of the whole place is much like Gaslight Square in St. Louis only authentic. The streets are mostly cobblestone. They crisscross many different ways, and must have been trod upon for hundreds of years.

Bill and I then went to a sidewalk café and sat there for about an hour over a beer talking and watching all of the interesting people.

The Cluny Hotel—a Parisian bargain at $2.00 a day!

We came back to the hotel about 1:45 and had to be let in by the night watchman or male concierge, you might say. He was trying to tell us something and it took us about 5 minutes to find out what he wanted. He understood my French fine, but the problem was understanding his. All he wanted was to find out what time we wanted up in the AM, and how we wanted our café. We talked about all kinds of things with him with our limited French—perhaps the best part of the day—at least, the most fun. He spoke German, Russian and French, *mais ne pas l'anglais* (but not English.)

Tomorrow we are taking the whole day at Versailles—and I'll tell you about it tomorrow night. It's almost 3:30 AM and we are getting up at 8:30—so I'll probably be tired. We are going to Brussels after we leave Paris, so mail might reach me there. I wish I'd brought that black V-neck sweater—it would have come in very handy due to the cold weather here.

Sorry I can't say more—there is so much I do want to tell about styles, hair, treatment of Americans, etc., but no room. Give my love to everyone—perhaps Randy[2] would like to read these letters. Until tomorrow—*au revoir*. Love, Tom

Paris—Friday, June 21, 1963

Hi–

Well, another day in France has passed very quickly and very much has happened. Today we went to Versailles and Chartres as well as visiting Les Halles when we returned to Paris. We got up around 9:00 AM and again had the breakfast of *café noir et croissants* brought by the little French woman. We left the hotel about 9:45 and started on our trip to Versailles in our new Volkswagen. There was a ticket on the car which we were advised to disregard and I am enclosing it in this letter. Versailles is a palace and grounds created by the French royalty at the height of its glory. It was begun in 1661 by Louis XIV, who wanted a magnificent palace. It is situated 13 miles from Paris, and it is a gigantic palace. It housed 5000 people, 1000 lords and 400 servants. Social life was ruled by the strict control of Louis XIV and very strict rules were set up to govern the court of 20,000 persons. Versailles was neglected under the Regency but again became fashionable during the reign of Louis XV. Louis XVI and Marie-Antoinette were the last of the sovereigns to live there. The Revolution scattered the beautiful furniture, and the palace was deserted and threatened with demolition until Louis-Phillipe paid 23 million francs to make a museum out of it.

It is truly one of the most impressive things I've ever seen. We first took a tour of the palace, which includes only the private apartments. I have never seen so many beautiful paintings, marbel [marble] statues and luxury in my entire life. There were many murals and beautiful works of art. Louis XIV had engaged the very finest artists of France to decorate it. It is almost beyond description. There is a chapel (where Louis XVI and Marie-Antoinette were married) which is beautiful. The rooms are really fantastic—beyond my writing ability to describe. Across the court of the palace are the Royal Stables, built for 2400 horses and 250 coaches. 368 persons were concerned with the preparation of the king's meals.

Our visit to Versailles was made particularly enjoyable because we met an American girl with her mother there in the palace. Dotty N. was her name and she had finished a year of study in Paris at the Sorbonne—she went to Sweetbriar back in the States, and they were from Greenville, S.C. She spoke French very well, so we enjoyed a French guide to show us around, since there were several of us who didn't speak French (including her mother) and the English guide cost $5, which was much too much for us to spend. Not only was Dotty cute, but very nice and intelligent too. So, we had a great time listening to all of the details about the beautiful palace. It seems that Louis XV was kind of crazy. One thing he did was have a peep hole

Taking in the splendor of Versailles

built through one of the walls overlooking the court so that he could watch the young girls go by, and seeing one he liked, would have his valet go down to the court to get her. He also was the king with 2 mistresses who lived on the same floor of the palace.

    He refused to sleep in the bedroom where he was intended to because it was situated across from the apartments of his 2 mistresses. So, he slept on the floor under them so that neither knew quite what he was doing. They couldn't see through the windows.

    After we had toured the palace, at about 1:30 we decided to get something to eat. We drove into the town of Versailles and stopped at a small restaurant where we had a delicious ham sandwich on French bread and a glass of beer for only about 60 cents. Obviously, not too many Americans had eaten there since we were regarded very peculiarly.

    That afternoon we returned to the Palace for a look at the gardens. They were even more impressive. They cover

250 acres, and include countless fountains shooting water from nymphs, lions, turtles and other statues. They are really unbelievable. They are the formal type and include symmetrically planned forests with tree arching lanes leading in all directions, beautiful colonnades and special garden courts for all purposes. There is an orange tree garden and a grand canal which can be seen from the palace. It all looks like a beautiful three-dimensional dream—very hard to describe. I hope I remember enough to tell you more about them when I return. (By the way, on the tour we also met a French woman who had lived in Chicago for 17 years and had never learned English very well. She was fun to talk to and I was having a real good time jaboring [jabbering] with her in a combination of bad French (mine) and bad English (hers). We left Versailles about 3:30 and headed for Chartres where la Cathédrale de Chartres is located.

Chartres is the "capital" or country town of the "granary of France," the Beuce (crop) country about 60 mi. from Paris. It is of course more well known for the beautiful Cathédrale there which was built in 1194. It dates back much farther than this however to the Gallic-Roman period (5th Century). It is strange that such a magnificent structure was built in a rural setting, but it seems that it was an important Druidical center, where ceremonies were held around a well. It was later a Gallo-Roman temple, where the statue of the Mother-Goddess was venerated. The 1st Christians saw in this effigy a prefiguration of the Virgin, Mother of God. The same statue stood in each successive building and people came from afar to venerate it. The crypt, the towers and the lower part of the east facade are all that is left of the 5th building erected on the same site. Kings, princes, barons, citizens, barons' peasants and laborers took part in the building, giving their money or their strength. The two tall spires can be seen for miles before entering the town, a pleasant site over the French country landscape. They are considered one of the finest examples of French religious art. The inside is immense and very beautiful. The stained-glass windows are breathtaking, and the blue that characterizes them is known as "Chartres blue." There were many people in the church praying and burning candles. There was a quaint group of small French girls who came scampering in the church to confession. They were cutting quite a caper until a priest in a long black robe came walking in and quickly quieted them down and instructed them to put something on their heads and to light candles. We also met a very nice Turkish couple there who spoke both French and English. I was asking a gentleman why one of the windows was unfinished in my broken French when the Turk came to my assistance. It seems that the people themselves had broken some of the windows so that more light could enter the church. (What a pity!) In back of the church was a wall which overlooks most of the town. The view from there was beautiful. There were small houses with red roofs which dated back to the 5th Century—interesting. I found this out from a lady sitting in the park there, and she soon became very bored with my lack of understanding. We left Chartres for Paris about 7:00 PM.

On the way back, we stopped in a small town called Ablis (population about 200) for dinner. This town must have dated back to the 12th Century because of the style of architecture and the streets which were no bigger than an alley and lined with buildings. It was very interesting. The restaurant where we had dinner was really terrific. For $2, we had a bottle of wine, steak, thousands of *frites* (French fries), a tomatoe [tomato] salad, ice cream and loads of French bread. It was also decorated very nicely—wood paneling half-way up, wallpaper, tablecloths, napkins, an old stone fireplace and small lights. We had a terrible time trying to talk to the waitress—she spoke no English and neither Bill nor I could read the menu. Finally, in exasperation, we almost gave up when she asked us if anyone spoke German. Karl bounced up and cried something in German, she squealed, and we were in business. The meal was delicious, and we went away from the place thinking how lucky we were to have stopped there. Freddy had been feeling sick, so he slept in the car while we ate. I thought that he might be homesick since he is having a hard time getting along with us and he has never been away from home before.

The highway we drove on is 3-lane, and really hair-raising. We had one close call while passing, so have decided to drive only 50 m.p.h. The road signs in Europe are all signal signs—and uniform throughout Europe. We got back to Paris about 10:00 and came back to the hotel to change and go out for a beer. We are staying in a very famous area for students and off-beats. From my window I can see not only the Eiffel Tower but also the many sidewalk cafés and shops lining la Rue de St. Michel. Nights there is much traffic and many people walking along the street. Tonight, there was a large student celebration which is held every year at the end of classes and on the 1st day of summer. The boys and some girls dress in elaborate masquerade costumes and go to L'Ecole des Beaux Arts (School of Fine Arts) where there is a ball. They drink and drink in the room where they are locked up—and at midnight they are released. They then run through the streets yelling and singing, grabbing women and girls, and carrying them in a parade up and down the streets. We saw a whole group of them go by under our window—and they seemed to be having quite a time. We met a couple of girls (not so cute) from Northwestern who are staying in our hotel and asked them to go with us in search of the ball. We never did find it, but we had fun going from place to place looking. We finally returned to St. Michel area, and met (in a sidewalk café) a French fellow who had studied in America for a year who was with an American girl who had known him in America. She was very pleasant to talk to and he was quite a character. He talked about lack of love in America and told us where to go to meet single French girls—a place called the "Slow Club." It was 1:30, but we took off to find it. It was across the Seine on Rue de Rivoli, but the cover charge was so much we decided to forget it. On our way back we discovered we were in the section of Les Halles.

Les Halles is a huge food market which handles all the food for Paris every day. It is located near the Rue de Rivoli and has been in existence since the 11th Century. There is no special place for it (that is, building or court), but it is located on the main streets where there are shops and buildings, etc. Several attempts were made to provide a place for it, but as the city grew, the congestion forced it to remain where it is now. Hundreds of trucks bring all their fresh food and leave the crates on the sidewalks and streets, where the farmers set up shop. This begins about 1:00 AM. The market opens at 2:00 and the food is bought by hotels and shops until about 5:00 AM. We wandered around through all the confused liveliness of crates, pushcarts and trucks until about 3:00. We then had a few beers and came back. After market hours, cleaners come and sweep, wash and scrub, and the next day, no one would ever guess that it wasn't an ordinary business district. It was really bustling in the middle of the night, and it has a real old-world charm. It seems very inefficient, but perhaps that is why 50% of the French national income is spent on food—and they seem to take great pride in it.

I am very tired—as it has been an exciting and terribly interesting day. I am sending my film to be processed, and I will appreciate you telling me the quality of the pictures since I haven't used the camera before. Until tomorrow—goodbye.

Love, Tom

Paris—Saturday, June 22, 1963

Hi–

It's hard to believe that another day has ended. So much happens and the time passes quickly. Today has been another good day, only much quieter than yesterday.

We were awakened at 9:00 by our little French friend again, but I didn't get up even for breakfast—we were up so late last PM—and we do need "some" sleep! So I slept till noon.

Today we decided to go in separate directions—Karl to American Express, Freddy and Rick to the Luxembourg Gardens, and Bill and I to the Eiffel Tower—a good 5 or 6 miles. We walked along the Seine—and this is fun due to the small vendors along the way selling books, paintings, post cards and trinkets. On the way we passed the entrance of "The Invalides"—a large building considered to be the finest architectural work in Paris and entered by way of an Esplanade which is like a Garden flanked with trees. It was built to house 7000 disabled soldiers before Louis XIV's time, but it never materialized that way. It was completed in 1676—and the Dome which adds further beauty to the building houses Napoleon's remains. There are only about 60 inmates there now and it is used for the relief of war victims and the Museum of the Army.

We finally reached the Eiffel Tower—and it is really quite a sight—the steel has rusted and it looks quite an eyesore up close—but still mammoth. It was built from 1887–1889 and is 984 feet high. It has almost been torn down several times but has been saved because of its usefulness for wireless communications. There are 3 levels—the first housing a restaurant, the 2nd, a restaurant and observatory, and [the] summit, observation. We went to the top, and spent about 2 hours there. While there, I ran into 6 people from Illinois—four I knew were coming to Europe this summer, and two I didn't know would be here. It was fun, and quite a surprise. It's apparent why Americans are disliked over here. They seem to have a "show-me" attitude and are at times very obnoxious. It's too bad, and also noticeable that the ones who knew no French have a much harder time. I saw 2 Alpha Gams, a Pi Phi and 3 AOPi's[3] who are nice, but the girls like Dotty, who spend a year over here seem much nicer.

After leaving Le Tour Eiffel, we walked across the Seine toward the main part of Paris where we wanted to see the Arc de Triomphe. By the way, the Tower is surrounded by beautiful gardens which are particularly nice this time of year. And the view from the top was really amazing. This city is very much lacking in tall buildings.

L'Arc de Triomphe is just as beautiful as it looks in pictures, and is surrounded by a circular square from which streets spoke out (much like Washington D.C.) It is of course located on the Champs-Élysées, the heart of the business district of Paris. The Arc has much historical significance which would take too long to adequately describe, so I will let it go. However, it is a beautiful sight.

We then walked down the Champs-Élysées, and watched the people shopping and sipping drinks in the colorful sidewalk cafés. This is truly the Michigan Ave. of Paris—only much nicer. Two gigantic rows of trees line the inside boulevard, and you can see for miles down to the Place de la Concorde—a large open space with fountains and government buildings, and the beginnings of the Garden of Tuileries. We turned off of the Champs onto Rue Marbeau, in search of a restaurant called "Valentin" which was recommended in the book—"Europe on Five Dollars a Day." We meanwhile had run into Rick and Freddy and they went with us to eat—but only had wine since they had previously eaten. Our meal there was the best yet—very French. We had red wine, the most delicious onion soup I've ever had (many onions with a thick cheese crust baked on top), *Canard a l'orange* (Roast duck with orange sauce), a bowl of fruit and coffee for only $2. Since we hadn't eaten yet today, we thought this was a good deal.

There were several Americans in the restaurant and we presume it's because of the recommendation in the book "E on $5 a Day." Evidently, the Americans are pouring into Paris en masse, and the Parisians are getting ready for them. It's really kind of funny.

A busy Paris street leading to the L'Arc de Triomphe

    Bill and I then walked back to the Champs-Élysées and took a Métro back to St. Michel. I decided not to go out tonight but to stay here and get caught up on writing and rest. Bill and Karl went to Montmartre with two girls and their brother, children of a very fine family we met at the Eiffel Tower. He just got back and they evidently had a real good time.

    About 11:00 tonight, while writing, Rick (who was also writing) came running into the room. There was an American Folk Singer playing the guitar and singing outside his window—and there were crowds of people gathered around listening. We leaned out of the window on the rod [wrought] iron railing (from our 4th floor) room and clapped with everyone else. He sang some songs in French and also "Michael Rode [Rowed] the Boat Ashore." Several people looked up and laughed and pointed at us—really wild! Our car was parked almost under the window and there were people leaning on it—as well as pointing out the red license plate—which obviously labels its owner American.

    By the way, Karl got to the car this morning and found another ticket. He took it to the police station where he found a policeman who spoke English. And the policeman kind of chuckled when he saw the ticket and said that it would be stupid to pay it—since we are foreigners and how would they ever get us. Karl chuckled too, and walked away happy. The ticket is enclosed—we just hope the policeman was right. It's very funny the attitude people have—very "I-don't-care-ish"—and very nice. The French are friendly and whoever doesn't have a good time in Paris couldn't have a good time most anywhere.

Our Paris parking ticket—still unpaid!

I have really and truly fallen in love with this city—and intend to come back. If not to school, to live. It's really the kind of place where I could get my teeth in my music and live in the ideal creative atmosphere. It is the artist's heaven!

I haven't had the chance to work on "The Creation,"[4] since there is so much to do and see. Hope to soon, however. [copy of ticket attached]

I'm afraid that I am going to run out of film, so will have to see if I can find some in Paris before leaving. I wrote Doug Scudamore[5] about my house bill, and he will send it to you. It really has to be paid—Dad was pretty upset, and rightly so, that I hadn't paid it or made arrangements.

Since these letters are taking a great deal of time to write, I would appreciate your letting Ann[6], Randy, Jeff[7], or some of my other friends read them. They are of course serving as my diary—and I presume you will save them all.

Did you receive the cablegram? What has been happening? I hope that someday you will be able to see Paris. It is really something. I priced perfume today and you will probably be getting some—it is expensive though—especially Joy. Until tomorrow night, *au revoir*.

Love, Tom

Paris—Sunday, June 23, 1963

Hi–

Another exciting day has just passed very quickly—it seems that everywhere we turn something new and different happens.

Rick, Freddy and I arose at 9:00 this morning since we had planned on going to Notre Dame for church. We had tea for breakfast instead of coffee because French don't make the best coffee and tea was something new. I'm glad of that decision because the tea was 100% better.

It was a beautiful morning—just the right temperature—and after eating, we hurried off to Notre Dame for the 10:00 mass. It was really beautiful. Notre Dame is an immense church and is considered one of the masterpieces of French art. It has been a religious site for 20 centuries and the present church was completed in 1345. Many historical events have occurred in the Cathedral, including the crowning of Napoleon by Pope Pius VII in 1804. The ceremony mass itself was beautiful and I was particularly impressed by the music. The double choir sang beautiful traditional Gregorian chants and the pomp and ceremony is I'm sure unequaled in most American Catholic churches. Much of the instrumental music was contemporary, characterized by discord and what sounded like use of whole-tone scales and alternation of various modes. However, the whole service was very moving. It was in Latin and French, so linguistically we got nothing out of it. However, just observation seemed to be plenty. The enormity and beauty of the church itself is enough to awe inspire one, so the mass just added to the specialness of the occasion.

After church, we walked across the island, and were intending to grab a quick bite and then spend the afternoon in the Louvre. However, we had a very pleasant interruption. We could see mobs of people gathered around a square near the government buildings—so decided to investigate. Lo and behold if it wasn't Le Tour de France, the famous bicycle race which occurs annually. All of the countries in Europe have a bicycle team competing and they race for thousands of miles all over France in a set plan. We pushed our way into the crowds (which turned out to be somewhat of a mistake, since thousands of people were pushing and yelling). It must have been 100 times tighter than a sardine can—everyone trying to see the teams get ready to start the race. Once in the middle of the crowd it was impossible to get out. We were literally crushed. In about 20 minutes we managed to escape to a stairway (only about 3 feet from where we were) and once down along the Seine we ran about 100 yards to another stairway where we ascended and found a better location to watch all of the festivities. Soon the teams zoomed by, one by one, and they were greeted with cries and yells from the crowd. They were followed by radio and television trucks as well as motorcycles—obviously part of the "referee" [press and support] crew. I managed to find out most of what I wanted to know by asking some old ladies who were standing by in my very scanty French. After the teams had departed and most of the excitement was over, we took a few pictures and went to a café to get a sandwich before going to the Louvre. I had a ham sandwich and a Coke for about 60 cents and it was very good (they use French bread for everything). After lunch we headed for Le Louvre.

Le Louvre is considered probably the world's finest art museum, and is so big that it can't be visited adequately in more than 3 or 4 days. It's divided into 5 sections, and we just scratched the surface of the Painting section today. I won't go into detail about what I did see, but it included many of the masterpieces I have long admired. I saw the Mona Lisa and many other works of Leonardo da Vinci as well as works by David, Rubens, Van Dyke, etc., etc. I thought of Randy when I was there and how much he loves the place. I have a guidebook to it, so further explanation would be silly. It is so well known as a museum because of not only the beauty of the building but because of the excellent lighting on the *objet d'art*. While there we met a real interesting gal from San Francisco who was an artist herself and knew much about everything we saw. Her name was Marcia—about 40, fairly attractive, and headed for Italy for the summer to study art. We left at 5:00 when the building closed.

Locals fishing along the Seine

We then strolled back home along de la Seine and ate at the Self Service cafeteria for about 85 cents. I was really dead by the time we got back and slept till about 10:00. Then Rick, Freddy and I decided to take a boat ride on the Seine, but the place was closed so we just walked around observing the sights. I bought some stamps to send the letters I've been writing and Freddy went back to the hotel.

Rick and I decided to have a beer, so we walked back to St. Michel Square and bought some peanuts, sat down with some beer in a sidewalk café, and watched people for an hour or so. There were two folk singers who serenaded us, one from London and the other from somewhere in France. Their friends passed the hat around while they sang… I presume their only income. I asked the boy from London how they were doing, and he said not so well. But what a carefree life they must have, traveling around Europe living off what they can beg.

About 12:30, things were closing up, so we walked back to the hotel. Rick and I then spent an hour talking to the old man I told you about before—the night watchman. He doesn't speak English, and very little French either, so we had an interesting time trying to converse. He has had quite an interesting life, from what I could gather. He lived in Russia till age 10, moved to Germany, then Austria, finally France, where he's been for 19 years. He doesn't like Kruschev [Khrushchev] or Kennedy or De Gaulle and lives very poorly. He told us about a public shower, where we could take a shower for 24 cents. He takes one there once a week. He asked me about different prices in the US and how they compare. He seemed pathetic, yet somehow happy. After an hour, he told us it was time for young boys to be in bed, so we laughed and came upstairs. It's now after 2:00 AM, so I'd better be closing this as soon as possible.

Tomorrow we are all going out on our own, and it will be a welcome break. I have to buy some stationery and envelopes, as well as perfume for you and Mary[8]. I'm going back to Le Louvre, since there is so much to see and so little time. In many ways, I wish I was spending the summer right here in Paris. I've fallen hard for this place!

I don't know how long I will be able to keep up writing these long letters every day, but they will be wonderful to have in future years.

Guess what! I haven't had a bath since I left Murphysboro[9] which has been almost a week. I have taken sponge baths, however, but a good American shower would be wonderful right now. I suppose I'll eventually have to break down and buy one. Seems funny, *n'est-ce pas?*

Well, will be looking forward to reading some news from home—as yet, I haven't heard anything. Do write long newsy letters. I would appreciate them very much. Until tomorrow night—*au revoir.*

Love, Tom

Paris—Monday, June 24, 1963

Hi-

Another very full and interesting day has passed in Paris. I got up very tired about 9:00 and spent most of the morning doing some of the necessities I must take care of: washing myself and some clothes; reading the guide book to Paris to make sure I see the important things before I leave, and relaxing. I left the hotel about 12:00 with a whole list of things to do—and didn't. I took a metro to the American Express area, which as I told you before is the very exclusive shopping area of Paris. Upon entering there, I saw that the lines were so long in the mail receiving area that it would take me hours just to see if I had a letter—which I wasn't sure of at the time anyway. So I left there.

I then did some shopping along Champs-Élysées and got the perfume, stationery and film I was looking for. Later on I walked to the Arc de Triomphe, and took the elevator to the top, where a beautiful view of the city can be seen. It has been a very beautiful day, weather just right, and sun shining most of the day. I also saw the light or flame that is always kept burning in honor of those who lost their lives for Napoleon in the French Revolution.

Nothing like a *jambon* sandwich and beer at a French café

After walking around, looking in shops, etc., I sat down in a sidewalk café along the Champs for lunch—this was a mistake. I now presume that you pay more in this area, because a ham and cheese sandwich and a beer cost me over $1.00. They say though that Paris is one of the most expensive cities in the world. So by this time, it was too late to go back to the Louvre, which I had intended on doing, so I took a metro back to St. Michel.

Rick was the only one home, so we decided to go back down to American Express area, since I wanted to check again for mail, and also, Rick had not seen that area. So we went back and I received your letter and enjoyed it very much. I wondered at what time you received my cablegram. I sent it about 2:00 AM your time. After leaving there, Rick and I stopped at a self-service place to grab something to eat. It was a real nice place—cheap, but overlooking the facing street. So we sat by the window and watched all of the people. My meal—steak, green beans, potatoes, dessert and wine cost only about $1.00. We then took a métro back to St. Michel since we wanted to go to the opera, and get there on time.

I wrote a few posts cards, got dressed, and we left for the Opéra Comique about 8:30. On the métro, we met some American girls from Wash. state… Seattle. They were also headed for the opera. "La Bohème" was really magnificent, the music by Puccini, the elaborate scenery, the voices, the orchestra and the costumes. I thoroughly enjoyed it. One funny thing, they sell beer and wine at the opera, just like it was soda pop. After the opera, we went to La Caverne de la Huchette, a night club in the Latin Quarter aimed at students. There was a jazz band, and the atmosphere was tremendous.

After leaving there, we went to this small out of the way place famous for their onion soup, and evidently a place where Hemingway spent a great deal of time while in Paris. We were all dead by the time we left, and it was about 2:30 when we got back to the Hotel.

And so ends another day. Thanks again for your letter—it was greatly appreciated and I'll be looking forward to another.

Until tomorrow, *au revoir*.

Love, Tom

Paris—Tuesday, June 25, 1963

Hi–

Well, my last day in Paris is over—and all I can think is that I must and will come back someday. Yesterday I got 2 letters back—that were too long for air mail—it's lucky I discovered it now rather than later—when it would be too late.

I didn't get up today until about 1:00 PM. We had come in so late last night after the opera, and I figured I needed the sleep—and besides, the museums were all closed today. As soon as I was dressed, I took a walk up St. Michel toward the Jardin de Luxembourg (Luxembourg Gardens), which is one of the nicer parks in Paris and very near here. It is a large park, with many trees lining its sand and pebble walks. The trees and grounds are very well kept—and there are hundreds of ice-cream parlor-like chairs lining its paths. In the center of the garden is a large fountain—and best of all, there were many children with sailboats and sticks running and screaming around the fountain. Today was rainy and cloudy, and the winds were strong enough to carry the boats quickly and swiftly through the water. It's really a charming sight. While sitting watching all of the activity, a lady approached me with tickets of some cost, and she wanted 30 centimes for it. At first, I didn't have the slightest idea what she was talking about, but I soon found out that I had to pay a rental fee for just sitting on a chair. So I smiled and gave her the money, which amounts to about 6 cents in American money, and about 15 minutes later the weather was so bad that I had to leave. I walked back to the hotel, stopping to buy a sketch notebook, so I can keep track of certain things, write myself notes, etc. I got back about 3:00.

Children with sailboats and sticks at the Luxembourg Gardens

We sat around for a while trying to figure out where we'll be the next ten days before Malmo, and we decided [that] if we were going to Montmartre, we had better get started.

We boarded a métro headed for Montmartre and were there in about 15 minutes. As I've said before, the subway system here is very quick and efficient. You can go anywhere in Paris for 11 cents or 55 centimes. The 1st thing we did there was go to Le Sacre Coeur (The Sacred Heart), a beautiful church costing the French 14 million francs in 1919 (the year it was completed.) It is situated on a hill (as in Montmartre) and from the church one can see a beautiful panorama of Paris (about 30 miles). We were there about sunset, so it was an impressive sight. We had 1st stopped at a small restaurant to get something to eat. I had chicken, fried mushrooms, wine, ice cream, French bread and butter, for about $1.75. That's really too high, but I hadn't eaten anything else today except for some French toast that I had bought at a bakery earlier.

After leaving the Sacre Coeur, we headed for the square of Montmartre, a very quaint place. It seems that Montmartre was at one time a small village, and was later engulfed by Paris. While there, we went into a very historical bar restaurant place where there was a pianist & singer. I ended up playing for about 20 minutes—and we had a great time there. The gal who sang was a real character, and she had a great time kidding us and making sign-language jokes. We then walked down from the Montmartre area into Pigalle, and saw Moulin Rouge, which seemed very modernized except for some of the Toulouse-Latrec [Lautrec] posters in the windows. After that, we came back to St. Michel and had a few beers at the Square, where we met some American from San Francisco who had been a piano student until he quit in April and has been bumming ever since. We then came back to the hotel and got ready for bed. More tomorrow.

Love, Tom

Luxembourg—Wednesday, June 26, 1963

Hi–

Well this has been quite a day! We got up at 8:00 and quickly packed while eating breakfast. We were anxious to leave Paris as soon as possible since we had a lot of ground to cover.

Last night we came in about 12:00 and were hoping to pay our hotel bill then so that we could leave earlier. So the old man got the woman who runs the hotel out of bed, and from there on everything was pure hell. She was rattling on and on in French and we had a terrible time understanding her. Then we found out that she wouldn't accept travelers checks, so we had to wait till the banks opened, which was 9:00. So after all the fuss, we agreed to pay in the morning and madame went babbling up to bed. We did have one consolation however. Our bill for seven days, including breakfast every morning was only 68.60 F, which is only $13.75. We were really surprised—less than $2.00 per night.

Anyway, this morning, after paying our bill, we loaded the car. It was quite a sight. There we were in the middle of the street, putting luggage on the roof, stuffing it behind the back seat, and cramming it in the trunk. Of course, we also had to put our tarp and rope over the luggage, and to top it off, there were hundreds of police gathered all around, getting ready for some kind of parade—or war march, or something. They had asked us to move the car and I kept saying, "*Un moment, un moment*" which means "In a minute." They were patient, though, and we at last managed to get everything and everyone in. Evidently, we were quite a strange sight, since people were pointing and smiling, and probably cursing the "strange Americans."

It took forever it seems to get out of Paris. The way Parisians drive is really unbelievable. But we finally made it, and took off for Reims, a small French town northeast of Paris, where is located a beautiful cathedral—La Cathédrale de Reims. About 12:00 we stopped for lunch in a very small farm village between Paris and Reims. By the way, the drive was really beautiful. The country is deserted, peaceful and characterized by rolling hills and foothills, and small medieval villages, with red slate roofs nestled in the valleys. This particular town was typical, and we had a delicious ham sandwich and a beer for only 60 cents. The small restaurant seemed to be one that catered to the same people every day. The waitress set out a certain number of plates—two at each setting, and sure enough, soon, farmers and truckers who seemed to know each other, came in for their two-course lunch. While eating, a little old hunched-backed lady came wobbling in with a whole armload of extremely long loaves of French bread. We said that she could have done the exact same thing 500 years ago, and even her dress probably wouldn't have been much different. It was fun.

We arrived in Reims about 2:30 and spent about an hour there, looking at the church and taking a few pictures. Rick and I met 3 very pretty girls in a shop there, and they spoke fairly good English. The one we talked to was in college somewhere and working for the summer.

We filled the tank with gas, and I drove from there headed for Luxembourg. This is perhaps the prettiest country yet, and the road was about deserted, except for a truck or car now and then. The quality of the road is similar to the one between Murphysboro and Ava,[10] very small and winding. There are tall trees spaced all along the road, and we wove in and out of hills, valleys and ancient looking villages. There was not a farmhouse to be seen anywhere. It seems that they all live in these small towns, and farm the land in the surrounding area. We drove through much of the Marne country, where much of the battlefield and action took place during W.W. I. There were many memorials and small military cemeteries dotting the countryside, and it seemed amazing that such peaceful land could have witnessed many horrible deaths and battles. All along the way are wild red poppies, and combined with the other wild flowers, often fields of yellow sunflowers (or something), the view is really beautiful. We stopped about 5:00 to change places and drivers. Surprisingly enough, the car is not uncomfortable at all for five—and the luggage fits quite well.

Postcard: Reims Cathédrale

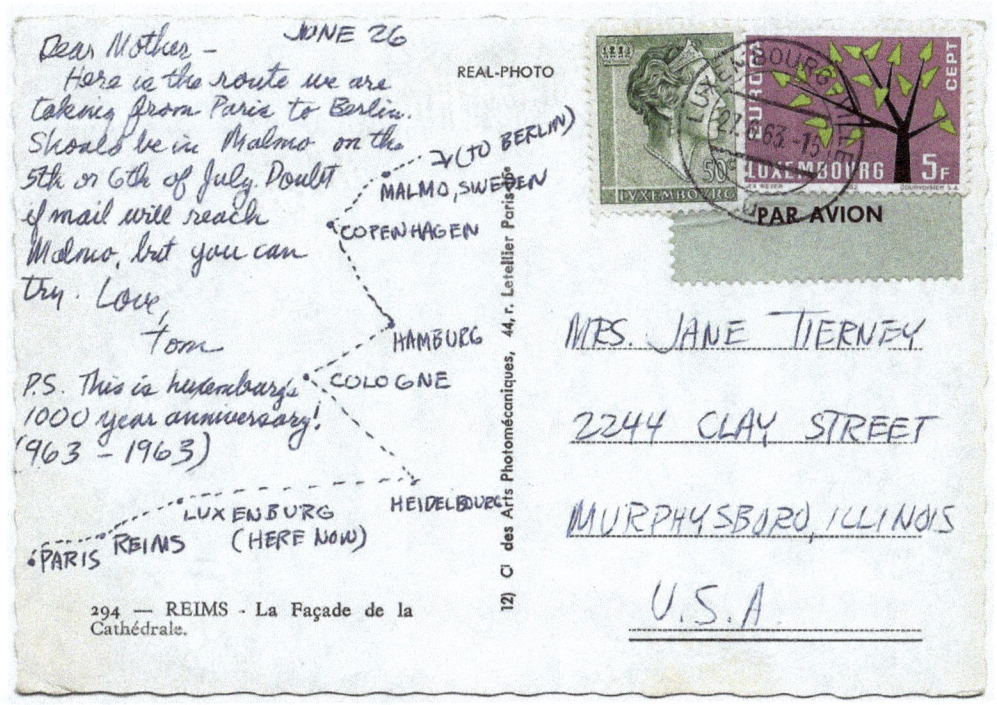

Side 2—Immortalizing the route: Paris to Berlin

    We finally crossed the border into Luxembourg, and expecting to go through complicated customs, we were surprised to be only asked to see the insurance for the car. The policeman smiled, and we drove in. Luxembourg is a country only 32 x 50 miles, and is situated right between France, Belgium and Germany. We arrived in the capital (Luxemburg) about 6:15. We noticed a change in the style of architecture here. The buildings are more Northern-European, not so frilly, and lacking shutters on some of the windows. They are built closer to the street and are charming in their own way.

    We first went to the main railroad station, the only place in town to exchange money (at least, the only place open at that hour). After getting $10.00 changed, we went to the airport to see if the gal there could find us a place to stay. Sure enough, she did—and it is perfect. It is called "L'hotel du Parc"—and there is a noticeable difference between it and the one in Paris. It is cleaner, somewhat larger, somewhat more civilized. English speaking and CHEAPER—if you can believe that. Our room, with breakfast is only $1.50 and we can even take a shower for 30 cents! Since I have not yet had one since leaving M'boro,[11] I feel the great need for it.

    I reflect and did I ever imagine myself being in Luxemburg. It seems very strange when I think of it—and yet, here I am, in Luxemburg. This is where Perel e Meseta [Perle Reid Mesta] was ambassador. It's very funny, I think! Also, *Call Me Madame*[12] was located here—remember?

Unloading the Beetle at our Luxemburg hotel

    After bringing up luggage (we're on the 4th floor), we decided to relax. We had a beer, and then took off for a place called "Stuff"—a restaurant recommended to us by the girl in the airport. Well, this place is out of this world! Not only is it the best food we've eaten, but the atmosphere, the service and the prices were just perfect. It is a German looking place, looks very old, and has high old wooden booths, a large fireplace and all kinds of odds & ends thrown in—like a beamed ceiling, a large tank of fish, so you can choose what kind you want, etc. We had a very congenial waitress and also some kind of waiter who helped her. Everything was served from silver dishes onto our plates, and the white tablecloths, candlelight and quick service added to its charm. We started out with Potage du Jour (Soup of the Day), which was a delicious consommé noodle soup, served in large flat soup bowls. We ate all we wanted of the soup, and then she brought the main dish—I had *pain de veau*—which is meat loaf, but it was really good. There were peas on top, and she kept bringing back all the French fries we could eat. The gravy was also delicious, and we topped the meal off with a dish of chocolate ice-cream with whipped cream.

And the cost—only $1.26 including tip. We left the place ecstatic—really unbelievably low prices. And beer here is only 12 cents/glass—and the glasses are bigger than they were in Paris!

We heard there was a military band concert on Luxembourg square—so we headed for there, and spent about an hour listening and watching. Luxemburg has a small-town atmosphere, and it's all very peaceful. One-fourth of the square is set up like an outdoor café, so we sat there for a while, sipping beer and listening to the band. It was a concert band, and they played serious music—and very well, too. We were all feeling lucky we had come here—low prices, peaceful, and really interesting. The people are friendly too, although they seemed to think our white tennis shoes looked very strange. I saw several people snickering and pointing—but who cares? I've never had such a good time in my life!

After the concert, we walked around and did some window shopping. This year, you know, is Luxemburg's 1000-year anniversary, so there is celebration all summer. Prices of clothes don't seem much different than the U.S., but the quality seems better. I'm going to do some exploring tomorrow before we leave Heidelberg about 1:00. I also hope to do a little playing—there is a piano here on the second floor the girl told me I could use—and I've been dying to play. I also hope to pick up some posters depicting this 1000-year celebration, etc.

I'll be very anxious to pick up your mail in Berlin. Do try to forward all mail I get from fraternity, etc. I haven't started on Stunt Show[13] yet, since I haven't received anything from Vicki, the girl who's working on it. We should be in Berlin by July 9.

Well, the Luxembourg chime just struck 1:00, so I had better get some sleep. Until tomorrow, *au revoir*.

Love, Tom

P.S. Aren't you impressed with my extensive letter writing? ☺
T.T.

GERMANY 2

Castles, Dungeons and Festivals Along the Rhine

Following its devastating loss in World War II, Germany tried to regain its footing. It struggled to build a thriving economy and once again become a proud European nation. Tourists returned to the shores of the Rhine River with its medieval castles and charming towns peaceably sprinkled throughout the beautiful unspoiled scenery.

Konrad Adenauer was the First Chancellor of the "new" Germany. In the 1950s, greatly aided by the Marshall Plan, the breaking down of trade barriers and the opening of global markets, West Germany, in particular, began to enjoy prolonged economic growth.

By the early 1960s, Germans would proudly display promising signs of recovery to visiting Americans. President John F. Kennedy came to Berlin in June, 1963 and made his famous "*Ich bin ein Berliner*" speech. Our guys missed the event but basked in the acclaim showered on their American president.

§ § §

Heidelberg—Thursday, June 27, 1963

Hi–

Well, we got up this morning after a very good night's rest in Luxembourg about 8:30. We went downstairs where they had breakfast for us all prepared. It consisted of coffee and rolls, and was served in a special breakfast room which had the "Old English" look, large fireplace, clean, with old brass pots, plates and paintings on the walls. The tables were set with white linen and coffee was served in individual pots with some kind of very fine china. They gave us two packages of butter, which was welcome since butter is not as customary here as in the U.S. However, the butter they serve is white and much better-tasting than ours.

It was raining this morning, so I spent the next two hours playing a piano, which they kept on the 2nd floor in a lounge. It was great playing again, but the piano hadn't been tuned in ages, so I could barely tell what I was playing. I was singing in English which must have been somewhat of an innovation to a maid who kept peering in and smiling, nodding, and muttering, "Ya, ya." I'm lost here language-wise, for everyone speaks either German or Luxembourgish, which is a weird combination of French and German. My French has helped me quite a bit, however.

On the road from Luxemburg to Heidelberg

    We packed and took off about 11:30. The people here are so very friendly and the city itself is really quaint (such an over-used word) and picturesque. Before leaving, we stopped in a book store where I bought a birthday card for Mary, which will be very late, and we also talked to a charming lady in the store who spoke fairly good English. She gave me a poster depicting the 1000-year celebration, and was very interesting in some of her bits of information about Luxembourg. In all the store windows are pictures of the Grand Duchess of Luxembourg, and we thought it was kind of funny that such a postage-stamp country should make such a fuss about their royalty.

Charming German villages nestled in wooded valleys

    On our way out of town, we stopped to pick up some salami, cheese, bread and wine, which we bought for a picnic on our way. About 5 miles out of the city we were driving through woods and hilly country, and came upon a beautiful shaded area overlooking a valley and a castle. So we stopped the car and walked into the clearing, sat down on the side of a steep slope and "broke bread." It was a peaceful, beautiful spot, and truly the high point of the day. We are getting along fine and seem to spend half of our time in hysterical laughter about not much of anything. We loaded back in the car, empty wine bottles and all, and proceeded on our way. We decided to change our route and not go to Brussels or Amsterdam until on our way back since we have to be in Malmo on the 5th or 6th—we thought this was best.

A picnic in the woods

The ride today was very long, very tiring, but extremely interesting and extremely picturesque. We took the back roads and went through countless small country towns. Surprisingly enough, at the German border we were only asked for our passports, and that was all. I suppose we all have honest faces, since we could have smuggled all kinds of things into Germany, and no one would have known. The back route is really back, and the roads are miserable. They are narrow, winding and full of trucks. The roads in Germany seem to be much more laden with traffic than the roads in France—perhaps indicative of a more industrial people (?). We drove, and drove, and drove. The country in Germany is beyond description it is so full of beauty. We were now getting in the more mountainous sections, and the hills and mountains were covered with large black forests. Sometimes we'd drive over a hill and behold some breathtaking sight of river valleys and small red-roofed villages nestled in the valleys. The drive has been like a continuous 3-dimension movie, only much better. It's really hard to believe at times that you're surrounded by such beauty, but every once in a while we would stop the car just to look at some of the beautiful surroundings—and then you can smell the fresh air and really know you're here. Of particular interest were the small German towns we passed through today. They seemed to be very old places, and obviously (from some of the strange looks we got), not passed through by Americans very often. The streets are mostly cobblestone and brick, very narrow, and even the main highway weaves in and out through these towns like some poor prisoner in an ancient labyrinth. The people seem contented, hard-working, and farm-like. The dress of the younger set is similar to ours, but many of the older people dress quite differently. Old ladies wear black stockings with long black dresses and usually some sort of white bonnet on their heads. Old men with Hitler-type mustaches peered at us with strange expressions as we whizzed past. They sit in rocking chairs or porches, contented just to watch the young wives pushing their babies and the younger children playing in the streets. The little boys wear lederhosen and look very mountainish and yodelish playing with their peers. We frequented many young women walking their babies along the highway on the outskirts of these small towns. We had some harrowing experiences at times driving over hills to meet not only an oncoming car, but also a whole troop of such women with their babies. After squeaking of horns, hustling of troops and heavy hearts, we'd sail by. They seemed to think nothing of it, though, and probably would have ignored us except for the pile of luggage on top and view of a very heavy-laden Volkswagen.

    We drove through Trier and Nonnweiler, where we stopped to get some beer and to change our money. We kept driving, and finally hit the Autobahn and passed by Worms and Mannheim, two very industrial sections of Germany. The Autobahn, built by Hitler in the late 1930's is a good road, very similar to the Pennsylvania Turnpike. It did show a lot of wear and tear, so was not as smooth as some of the newer roads in the Chicago area. We finally arrived here in Heidelberg about 9:00 PM.

    We were immediately impressed with this town. It has a rare combination of progressiveness, quaintness and cleanliness, which is certainly in its favor. It is situated between two very high mountains in the Neckar River valley. The river, the bridge, the castle over-looking the city from the bluff, and the red-roofed houses and buildings dotting the valley combine to make this place truly impressive.

The Heidelberg town gate welcomes the five guys.

Since it was so late and our usual hotel recommendation place (a local airport) was not open, we went to a hotel recommended in our Bible "Europe on $5 a Day." They were filled, but a waitress invited us all in for a beer while she called another place to see if they had room. Sure enough, they did, and she told us that the fellow who ran it would drive over to show us the way. He was there in 5 minutes, and we were led to what is an old house changed into a living quarters for Heidelberg professors and a hotel in off-season. It is a late 19th century house, beautifully decorated and complete with large spacious rooms with a balcony, large desk, great big soft beds and huge closet chests. Even the bathroom has stained-glass windows!

The fellow who runs the place is young and extremely congenial, but speaks no English. We're very lucky to have Karl, who speaks perfect German. It's terrible not to be able to communicate with people, not even the simplest things. It's a very helpless feeling! By the time we unloaded and got settled, it was about 10:15, and we were all famished, since we hadn't had a bite to eat since our mountainside picnic. We had dinner at a hotel restaurant. I had pork, French fries, green beans, spaghetti, ice cream and a beer for only about $1.90 including services. It was delicious! The Germans certainly do know how to cook—and their method of serving food—out of silver platters, is very much superior to any U.S. method you normally see.

After dinner we explored a little, but then returned to our place, since we were all tired after the long day's drive. I read for a while and here I am writing.

Until tomorrow, *au revoir*.

Love, Tom

Heidelberg—Friday, June 28, 1963

Hi–

Well, Heidelberg is a friendly, peaceful and scenic place, and it has really been a beautiful time here—except for the weather, cold and rainy this morning. I got up about 9:30 and spent most of the morning polishing shoes, goofing around, etc. When we awoke, the sun was shining—indicative of what we thought would be a beautiful day. So we set out to do some exploring of the town, and hadn't walked 2 blocks when it started raining. So we trotted back to our place to pick up umbrellas, raincoats, etc. Rick and Freddy were hunting for a current converter for their electric shavers and I was hoping to find a piano somewhere where I could get some playing in. Our hotel, by the way, is located in a very nice, quiet residential section. The houses are similar to the ones in New Orleans, large, late 19th Century Victorian style, and surrounded by trees and gardens. They all seem to have a rod [wrought] iron or stone wall lining their borders, and are entered by some kind of gate.

On the way toward town, we passed a music shop, which was very lucky, since I not only found a piano but we found out about a Brahms and Bartok concert to be given at Heidelberg Univ. tonight. The lady in the shop spoke English very well and she told me that I could rent a piano in their tuning shop from 5:00 to 6:30 tonight and tomorrow if I liked. She also sold us tickets to the concert and was overly friendly and polite. She even gave us some posters that they had had in their windows.

It was a miserable day for walking, the rain was heavy and it had turned very cold. We crossed to the other side of the river, and after eating lunch in some small cheap restaurant (similar to the Kitchen),[1] we took a trolley to the castle. The castle is a world-famous ruin, former residence of Electors Palatine (13th-17th Centuries), gothic, renaissance and baroque elements in its architecture. It's really an awe-inspiring sight and makes one want to just stare at it and think for hours. We climbed a very steep narrow road to the castle itself and found out later we had entered from the back. It is built like a fortress, and all along its surrounding walls were holes for defense by cannon and you could see in the throws [throes] of the buildings dark barred windows, obviously used as dungeons. We climbed then onto a terrace which overlooked all of Heidelberg, and it was a non-describable [indescribable] sight. We went to an exhibit of Elizabeth Stuart[2] paintings, lectures, and coins borrowed from a museum in Windsor, England. It was very interesting, especially some of the old letters written as far back as 1616. Most of them were in English or French, so I managed to decipher some of them, but not all. After spending about an hour there and meeting a very interesting couple from Windsor, England who had heard about the exhibit and were passing through to check it out, we walked through the castle gardens and out over a bridge-like wall built on the side of the mountain, where the view was again breathtaking. The rain was so bad by this time that we decided to go back into town, see the Holy Ghost Church, and return home. It was already about 3:30, and the church was closed. Walking back, we passed a small restaurant that had a very tempting pastry display in the window. Unable to resist, we went in for some cheesecake and coffee, and it was delicious. It's terribly exasperating having to use sign language for everything, and still not always be understood. But when we have money to spend, they somehow manage to understand—so in the end, everyone's happy. We took a trolley back to the main section of town, and walked the rest of the way back to the hotel, stopping along the way to window shop, etc. We got back about 4:00, and I changed clothes, and cleaned up my shoes, which are really taking a beating in this weather. I then went back to the music shop and practiced from 5:00 to 6:30. I started some new music about Paris Fountains, and spent most of my time working on that. The piano was in perfect tune, and it was great being able to play a decent piano by myself for a change.

Rick met me at 6:30 and we then walked along the Neckar River. It is truly a beautiful walk with the castle ruins, mountains, valley in the distance being part of the surroundings, and the University rowing teams practicing in the river. There were also many barges, small boats, and excursion boats peacefully making their way along the river. By this time, the weather had cleared up, the sun was shining, and the town had a real inspiring charm. We walked down to the old bridge, crossed it, and found a restaurant where we could get something to eat.

We had sort of an interesting experience there. We sat down with only about 45 minutes left before the concert started, so we told the waitress, and she then informed us that the restaurant was closed. It seems that they were feeding a special group of American tourists (students) and had prepared only enough for that group. So to show you how nice they were, she said we could have some soup. Not only did we get a delectable bowl of noodle soup, but also a delicious lettuce and tomato salad, big bowl of French fries, big platter of pork with mushrooms and gravy, a beer and some ice cream with peaches for about $2.00. The service was tremendous, and she made sure we were finished eating in time. While there, we made some observations of the touring group, and thanked our lucky stars we weren't part of it. They were flitting from place to place (Rome for one day, for example) and everything was preplanned for them, food and all. They had a bitchy looking chaperone who kept complaining about the food, and some sweet man who kept apologizing every time he turned around. We got a big laugh out of the whole thing—and felt very lucky, too! We thought how they missed so much of the very heart of Europe, passing thru small towns, staying there, etc.

Postcard: The Heidelberg bridge beneath the old castle

    We then took off for the concert, which was given in what looked like a very old, traditional-type lecture hall. There we ran into Karl, Bill and Freddy who had decided to come to the concert. The concert itself was extremely well done. Sung by a quartet, they were all excellent musicians, and the music by Brahms and Bartok was well-selected and thoroughly enjoyable.

    After the concert we investigated some of the student hangouts of Heidelberg, and it turned out to be a most, shall we say, happy occasion. We started out at the most popular place, very traditional with beer for only 12 cents a stein, and rubbed elbows with some of the Heidelberg students, one of which I talked to. He was quite high, and told of his father who had been a Natzi [Nazi] and praised the U.S. Next we went to a small place and met some students from Berlin. We then sang German drinking songs as well as some of our own—and had a really tremendous time. We talked to one girl who had studied in England and spoke English perfectly. She was quite a character and told stories of their travels etc. It was quite a fun time!

    We ended the evening at a place where they had a band, and they even let me play the piano, Bill the drums. We sang, watched the band (the men wore mountain hats and lederhosen and the drummer was a big German blonde girl) and had a tremendous time there too. Two American fellows joined us there—they are stationed at the local U.S. air force base. At about 2:30, we made our way back across town, and I was rather high—too high. Anyway, it was a great evening, and one we'll always remember.

    A few last words about Heidelberg. "Its favorable situation has made it a commercial and cultural center since

Roman times. The surrounding landscape, perfect setting for that light-hearted marvel, the castle ruins, bestows a special distinction on the town; its university is Germany's oldest and most memorable; its industries and their products, and with them Heidelberg's name, are known throughout the world; to the various publishing houses the world's best minds entrust their works, the inhabitants are hospitable and show a lively interest in cultural activities; and finally, the play *The Student Prince* has traveled round the world in many guises awakening in its audiences a nostalgia for Heidelberg. Perhaps it was the Englishman, John Boynton Priestly, who best expressed Heidelberg's enduring fascination: 'I will stay here forever, for this is the town I have dreamt about when I have awakened to find myself miserable in my own world.'"—from booklet on the city.

Until tomorrow—*au revoir*.
Love, Tom

Mainz, Germany—Saturday, June 29, 1963

Hi–
Today's letter won't be too long, since we did little today except drive. I got up about 10:00, packed, paid my bill, polished my shoes, and took my luggage down to the car. I had a terrible time talking to the hotel owner's wife, who spoke no English and I spoke no German. So we played charades and after 15 minutes of sign language managed to pay the bill. I then went back to the music shop and practiced from 12:00 to 1:00. We couldn't leave Heidelberg until 2:00 since Bill had had some shirts laundered there. After playing, I walked along the River, taking pictures (it was a gorgeous day) and pondering the view. I then ran into Bill who was doing the same thing and we decided to take what they call the "Philosopher's Walk"—a path high on the mountain overlooking the whole city. The view from up there was truly majestic and we spent about an hour looking and walking—and climbing.

I grabbed a quick sandwich and we took off about 2:30. We drove all day, and the scenery was even more beautiful today than ever before, probably because we are in the Rhineland, and the mountains, valleys and streams are more plentiful than ever. We stopped at the particularly scenic spots and changed drivers as well as stretching a little.

We stopped for dinner in a small town and had a delicious meal for about $1.50. We're now in Mainz, a university town, and we arrived about 9:30 tonight. We took forever trying to find a place to stay, trying everything from religious foundations to Youth Hostels. We finally ended up at a 5th rate hotel on the 5th floor—but we were all so tired, it didn't really matter where we stopped, just to get some rest.

It's pretty late, and the day has been rather uneventful, so I'll close. Until tomorrow, *au revoir*. Love, Tom

P.S. I'm going to have my film developed in Berlin—and if the pictures are good, fine—if not, I may buy a new camera, since they are cheap over here, and very high quality. Give my love to everyone at home. If you wrote me in Brussels, I won't be there until August.

Love, Tom

Ehrental, Germany—Sunday, June 30

Hi–

What a wonderful day it has been—perhaps the best yet! We awoke about 8:30 this morning in Mainz and left there about 9:45. We all put suits on in hopes that we'd find some small church along the way where we could observe true German Lutheranism. After paying the hotel bill which amounted to about $1.95 we began again our trail blazing.

We have traveled all day along the Rhine, and this drive is unsurpassed in beauty in comparison to anything we've seen so far. There are majestic low mountains on either side of the river, which winds its way along the German landscape. We stopped about 10:00 in a small town to attend a church service. The church was about the size of the one in Cora[3], with an attendance of 158. Of course, the service itself was all in German, and I was kind of embarrassed sitting there, not saying a word. I sat in a pew by myself next to some regular parishioner and he offered to share his hymn book with me, which was certainly a nice gesture, but really hilarious because the words were in Old English text which is hard enough to read in English, let alone German! So I sat there stammering and stuttering over the songs while my German friend on the right must have thought I had just escaped from an institution. I had that feeling myself. Karl, of course, knowing and worshipping the language so well, was having a wonderful time. After the service, I asked the fellow if he spoke English, and he said "a little" but then only smiled and wouldn't say anything else—I presume it was because he couldn't think of an appropriate phrase—but it was all very comical.

After church, we headed for the river, in search of the road which follows the contours of the river. We were on the West bank, which was more crowded and had heavier traffic, so decided to cross to the East bank. We took a ferry across at Bingen and proceeded North along the bank, stopping at Assmannshausen for lunch. We spent quite a bit of time there as it was a very old town and well preserved for tourists. We ate in a quaint old restaurant, and I ordered the cheapest thing on the menu, which turned out to be liver—and that being one dish I can hardly stomach—I filled up on potatoes. While there, Rick bought a camera for about $60.00 and I picked up some stamps and a postcard. Enclosed is the menu and the check from the place where we ate!

The drive along here is really the kind of thing you dream about. The river is wide and commercially very busy, with many barges and various boats making their lazy way through the water. What really makes the drive so wonderful, though, are the castles that line the rim of the mountains. Most of them date back to the 12th Century, and they loom in the distance overlooking miles of winding river, with the appearance of medieval grandeur and "knight on white stallion" majesty. We spent most of the day stopping to investigate these medieval wonders, and to me, this was the most thrilling experience. We stopped first at Castle Gutenfels, a very mysterious looking place. We drove the car up very narrow winding roads toward the old place, stopping about 100 yards from the entrance. Karl and I walked up the deserted path, and approached the large gate to the place. The gate was locked, so we took another path which wound in and around behind the place—and we both felt like we should have been adorned in armor and riding a horse, carrying gauntlet and shield. The view from the castle surroundings was really amazing—and particularly beautiful was "The Pfalz"—an 11th Century structure built on a small island in the Rhine—which we overlooked from the castle. The stories told about all of the barons who owned such castles is that they stopped each boat along the Rhine with huge long chains, demanding of each boat a tariff for passing his castle. Since we couldn't get inside the old monster, we decided to try our luck up the road at another castle. These old places are built very steeply and highly along the cliffs, and it seems amazing to me how they actually engineered such things—probably no more amazing than it is today.

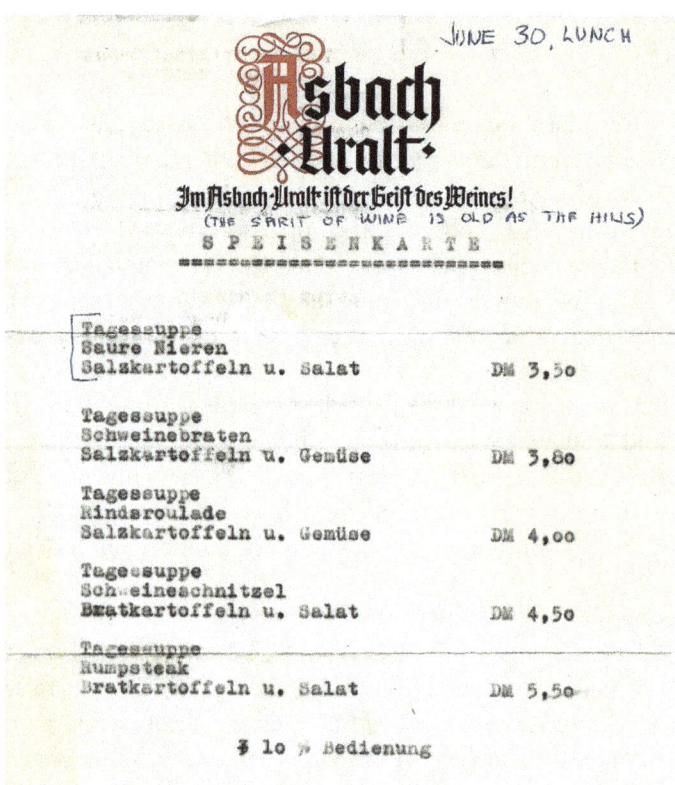

Liver on the menu in a quaint German town

We then passed the Lorelei, a huge mass of basalt rock, made famous by Heine's song about the sirens on these rocks who lured boats and their crews to their doom on the rocky shores.

We next stopped at the town St. Goarshausen, above which loomed the Castle of Katz, built in 1393, rebuilt in 1898. It was similar to the other, except it showed signs of life. We made our way near the summit in first gear, the Old Volks[4] (which we call Victoria Windsor) (VW) trustily trudging along. We had much better luck here, as we were able to get inside. It was the residence for a private school located in this town, and a beautiful girl gave us a guided tour of the living quarters, dungeon and tower. The section where the students lived was rebuilt in 1898, and she told us that the old section was kind of dangerous, as sections of it often crumbled. She also said that the upkeep of these old places is very expensive, and most of them are either hotels, hostels, or government owned. It's great to have Karl along, for he does a beautiful job of interpreting—also we learn things we otherwise would be ignorant of if we didn't have him. The view from these places was so moving that description is not adequate. I hope the pictures we're taking do it justice.

After leaving here, we drove through Wellmich, where we stopped to find a place to stay. There was "no room in the inn" so to speak, but we were told of a "stable" in the next berg called Ehrental, which proved to be open, and here we are. It is a very small place, situated below a large castle called Castle of Mouse. Its real name Deuemburg, received the nickname of Maus from the Courts of Katzenberger, in contrast to the Katz (Cat and Mouse). We're staying in a little *gasthaus* (called German Gasthaus), actually a private home. It is clean, neat and very homey, the people (old couple) being very friendly, and the prices very low. I slept for a couple hours after unloading the car, and awoke about 7:00. Karl, Rick, Bill and I then walked up the road to a small restaurant, where I had delicious Hungarian goulash, fried Lyonnaise potatoes, salad, fruit and coffee for about $1.35. After dinner, we walked on up the road, and I experienced what is perhaps the most aesthetically beautiful emotions I have ever felt. The sun was setting over the mountains, the river was calm, and the breeze was just right. I can't really explain how impressed I was, but we walked for about an hour, just gazing at the whole thing—I'm still a little dazed by the whole experience—and wonder how many times something equally as beautiful can happen.

Admiring the scenic beauty of the Rhine

If those old Rhine castles could talk…

We came back to our *gasthaus* and then took a jaunt in the car back toward the castles we had seen earlier. They were illuminated with yellowish lights, and were very alluring looking—the feeling is similar to the song "Follow Me" in *Camelot*[5]. These castles have a strange way of arousing your imagination to its fullest. The castle that looms above us is deserted, so there were no lights, but from our back door, you can see the towers looming toward the sky—very black and mysterious looking. It makes one wonder about all the people through the centuries who have gazed on the same sight—of the tales the ghosts of these houses could tell. This is the Europe you dream of.

    Until tomorrow—good night.
    Love, Tom

Somewhere in Northern Germany—Monday, July 1, 1963

Hi–

Time certainly flies—it seems impossible that July is here already! We got up about 8:00 this morning, got dressed and packed, and sat down to a terrific breakfast of coffee, rolls, ham, eggs (which I didn't touch), delicious broth and jelly. The place where we stayed was run by a family, and was actually a private home. Even though we couldn't understand a thing they were saying, one woman kept fussing around the breakfast table, smiling, and blabbering in German. We ate right in their living room, and their daughter of about 19 was busy finding American radio stations on their radio, while we kept stuffing ourselves with food. There were actually two small houses, one facing the Rhine where Rick and I stayed, and one in back where the other three stayed. Before leaving the place, we took a picture of us with the whole family—and then they asked us to send them a print. They were very warm and friendly, and seemed excited to have us. It was a real production leaving the place, everyone waving and giving advice about the car, etc. For such an inexpensive place, we had a wonderful time. And the breakfast was enough nourishment to last at least a good long morning!

Bidding *auf Wiedersehen* to our Gasthaus family and Germany

We then proceeded on up the Rhine and again were amazed by the beautiful landscape and castles. We saw one that looked particularly interesting called Marksburg—so decided to stop. It was run by the German Society for Protection of German Castles, and was the most unusual and beautiful of any we had seen. We were given a guided tour by one of the fellows that worked there, and this proved to be a real treat! One thing about this place that made it so interesting was the superb upkeep and the very interesting items it contained. We were first shown the armour [armor] making shop, which looked like not much more than a glorified ancient toolshed, and we were then led to a fortification wall, with small holes dotting its length, behind which loomed ancient cannons. It seems that Marksburg has been one of the most militant castles along the Rhine, at one time responsible for the protection of the whole Rhine area. It was especially useful during the 30 Years War, and was also used during World War I for protection of the Rhine area. The particular cannon he showed us was filled halfway with gun powder and then loaded with two mammoth stone cannonballs—which, as our guide said, sometimes got stuck in the barrel of the cannon, sending the cannon exploding back some 180 meters.

We were next led into a room containing knight's armour [armor] and weapons ranging in age from Greek, Roman and Gallic armour to 15th Century equipment. How they ever wore some of that stuff is hard to imagine. One "suit" weighed so much that it was compulsory for the knight to stay on his horse once it was donned—for one fall, and he couldn't get up. He would just have to lay there like a bug on its back! That could be a disastrous blunder! Some of the weapons were deadly enough to cause shudders in the spine, mostly clubs and sticks with heavy metal prongs on their ends or ball and chains dangling from them. It made you glad you didn't meet a knight charging up the hill—even though it had originally sounded very romantic and exciting!

We then climbed up a dark, narrow, winding stairway and entered a living-dining hall that was used for parties, banquets, marriages, etc. It wasn't a large room, but seemed very comfortable, complete with large fireplace, eating nooks that were actually dormers, and old wooden furniture that didn't look luxurious, but probably comfortable enough. The room itself overlooked the river, and had a small room right in the middle, which we were informed was a john—put there for the convenience of the lords and knights during wine parties and banquets. All it was was a hole in the wall overlooking about a 1000 ft drop—quite comical! We were then shown a small chapel, which was octagonal in shape and whose ceilings contained religious murals which were only recently discovered under about 5 coats of dirt and white wash.

We then went down a flight of stairs into an immense kitchen. The fireplace (walk in type) was big enough to cook an entire steer on a spit. There were interesting pots and utensils around, and even a 14th century mousetrap! Adjoining this room was a food storage room. Those who actually made use of these places had to hang all of their food and meat from the ceiling so that it wouldn't be devoured by hungry rats and other rodents. Heading down from this room was a dungeon, but we weren't allowed there because of the danger of falling rocks.

Our guide then showed us a whole bevy of torturing devices that were common to these castle dungeons. Among them were the body stretcher, various head, arm and leg locks, and even an honest true-to life chastity belt, used by the head baron when he wanted to leave the castle for a few days and make sure his wife remained true. Stories have it that he gave the key to his best friend so he would know who to smite if any hanky-panky was uncovered.

After seeing the wine cellar and a bedroom containing a 14th century baby cradle, we roamed about the place for quite a while before leaving. This was the castle that Walt Disney used as a pattern for the one in "Snow White and the Seven Dwarfs." It was really a beautiful and interesting place.

We then continued up the Rhine, stopping to buy some groceries for lunch in Koblenz. It is a large, prosperous looking city, and very American looking. We stopped at Rutzel to eat and had a real good lunch very cheap. We've found we can save a lot of money by stopping to buy food in a grocery rather than going out to a restaurant. We then proceeded up the East bank to Remagen, where we ran into the beginning of a Hunting festival. The houses and streets were all decorated with flags and greenery, and a group of about 30 men, very impressively uniformed, began to line up. There was even a brass band, and we spent about a half-hour there, taking pictures and following the procession. It was such a great surprise finding something like this. We finally left Remagen, a little dazed by the impressive happenings. We then drove on to Bonn, the present capital of West Germany. We spent about an hour there looking at the government buildings and walking along the riverfront. It was a very modern looking city and the official buildings were contemporary, fairly attractive, but rather temporary looking. On the riverfront there was a cross, very simple in style, with a saying inscribed on the rock below: "we are waiting, comrades." It was a meaningful symbol, and opens your eyes to the troubles that the Germans have over their divided fatherland. It was sad in a way.

Hunting Festival in Remagen on the way to Bonn

The highly decorated festival leaders

We left Bonn and headed on the Autobahn to Köln (Cologne) where we hunted unsuccessfully for a place to stay, looked at the beautiful cathedral there, and went on our way toward Hamburg. The cathedral was the most beautiful we've seen outside of Chartres, and although having some war damage, was surprisingly intact. It is obvious that when bombing these cities, they were as careful as possible to avoid hitting these beautiful churches.

We drove on the Autobahn until about 10:00 when we decided to try to find a place to stop for the night and also to get some food in our gullets. We ended up in some small town, the name I don't know, and got a delicious meal of beans, toast, cheese, fruit and beer for about $1.75. The gal who was our server was a perfect grandma type and kept bringing us more lager to drink. It was the best service we have had. It's a joy to see such friendly service here.

The place where we are staying is clean and a very nice place.

We're hoping to make Hamburg tomorrow, and Copenhagen the next day. The Autobahn does wonders for quick travel.

It's getting late, and I must sign off. Until next time, good night.
Love, Tom

WINDOW SHOPPING IN HAMBURG

3

"Hope you're not offended!"

This chapter reveals a truly coming of age moment. It needs no further context.

§ § §

Hamburg, Germany—Tuesday, July 2, 1963

Hi–
Well, here we are in Hamburg, Germany, and it has been an interesting day in more ways than one. We got up this morning about 8:30, ate breakfast, and got back on the Autobahn, heading for Hannover and Hamburg. We woke up to a view of a colossal garbage dump this morning, which came as a surprise since we had arrived in the dark last night. But I guess we can't always have views of the Rhine! We drove through the morning until about 12:00 when we pulled off the Autobahn into Herrin, where we bought some groceries, ham, cheese, apple cider and bread. We got back on the Autobahn and stopped about 1:00 at a *Restplatz* to eat. We then continued driving through Hannover to Hamburg on the Autobahn.

> We've worked out a fantastic maneuver for changing places in the car, and we have it down now to about 10 seconds. We call it our "big switch." It's diagrammed as follows: [diagram] Today on the Autoban at one place where we "switched" we really mystified a group of German truck drivers. They probably wondered what the hell was coming off!

Beetle "switch" diagram—10 seconds to move 5 guys every hour

Karl calls it our "Keystone Cops scene." We arrived in Hamburg about 5:30 and went immediately to the railroad station to find an inexpensive place to stay. Freddy and I sat out in the car and watched the rush hour. We were parked right in front of some office building and it was interesting watching all the people leave it on their way home. There were all types of people who passed by, from beautiful young co-ed types to old beaten looking men and women. We saw one fellow who looked just like Tom Winings[1] and I saw another who was the spitting image of Dad when he was younger. It was such a strange resemblance that it was almost uncanny.

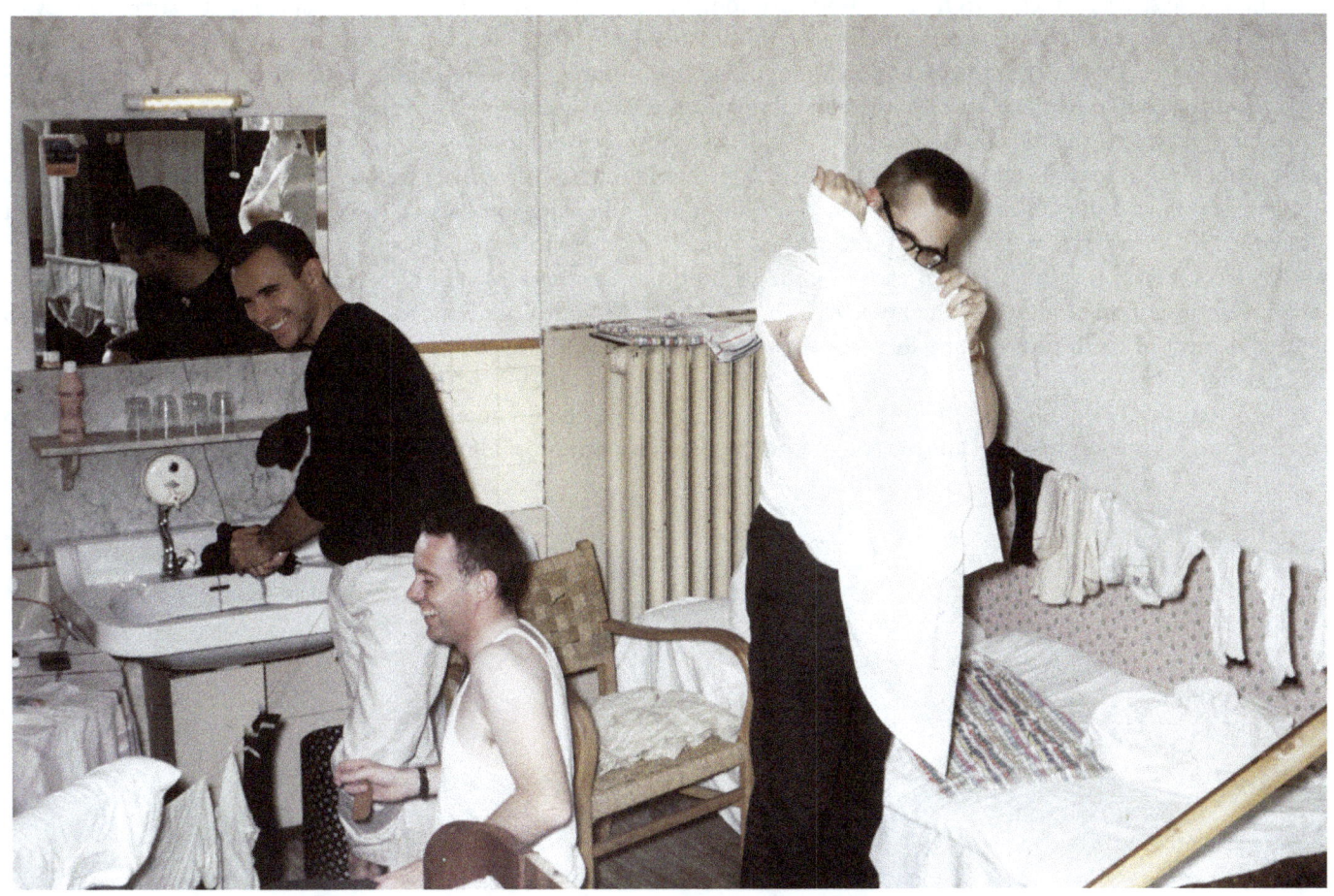
"Self service" laundry at the cheap Hamburg hotel

    Sure enough, we got the cheapest hotel in town, and it was really a dump, run by some German gal who was, to pardon the expression, a super bitch! We spent the next couple of hours relaxing and washing clothes, and we went next door to a small restaurant for dinner about 8:30. We all ate fried chicken and French fries, and it tasted great! We then struck out for the nightclub district of Hamburg, located on the other side of town. We walked along the wharf, where there was quite a bit of activity. We stopped to look at an English ocean liner which happened to be in port at that time. Hamburg is a true port town, and it was evidenced by the many sailors roving the streets, and all of the rough looking bars and night clubs. We went into one, which seemed more like a tourist trap than anything very authentic, and spent about an hour there, watching the stage show and dirty movies they showed between acts. It was a sleazy place and the girls weren't much better. The street where these places are located is called the Reeperbahn, and it is world famous for a side street where only adults are allowed. Since we are adults, we decided to see what it was all about, and after entering, we saw the most amazing sight we've ever seen. The whole street is lined with houses of prostitution, and the "girls" sit in the windows all along the street so they can be looked over. It was like a whore department store if that seems possible. The women and girls were of an amazing variety, all sizes and kinds. There were some who were quite pretty and innocent looking, and others who were the opposite. There were crowds of people roaming this little street, talking to the girls, and going in every once in a while. There were even women and girls with their escorts looking at the spectacle, and I'm sure that the objects of their stares knew they were a tourist attraction. In many ways it was a very pathetic sight, seeing these girls subject to the ridicule and fun-making the way they were. I walked along looking at them, and every once in a while one would catch my eye, and turn away quickly, with an ashamed look on her face. I suppose she realized we were only there to watch. Just for the fun of it, I priced one, and it was 20 marks, which is about $5.00. Breathe a sigh, Mom, I didn't go in—I was only "window shopping" shall we say! But it was a very interesting sight, and one I'm sure I'll never forget. On our walk back tonight we passed many prostitutes on the streets, most of them very fat, heavily made up and ugly. We got back to the hotel about 2:30, and since I'm very tired, I'd better sign off.

    I hope you're not offended by this letter, but I thought it was plenty interesting enough to describe. Be careful who you circulate this one to, but let Ann read it—she might get a kick out of it. Until tomorrow, *au revoir*.

    Love, Tom

SCANDINAVIA
4

Celebrations, Conflicts and a Welcoming Swedish Family

Scandinavia is generally thought of as comprising Denmark, Norway, and Sweden. Each of these countries fared differently in World War II. Denmark, more strategically located than its neighbors, declared itself neutral. However, it became a protectorate and an occupied territory of Germany. Norway was also occupied by the Third Reich. Sweden was officially neutral but continued to export iron to Germany throughout the war.

By the sixties, Copenhagen, Denmark and Stockholm, Sweden were both thriving cities. Sweden could boast of being the birthplace of two giants of the film industry: Ingrid Bergman, world-renowned actress; and Ingmar Bergman, director extraordinaire. Tivoli, the sprawling amusement park in the heart of Copenhagen, was the inspiration for Walt Disney's Disneyland.

Today, IKEA is synonymous with Sweden. This world-renowned store, with its uniquely Swedish style ready-to-assemble furniture, was founded in 1943 by a seventeen-year-old Swede. IKEA opened its first store outside of Sweden in Norway in 1963. But I do not think our young Americans had furniture on their minds that year.

§ § §

Slagelse, Denmark—Wednesday, July 3, 1963

Hi–

The days are really whizzing by, and we've been gone now about 2 weeks, exactly 1/5 of the trip. So much has been seen on this first fraction that it seems impossible to actually see much more.

We slept late this morning—till about 10:00 because of our big night last night. To prove what a complete ass the landlady was at the hotel, listen to this: When Rick, Bill and Karl returned to their room last night, their wet clothes had been thrown all over the room, clothesline and all. She had obviously come into the room, seen the miles of clothes strung all over, and in a rage, thrown them all around. I'll admit the room looked like a miniature Chinese laundry, but what right did she have to pitch them that way—we were cussing about it this morning, but decided it wasn't worth causing any trouble. Another thing she did last night that irritated everyone was refuse to let us leave the hotel—even for dinner (!) before we paid the bill. Quite a time! She was threatening to call the police!

We left Hamburg about 11:15 and took off for Denmark. The roads weren't bad and the countryside was very picturesque in this part of Germany. We stopped about 12:30 in some small resort type town, and bought some cakes, cheese, bananas, macaroons and milk (my first since leaving the U.S. and pasteurized) and spread it on the hood of the car. We were parked right in front of an exclusive sidewalk café type restaurant and we kept getting strange stares from the waiters—it was a funny sight. A group of five gathered around their overloaded Volks peeling bananas, talking loudly and laughing hysterically.

We then drove on toward Flensburg, and crossed the border into Denmark about 7 KM beyond that town. At the border, they checked our car and our passports, and let us go without any kind of trouble at all. We've been disappointed at the lack of formality at these border crossings, having fully expected to be questioned, searched, etc. There had been even less trouble getting into Luxembourg and Germany.

Denmark is certainly beautiful country, characterized by small hills, fields dotted with small mounds of hay, and much greenery. We drove up Denmark on Route 10A to Kolding, where we took the bridge across to the island, proceeding east through Odens to Nyborg, where we decided to take a ferry across to the peninsula, since it was only a 45 minute trip, and we would have that part of it out of the way. The ferry trip was one of the better things we've done so far, as it was a beautiful time of evening (sunset), and there were thousands of seagulls flying next to the ship, begging crumbs from the passengers. The ferry was unusually large, about the size of the ship we took to Michigan from Mackinac Island. The best part of the trip, however, was the hoard of birds that kept gliding and flapping within inches of the boat. Several people were throwing out breadcrumbs to these creatures, and each time there would be a big squabble, but the crumbs never did reach the water—they were always devoured before having the chance. The combination of the salty breeze, the beautiful gliding birds, and the sunset over the water was really a gorgeous sight. Rick and I took a trip to the top deck, which I later regretted because one of the damned seagulls flew right over my head and let me have it in the face. Everyone around laughed, and I borrowed a handkerchief to wipe the stuff off—messy, but funny! We landed on the peninsula about 8:30 and decided to stop as soon as possible since we weren't that far from Copenhagen, and we were all hungry and tired. Rick and I had the great idea of taking a side road to some small seaside town for the night. This we tried but had no luck. The people didn't understand English, German, French, or Spanish, so we gave up. We got back on the road to KOBENHAUN (as they spell it) and ended up staying at Slagelse, a town of about 25,000, very neat and cheap. We stayed at the Regina Hotel and ate dinner across the street in another hotel. We had a wonderful meal there for about a dollar, consisting of breaded veal, mounds of fried potatoes, milk, ice cream and strawberries, and an *hors-d'oeuvre* of lemon slices with herring. After the meal, we had a terrible scene with the waitress, since we didn't have any Danish money, and were trying to pay in marks and dollars. She didn't speak any of our languages, and it must have taken 20 minutes to finally get things straightened out.

We then went back to the hotel, and here I am on my nightly letter. We should be in Malmo by Saturday, Berlin by Wednesday. The next towns you can write will be Vienna or Salzburg after Berlin. Until tomorrow, good night.

Love, Tom

Copenhagen, Denmark—Thursday the 4th of July, 1963

Hi–

A national holiday—hooray!—and yet it seems a very normal working day over here—no fireworks, no drinking, no mad celebration.

We got up this morning about 8:30, ate a very good breakfast of coffee and rolls with butter and jelly, and took off for Copenhagen. Before leaving Slagelse, we changed our money into Kroners (the Danish unit) and Karl and Bill bought themselves pipes.

We left there about 9:30 and took off for Copenhagen. We sang most of the way, trying to think of all of the American songs we could, since it was the 4th, and we had to celebrate in some way! The Danish landscape was very green and peaceful looking, and the road was excellent. We had patches of 4 lane highway all along the way, and even places where the road was not 4 lane, it was plenty wide enough for 3 cars. We pulled into Copenhagen about 11:15, and headed for the railroad station, where we hoped to find a place to stay. We did find a place, and headed for it immediately, as we were all anxious to settle down for a couple of days and try to get reorganized. We are staying in a private home on Christen Berge. It's a very modest, clean place, the people are friendly, and it is very inexpensive, less than $2.00/night.

We have run into a great deal of difficulty with Freddy, who is having a terrible time fitting into the group. All the way to Copenhagen today, he was in a miserable mood, not saying a word the whole way or joining in the singing. Don't misunderstand, this hasn't happened too often. The other evening in Hamburg, I reached my saturation point, and was burning with disgust and anger for about an hour. I realize that this doesn't help matters any, but I really don't know how to get through to this kid.

I spent most of the afternoon sitting in the park, and it was good to get away from things. I wrote for a while also and returned to our house about 5:30. Bill and Freddy returned shortly, and the afternoon had obviously been profitable for the Freddy situation, for he was in a fine mood. At times it is very easy to get along with him, but I wish they occurred more often. Bill said they had had a very enjoyable time at the zoo, which was good to hear. I just hope that the entire situation improves!

We read in the *New York Times* about a concert given in the Tivoli Gardens about 9:00, so decided to go there after dinner. We all put suits on and headed for downtown Copenhagen on a trolley. Copenhagen is a prosperous looking city with extra clean streets and very friendly people. It has that strange but pleasant combination of modernness and tradition. You see ancient looking church steeples towering over brand new modern buildings, as well as many trucks and railroads.

We had a delicious meal in the Wivex Popular, a restaurant right next to the Tivoli for a little over a dollar. I had beer, roast beef, French fries and bread, and there was a delicious cheese sauce over the roast beef. After eating, we went next door to the entrance of the Tivoli. This is a large, elegant amusement park, set up on a permanent basis, and quite an amazing place. The fountains have sparkling bubbles in glass tubes of various sizes protruding out of their waters, and there are thousands of magic Japanese lanterns dotting the paths. Many of the trees are equipped with blinking lights (like Christmas tree lights) and the sidewalk cafés, restaurants and buildings are very luxurious and interesting. They are colorful, both in color and in lighting, and are truly a beautiful sight. As we walked into the place we passed a small orchestra playing light classical music, and then a glorified hot dog stand. The funny thing about this amusement park is its cleanliness and wholesomeness. It seems to be a place to come in suits, and even the people manning the booths look like upstanding intelligent people. There is nothing in poor taste about this place, and it looks like a glorified never-never land. We spent the next hour or so riding the roller coaster and Ferris wheel, wandering through all the concessions, and watching all of the interesting looking people. The variety of types of places was really amazing. There was a dance hall crammed with people dancing to the music of some dance band, and at the end of the park is an immense concert hall, very modern and beautifully lit. There are classical concerts given there each night, and I hope to see one tomorrow night.

We next entered a beer garden, and met some really interesting people. We passed some Americans with a 4th of July cake (iced like the flag), and they insisted that I have a piece. We sat down with some Danish people who spoke a little English and we spent about an hour singing songs like "Swanee," "Grand Old Flag," etc. There were also some Canadian sailors there, and an English speaking guide to Copenhagen who had led quite an interesting life. He had worked for a U.S.

travel agency before the depression, and had made more than thirty 2-month tours of Europe with American tourists. Then the best thing of all happened. An American gentleman with wife and two beautiful daughters came over to the table and we asked them to sit down. The pretty daughter sat right next to me and we talked for about a half-hour. They were living in Paris, and spent weekends and short vacations away from there, touring all of Europe. She was a gorgeous creature, only 18 and entering Northwestern this year as a Freshman, and I'm going to try to get a date with her for tomorrow night.

We returned to the house about 12:30 and hope to get up early tomorrow, but since it is now about 2:00, I'm not sure if I can make it. So, until tomorrow, good night.

Love, Tom

P.S. It turned out to be a fine 4th after all, and the Tivoli seemed to be very appropriate. Meeting Joyce Taylor made it even more interesting! What did you do today?

Copenhagen—Friday, July 5, 1963

Hi–

"Wonderful, wonderful, Copenhagen, Salty old queen of the sea. With your Harbor lights, that you wear at night." As the song goes, so does Copenhagen. This is truly a great place!

I slept till about 10:00 this morning till I decided that if I wanted to see this place I'd better get moving. The other fellows left about 10:15, and I decided to stay and polish shoes, read letters, etc. I left our house about 11:00 and walked down toward Valby Langgade, the large street we are about 3 blocks from. I went into a bakery and bought 2 Danish pastry rolls for about 10 cents, and continued strolling down this street, window shopping and observing people. I stopped in the post office to mail a letter, and then caught a trolley for downtown.

I decided that since we were going to be here only a short time that the best way to see this city would be to take a sightseeing bus with an English-speaking guide. I asked the trolley attendant where the tour left from, and then spent about 15 minutes looking for the right spot. While hunting, I ran into Karl, Bill and Freddy, who were doing the same thing, and we shortly found the spot where the tour trolley departed. While waiting, I ran across the street to American Express, hoping to find some mail there from you, but no luck! I guess I never did make it explicit about being here in Copenhagen—it was sort of a last-minute decision, to tell the truth.

The tour trolley arrived on the scene about 12:20, and we began our hour-and-a-half tour. It was a very interesting jaunt, the guide pointed out statues, government buildings, parks, churches, palaces, museums, harbors, etc., and it all made you realize how much you were missing by not staying in Copenhagen longer. We stopped at one church, completed in 1949, called something which I now can't remember, but none-the-less was truly impressive. It was a majestic modern structure with a definite Gothic influence, Lutheran in sect, and built by ten men only over a period of 19 years—and designed by a famous Danish architect. Each brick of the church was hand-polished, and it was a welcome change from some of the other ancient cathedrals and churches we had been seeing.

Modern Lutheran church in Copenhagen

A few of us at the church entrance

    I was sort of depressed after the tour because I realized how very much there was to see, and no time at all to do it. We are meeting Freddy's friend tomorrow in Malmo, so extending our days here is impossible.
    After the tour we ran into Rick, who had taken the same tour on a different trolley, so all five of us went to the Copenhagen University for lunch. Here in Denmark they serve what they call SMORGESBROD [smorgesbord], which are delicious open-faced sandwiches of all kinds and sizes. They serve them dressed up with all kinds of condiments, fruit and mayonnaise sauces, relishes, cucumber, fried onion, tomatoes, etc. I had three roast beef smorgesbrod [smorgasbord], which they topped with a mustard relish, French fried onions, and tomatoes, and 2 sodas. The sandwiches were only 17 cents each, and actually worth much more. After eating lunch, I walked back by American Express since they had a new assortment of mail, and again, no luck! We then browsed through a bookstore, looking at their fabulous selection of English books. Here in Denmark, most of the students learn English, French and German, since there are so few books actually printed in Danish.
    Freddy, Bill and Karl then took a bus out to the harbor, and Rick and I started back home, stopping to pick up some

posters from the Tivoli. Rick had to pick up some new glasses, since he had lost his in Heidelberg, and we stopped there to get them. They were so inexpensive (only about $7.00), that I decided to splurge, and got some prescription sunglasses for only about $6.00. It seemed like a very decent place, so we figured they must be pretty good quality. They are going to send them to Berlin for me, at no charge, if they aren't ready in time before we leave tomorrow.

    I decided not to call my girlfriend since I wasn't sure of the name of the hotel, she was very young, and money is precious! So, what did I do? Rick and I decided to splurge and go to a fancy restaurant in the Tivoli. It turned out to be a very good thing. As I said yesterday, the Tivoli is an unbelievable place, combination amusement park and fashionable wining and dining hangout. We ate in one of these outdoor sidewalk café type places, and it was something like only Renoir could paint—colorful, bright, chattering people (certainly not English speaking), and thoroughly elegant! We ordered white wine, lobster and strawberries with cream for dessert, and it was by far the best all-around meal yet. Our waiter must have been trained in some very exclusive waiter's school, for when he brought the wine, he decorked [uncorked] it and poured a very small amount in my glass, giving a smiling nod of his head. Dumbfounded, I sat there a moment, smiling and nodding back, when I realized that I was supposed to taste it to see if it met with my approval. So I laughed embarrassingly and took a gulp—sure enough, it met with my approval. About 10 minutes later he brought a large silver platter over to our table, unveiled the serving dish (also silver), and asked me if the lobster looked all right. Did it look all right? I could have devoured it right there on the spot! It was lobster served in a cheese and mushroom sauce, resting in the lobster shell, and he served it to me, putting some kind of greenery on top. It was very rich, but it was the best-tasting dish I've had in days. After gobbling down the last morsel of lobster, we ordered the strawberries and cream, which was served in separate containers, a large heaping bowl of fresh strawberries and a generous pitcher of cream. It was delectable. The meal cost only $4.30.

    After eating, we headed for the concert hall, where the Copenhagen Symphony Orchestra was giving a free concert. They did Prokofiev, Tchaikovsky and Sibelius' Finlandia, which was great music, although the musicianship wasn't as good as I expected. They also did a Strauss Waltz, which was labeled "extra," and sounded about the same—unrehearsed. Don't misunderstand, it was a good concert, but not as good as possible. This concert hall is really amazing. It is very modern, acoustically perfect, and decorated very simply and beautifully.

    After the concert, we ran into the rest of the group, and went to the dance hall there, which I told you about last night. The band was swinging, the girls were beautiful, and we were sorry as hell that we didn't have dates—and I could have really kicked myself. We then wandered onto another dance pavilion, where we watched for a while, and finally ended up in a beer house overlooking one of the Tivoli lagoons, singing and watching the girls. There were hoards [hordes] of people there, many of them American, and when we sang "Auld Lang Syne," everyone stood up, raising their beer mugs to the sky. We left there about 12:00. On the way out, I took a few last glances at this overwhelming place. There were beautiful garlands of blue and red lights lining the edge of the lagoon, their mirrored reflections dancing in the water—and the sparkling fountains, pagodas and magic lanterns were one gorgeous blur of excitement, color and beauty. It is hard to describe.

    We boarded the trolley, Bill and I singing "Wonderful, wonderful, Copenhagen," and made our way back home. We stood in the back of the vehicle with the conductor and some old man, who were enjoying immensely our concert, and even asked us to sing "When Irish Eyes Are Smiling" and "Show Me the Way to Go Home." The conductor was terrific. He had a great big friendly smile and a wonderful sense of humor, and would mimic each passenger as they got off, in the Maurice Chevalier[2] manner, giving us a twinkling smile out of the corner of his eye. By the time we got off, we were all buddies and he waved a friendly "Cheerio" as we stepped off the trolley.

    It has truly been a wonderful day, and I'll never forget Copenhagen—and hope to come back someday.

Tomorrow we are taking the 11:30 ferry to Malmo, where Ann (Freddy's friend) will meet us to take us to their summer home. I'm hoping this can be sort of a vacation away from the vacation, a chance to write, relax, practice if I can find a piano, and catch up on sleep.

I'm very anxious to hear from you in Berlin, and also hope to find out about Stunt Show, so that I can start on that! I'll try to send the music to "The Creation" as soon as possible. Perhaps I can get to it in Malmo. Until tomorrow, goodnight.

Love, Tom

Torekov, Sweden—Saturday, July 6, 1963

Hi–

How can life be so wonderful! We are here in Sweden with the most hospitable and friendly family imaginable and it is a refreshing experience.

I got up this morning about 9:30 before any of the others, since I had a letter to mail and my sunglasses to see about. I walked down to the main street near our location, and after cashing a travelers check, bought four delicious Danish rolls and a pint of milk, which I devoured right there in the "Bageri," as they spell it. After that I went to the optical place to see if my glasses were ready. They weren't so I arranged to have them sent to American Express in Berlin. I then returned to our room about 11:00, since it was almost time to leave for the ferry trip, from Copenhagen to Malmo. Karl and Bill had made reservations for the one that left at 11:45, and we were supposed to be there a half-hour before it left. We gave ourselves only 15 minutes to get there, and it turned out to be quite a mistake, since we had first to pass through the main part of Copenhagen in the midst of all the city traffic. About 11:15 we were completely lost, and had to stop several times to ask directions. We ended up in the wrong spot and didn't actually find out where we were going until about noon. We had been directed to the port where passenger boats only travel to Malmo, and the spot we actually desired was "Frihavre," or Freeport, where the automobile ferry leaves. We got there about 12:15 and found out the next boat didn't depart until 1:30. While there, we ran into an American family, doctor, wife, son and friend of son, who were also motoring around Europe. They were very friendly and had been to many of the places where we were headed. They gave us hotel tips, and other suggestions, and we had a good time talking with them.

Rick and I had as yet not seen the mermaid in the harbor, for which Copenhagen is so famous, so we decided to walk that way, since we had plenty of time. Copenhagen's harbor is very beautiful, much more so than Hamburg's. The mermaid is not as big as she might be imagined, but is impressive in her own way. She sits perched on a large rock right in the water where the waves break, and she has a modest unimposing pose. She is simple and very charming. We had not much time to look at her, so we returned to the ferry, stopping to buy some postcards and a Coke.

Copenhagen's famous mermaid (before she was stolen!)

We boarded the ship at 1:30 and sailed for Sweden. I was excited to think that this was the first time I had crossed an international border on a ship. The vessel was similar to the one we had taken in Denmark, but missing so many hungry flapping seagulls and the sunset. There were seagulls, however, but not nearly the great amount there were on the other ferry. The water was fairly rough, and the boat rocked some, but not enough to cause any alarm. They sold cigarettes on the boat not subject to any tax (since it was between countries), and they only allowed one pack per person, stamping your ticket when you made the purchase. So I proceeded to gather 8 tickets from people who were not buying cigarettes, and bought that many packs of Winstons. By the way, I didn't quit smoking. It is too enjoyable having a smoke every once in a while over here. We grabbed a bite to eat on the boat, and changed some money into Swedish kroner, which we would be needing once we docked. The ride took about an hour and one-half, and we docked in Malmo at about 3:00.

We now had a new task ahead. In Sweden, as in England, cars drive the left side of the road instead of the right. It all seemed like a backwards movie, and there was the constant temptation to get in the right lane, but we did finally manage to get to Ann's apartment with no mishap.

All five of us trudged up to the door, and shortly, a tall, good-looking, smiling and friendly blonde (Ann, herself) came to the door, and rolled out the red carpet, upon which we are presently enjoying immensely.

Ann Bruzilius is her name, and she and her mother were both there to greet us. The apartment was extremely tasteful, roomy and very warm in feeling and décor. Ann and her mother are both very warm, congenial persons, and Ann speaks almost perfect English, although it has been a year since she has spoken it. Her mother also speaks English well, although her vocabulary does not measure up at all to Ann's.

They first sat us down to some piping hot coffee and Swedish pastries and cookies, which Ann herself had made—it was great. They next insisted that all five of us take baths—and no, it wasn't because they thought we needed it, although I did very badly, but because they realized that baths are a rarity in most European hotels, especially the variety we had been patronizing. We then proceeded to take them up on the proposition, I deciding to go last, since they had a piano and it had been since Heidelberg that I had played. We finished our baths, and blissfully and cleanfully took off for their summer home Womenok, her mother taking Bill and Rick, the rest of us with Ann in the Volks. Freddy drove, and did very well on the left side, and we talked and laughed about the left side driving business for about an hour, when Ann suddenly put her hand to her mouth, exclaiming, "Ah, no!" It seems that we had taken a wrong turn somewhere, and been going in the opposite direction now for almost 45 minutes. So we stopped, Ann asked directions, and we then proceeded West across Sweden through small towns and back roads—the only possible way to get where we wanted to go without taking more time. It was a real enjoyable trip, for Ann was able to tell us bits about the countryside, including agriculture, architecture, etc. We finally got here about 9:00. Before going to Ann's place, we stopped at the home of one of her girlfriends, who was to go out with us tonight. She is a real interesting girl, sort of pretty, and called Monica. She speaks very fine English, as she spent 8½ months in England, but her accent is extremely British—almost to the point where it sounds affected. But Ann said later that Monica comes from a very wealthy family.

This village is located right on the coast, near the Baltic as well as Atlantic. I've said this about every place we go, but this has been by far the best, most beautiful, and most fun. Ann has two younger sisters, Marianne 18, Ingrid 13, and a young brother Anders, 4. Her father is a bright eyed, intelligent and young looking person, with loads of charm and many questions to ask, funny comments to make, and plenty to talk about. He also speaks very good English, lacking only in vocabulary. Her sisters have also studied English, and do very well. Ann's brother is the cutest kid I've seen in years. He has white blonde hair, bright blue eyes, and is always laughing and talking. When we came in he was on his way to bed, and they had just taught him to say "goodnight," which he was doing so vehemently, as would most four-year-olds. The whole family is so wholesome, so young and full of life and love, that it is a refreshing observation.

The welcoming Swedish family

 Their home is located right on the ocean, and is simple, but quite tastefully decorated. They have five rooms and a bath, living room, bedroom and kitchen downstairs, two bedrooms upstairs. There is a fairly large hallway upstairs between the two bedrooms that is much like a sitting room, with windows and a balcony overlooking the ocean. The living room is painted white, and much of the furniture likewise, with the color in the room made up by such things as the red brick fireplace, the pictures on the walls, the curtains and upholstery on the furniture. It has a very contemporary and clean look, without losing any of its warmth. The rest of the house is decorated similarly, using contrasts in color to make it seem so complete, clean and comfortable. They live here from the end of May to the first of September each year. Ann says that, at least in their circle of friends, it is common for the father to live at home during the week in Malmo, coming here only on weekends and vacations. Her father, by the way, is a CPA in Malmo.

But the real important thing about this place is the ocean. The sounds of the waves breaking on the rocks is constantly heard, as are the wails of seagulls as they fly overhead.

In the back of their house is a garage and connected to this is a small bedroom, with 2 bunks, table and chairs. This is where Karl and I are staying, and we have a beautiful view from the room of the ocean and villages. There is no electricity in this room, so I am writing by candlelight, and I can hear the wind howling around the building and the water breaking on the rocks. You feel like you are the only person left in the whole world, and it is a funny feeling—but very peaceful.

After getting settled, we sat down to a tasty meal of Swedish meatballs, potatoes, salad, coffee and homemade shortcake with piles of whipped cream and fresh strawberries. We then put suits on, the girls dressed up, and we headed for a night club type place about 15 minutes up the coast. We stopped to pick up Monica on the way, and even borrowed her car, since there were so many of us. Here in Sweden, there is no such thing as dating, but the kids do everything in groups, so there were five of us, and three girls, Ann, her sister and Monica. When we arrived at the place, there were too many people downstairs, so we got a table upstairs, and made the mistake of ordering lobster and salmon as hors-d'oeuvres—it was a mistake because the bill amounted to about 192 kroners, which is about $38.60. We didn't know that it would be so expensive! But the girls chipped in, hurting our pride, but at that point, pride had to be forgotten. There was a band there, and we danced and really enjoyed ourselves. At 12:45, we went downstairs where most of the young people hang out, and it was so very crowded, that we had no room at all to move, so we left about 1:30. The stories of how beautiful the Swedish women are have all proven to be true. I have never seen so many luscious blondes in my life, and they all seem to wear their hair long and stringy—very sexy!

On the way back someone suggested that we go swimming upon returning, an idea which sounded strange to us in weather of about 68 degrees, but they all seemed to think that it was quite the normal thing to do. But since it was so late and we wanted to get up early we finally decided against it, a decision I was somewhat happy to hear.

Bill, Monica, Marianne and I drove back in Monica's car, and decided to walk from her house to Ann's. After bidding her goodnight, which was a production in itself, she muttering in that fantastic British accent such things as "Sleep well; see you in the morning," etc. and we laughing to ourselves trying to believe that this could all be true, we started walking along the beach. It was about 3:00 AM and there was a bright white full moon, few clouds and the sun already rising in the east. We walked through a campsite, which was completely silent, and on around the coast, passing the fishermen's small houses and the villages. It was about a half-hour walk, and quite beautiful. It was very light in the sky, and it seemed strange to be so at such an odd hour. We had some trouble talking with Marianne since she wasn't up so much on her English, and had a hard time understanding our questions. We would constantly rephrase everything until she would finally recognize the word or synonym that she had studied—it was fun.

We got back to the house after about a half-hour, and it was already 3:00. We decided to go to bed then so we wouldn't sleep all day tomorrow. So here I am, reflecting on these very wonderful people in these beautiful surroundings. Until tomorrow, good night.

Love, Tom

Torekov, Sweden—Sunday, July 7, 1963

Hi-

We slept in this morning, until about 11:00, and it was a very restful sleep. We walked over to the house, sat down to a filling breakfast of bread, cheese, cereal, coffee, milk and jam, and spent the next half hour or so discussing what we would do today. This family is so very hospitable and friendly that we are really taken aback!

It was a cold day and kind of rainy, but we decided to go swimming this afternoon in spite of it all. Up here the Swedish people seem to think nothing of jumping around in icy water like Polar bears. And you know the old saying, "When in Sweden, do as…" So this afternoon we went swimming. Their home is set back from the coast about a quarter mile, although it's not out of "seeing the ocean" range. We walked down the road toward the water, through an old wooden town-gate, and along the coast heading north where there is a long swimming pier about a mile away. We also had to walk through the old fishing village which is now filled with swarming city folk from either Malmo or Stockholm. We had our swimming suits on under our clothes, and when we got to the spot, everyone strips, doesn't take time to think how cold he is, and makes a running leap off the end of the dock. Then it's too late to try to get out, and surprisingly enough, the water is warmer than the air, and feels terrific. Karl and I stayed in longer than anyone, and it was great fun, as it had been ages since I had been swimming. After climbing shivering out of the water, we got dressed right there on the beach. You use a robe, a great big roomy one, and the whole matter is very simple, although hard for most Americans to get used to, so they said. It didn't bother me in the least!

After we got dressed we sat around on the rocks talking, and I even got a Swedish rubdown from Ann, who is indeed a perfect girl. She cooks well and looks well. It rhymes, and it should. She's a doll. If only Freddy hadn't dated her—whoops. I'd better get back to business.

We went back to the house, stopping on the way back to buy Anders (Ann's little brother) a shovel to play with in the sand. Dinner tonight was really delicious—eating out has been fun, but these homemade Swedish dishes are the best yet! We had sausage (great big pieces which were covered in a really tasty cheese sauce), beer, cauliflower, potatoes, salad with sour cream, vinegar and sugar—and Libby's pineapple for dessert. They all laughed about the brand. The meal tasted tremendous, and being back in a family atmosphere was such a welcome change. Mrs. B. is a wonderful, wonderful person and words are hard to find in describing her. She speaks just enough English to make her very cute, and she has a sense of humor that is tops. She and Mr. Bruzilius make a very lively, fun-loving, witty couple, and as I said last night, they are doing their most to show us a good time—without putting on any airs at all. From what I can gather, they frequently have a house full of guests, so the five of us are not the burden we seem. At least, Ann keeps reassuring us that we are not—I'm not going to worry about it.

After dinner, we decided to go to the cinema, as they call it. There is a very small movie theater in Torekov, and after seeing it, I agreed especially to the very small part. The machinery is not what it should be, Ann says, as it often broke down in the middle of the movies, sometimes in the very tender love scenes, and Ann says that at that time, there are catcalls and all kinds of ruckus until it is again fixed. We had a great big gang to go—the four of us, Marianne, Monica, Ingrid, and Ingrid's friend Bodel. Ann and Freddy didn't go because Freddy woke up today with sore eyes from his contact lenses, and he couldn't see, they had to take him to the hospital, get medicine, and go through a lot of malarkey which sort of repulsed me, because it couldn't have happened to anyone else. The whole family huddled around him with pills and ointments all day.

Anyway, Ann stayed home nursing Freddy (damnit!) and the rest of us carted off to a movie we wouldn't be able to understand anyway since it was in Swedish. Fear not, all is not lost! I had a good time anyway. Ann's sister, Ingrid, a lovely young thing of 13, had studied English for 2 years, so she sat by me in the show and tried to translate. She didn't know much English, but what she did know helped a great deal. Moreover, the film—being a mystery thriller that was so much killing, murdering, finding bodies, walking in tombs, etc.—was very self-explanatory in most parts. It was interesting.

We walked back after it was all over, and when we walked in the door, there was not only a roaring fire in the fireplace, but a table filled with hot coffee, bread, cookies, butter, cheese, and other things to feed on. After doing so for the next hour or so, we decided to retire. I had everyone kind of scared, pulling a monster type act. It was really not very good, but the fact that I could hold it so long without laughing was the real convincing part, and the girls seemed indeed convinced—almost to the point that they wondered if perhaps I was crazy. And it was especially effective after the movie—which was most conducive to rousing the horror type emotions in one.

So here I am and it is late—and the candle is running low. It's strange how it hardly ever gets really black here. Sun is rising so soon after falling—and from the window I can see the ocean, the white waves breaking over the rocks. Beautiful and eerie. Until tomorrow, good night.

Love, Tom

Torekov, Sweden—Monday, July 8, 1963

Hi-

Another very fine day—oh, how can one be so lucky. To think that it was doubtful that I took this trip seems like a dangerous thought. I have learned so much, had so much fun, really become inspired by all the beautiful and interesting things I've seen, that the thought of not being able to make it is sickening. I feel very lucky.

I got up this morning about 10:00, to find everyone already up and gone. So I went in, sat down to the typical Swedish breakfast of bread, cheese, coffee and jam, and then found out the others had just gone down to the house where Ann and Marianne were sleeping to roust them. I decided that this was perhaps a good day to wash clothes, and before I had a chance to even try, Mrs. B. insisted on washing them for me, which was just fine, but I hated for her to do it—but as much as I protested—she wouldn't budge. So she washed my shorts, undershirts, shirts and socks. To tell the truth, I was kind of embarrassed to have her wash my clothes since they were all stained and extremely filthy. I had held off washing for several days, and had arrived in Sweden in very stiff clothes. You know—the kind that stick to the ceiling. Anyway, the clothes got washed and that is one thing off my mind.

The guys with Ann and Marianne overlooking the beautiful Baltic

Today was another rainy day, and after a lunch of fried potatoes and sausage, we all decided to go to Bastad shopping. So seven of us took off in the Volkswagen right after lunch, the five of us and the two girls, Ann and Marianne. Believe me it was a cozy fit. On the way to Bastad, Ann knew of a beautiful area along the coast, where the shore is mostly cliffs and beautiful high rocks and formations. So we stopped and went walking there along the coast, and it was indeed as beautiful as we had been told. We walked along the cliff, perhaps several hundred feet above the water, and the waves were splashing on the shore, the breakers spreading their white foam on the sand and rocks, and the water forming its beautiful endless patterns—waves continually piling on top of one that has had its cycle and is retreating. It is fascinating to watch the water of the ocean, the waves which look different and do something different each time around. Also the pattern of the foam on the beach and rocks is so interesting to watch. And the most thought-provoking, inspiring thing about the sea, and especially when you sit alone watching it, is the fact that it has been just the same beautiful thing for centuries ad infinitum, the same sight to men who lived in untold times, the same sight to those who existed before me. Sitting alone like this, and thinking like this sends a small chill up the spine, and even though this sounds cliché-ish and silly, I even felt tears in my eyes—not really sad tears, but tears for a different reason—perhaps for the beauty, perhaps because you realize how ridiculous so many things in the world are—so many things that are considered important. You realize how really unimportant these petty things are. It really is impossible to try to express the feeling—but this might suffice. But the wind roaring around you, the sound of the water and the blue horizon of water is probably more reason for tears.

Back to ground—we walked along the cliffs for about an hour, running in a wood to get out from under a sudden rainstorm, and then loaded back in the Volkswagen. We drove on to Bastad, parked the car, and headed for an old shop that had been there since 1770. It was an old home that had been converted into a shop for the sale of hand made crafts—cloth and dishes. The cloth in particular, hand made scarves, placemats, tablecloths, napkins, etc. were really beautiful, and if I had had a lot of money, I would have bought them. And their prices were particularly low and well worth taking advantage of. But since I've already spent quite a lot of money, I couldn't afford it. But there will be a next time.

Bastad is a clean, bright and extremely traditional town, very well preserved and fun to browse around in. Bill and Freddy bought yarn there, since the girls offered to knit them sweaters, and I was green with envy, but managed to control my jealousy so they didn't notice. But later Ann said that she would do the same for us if she found the time—so all was not lost!

We headed back for Torekov about 6:00, and got back just in time for dinner—which consisted of a delicious cabbage and ground pork casserole served with lingonberries (similar to cranberries, but not so bitter), salad, potatoes, beer and famous Swedish pancakes with strawberries for dessert. Here in Sweden pancakes are always served as dessert, and are never served with syrup or as a main course. The cabbage stuff was particularly good and we all talked about taking the recipes home, but later forgot all about it. Mr. Bruzilius was not with us tonight, as he had left early this morning for his work in Malmo. He left the message that he was glad to have met us and talked about politics, Kennedy, etc, and that we are welcome to come back anytime that we feel like it.

After dinner, there was a mad scramble to get things cleaned up, as we were planning on going to a play given at the church. At this moment, the sun was setting over the ocean, so Rick and I decided not to go and to instead go down to the shore to watch the sunset. I ended up going alone, and spent about 2 hours there, walking along the water, watching the sea, and thinking. It was at this time that I felt most humbled by the natural spectacle of the sunset, water and sound. The wind was strong, and that with the combination of the roar of the waves as they broke, one by one, on the rocks, was a sound that seemed to close out the rest of the world. I didn't want to leave—but Monica had invited the whole crew to her house after the play, and Rick, Marianne and I were planning on walking to her place about 9:00.

The sun still hadn't set by this time, but it was almost through. One interesting thing about the sunset, and especially when there are quite a few clouds in the sky, is the constantly changing patterns formed by the sun rays as it shoots through holes in the clouds as it makes the journey downward. At times, there would be a perfectly symmetrical pattern of light rays clearly seen as a halo several miles out at sea—and at other times there would be only one glorious group of rays shining through on the shore or the hills in the distance. It was a beautiful sight.

The three of us left the house around 9:00 and headed along the shore to Monica's house. It is about a half-hour walk, and a very impressive one. We walked the same direction we did yesterday toward the swimming pier, through the village, and around several inlets—even through a campsite and a golf course. We saw Monica's house perched on a hill right on the ocean, on a small peninsula. It was an old shepherd's house that her parents had bought and fixed up. Upon walking in, we were immediately impressed with the feast that lay before us. The small living room was all lit in candlelight, and on the table were all kinds of pastries, cakes and cookies, as well as a steaming pot of hot tea—and it looked great since we were kind of chilled, after walking along the windy shore.

I was extremely impressed with the way the house was decorated. Even though small, it was almost as if it had been a movie set with extremely expensive taste used throughout. The living room was all painted white, and much of the furniture likewise, with fruitwood chairs, etc. used as a complement. The windows were particularly interesting, as the walls of the old house were about a foot-and-a-half or two feet thick, thus causing the windows to be set out from the side walls. The furnishings, such as a beautiful miniature sailboat, interesting sea painting (original or inherited) and unusual candle holders, really set the place off.

The food was something else again. The pastries and cookies were special Swedish type, and some of them from a shop that refused to give out recipes. Mrs. B. had baked a delicious pound cake with almonds, and with this combined with the piping hot tea and everything else, we stuffed ourselves for the next few hours. It was really a beautiful evening. Ann and Marianne were knitting, we sang song after song, including most of our school and fraternity songs and Broadway tunes, etc, and talked about everything from Swedish and American customs to politics and Kennedy. The Swedish people, although claiming to be neutral, are actually very dependent on the United States—Mrs. B. made it a point to emphasize this to me. Monica is such a very funny girl—typical female, but so much nuttier with her wild British accent and scatterbrained mannerisms. She is quite a character! We left her place about 12:30, very reluctantly, since it was such a perfect evening. I can't remember having such a good time in quite a while. We came back in the car, Freddy and Ann deciding to walk back.

It's now late, and I must go to bed. Until tomorrow, *au revoir*, *bon soir*, or something!

Love, Tom

Somewhere on the Baltic Sea—Tuesday, July 9, 1963

Hi–

Today has been quite tiring, so this letter probably won't be too long, but the way I ramble, you never know! We got up about 10:30, ate another typical Swedish breakfast, and got ready to depart. We had set our departure time for about 1:00, but we all know that it would be later than that—it always seems to work out that way. After breakfast, Mrs. B. insisted on ironing my shirts, and even though I had intended on doing them myself, she persisted, so what can you do. These people are so hospitable! During this time, three of us walked down to get Ann and Marianne, and it looked like it was going to be a beautiful day. The weather would get nice just when we are leaving—that's the way it goes, I guess!

We returned, and I was running all over the place trying to gather shirts, underwear, and all kinds of other stuff that was scattered here and there over the household. The girls then decided it would be a great idea to go swimming, and so they took off in the car with Freddy and Rick before Bill and I were ready. Karl decided not to go as it was a nice but chilly day—but Bill and I went along with the crowd and walked down to the swimming dock along the beach. By the time we got there, they had already been in and out of the water, and said that it was ice cold. But Bill and I, too proud to chicken out at this late date, stripped our clothes and went running down the dock, not waiting to see if they were right, but diving right in, finding out first-hand that they were absolutely right. That water was so cold, I must have turned five shades of lavender and purple for all the cold-blooded fish, and I did a few churns and got right out. Even though it was ice cold, it was really an eye-opener, and I was amazingly alert and awake after that dip. Before I had been kind of groggy, probably due to all the food we had eaten last night.

After our swim, we returned, got packed and sat down to a delicious lunch of ham and tomatoes in cheese sauce, salad and beer. After meals it is a custom for each member of the family to shake hands with the mother or father, and say *"Tak so muks,"* which means "thanks so much for the food." Ingrid proceeded to do this, and I feeling in a jovial mood, followed suit. Well, this got the biggest laugh of the day because in doing so I curtsied as Ingrid did, when actually the fellows are supposed to nod their heads. Well, the whole family thought that this was very funny, and they chuckled about it for quite a while—and I couldn't help but laugh myself—they say that ignorance is bliss!

As I expected, we didn't get away at 1:00, but did manage to leave by 2:00. Before we left, we had to take pictures, hug, shake hands, and go through the usual farewell procedures. Truthfully, we all hated to leave since it had been such a wonderful time, and I'm sure I'll look back on these three days as one of the best times all summer. Before leaving we performed our "switch" for them, and went tearing down the road leaving a cloud of dust where they were standing. They were waving until we rounded the bend in the road, and the whole thing was sort of sad. In another way, we were glad to be back on the road, and headed for such fascinating sounding places.

I was behind the wheel, and we were on our way back to Malmo. It was still difficult getting used to driving in the left lane, and we all dreaded driving in the British Isles, which have the same kind of setup, road-wise. We got to Malmo about 3:30, and upon arrival, parked the car, bought ice-cream cones, and set out to do some window shopping or buying. I bought this new pen today since I have been dying for a fountain pen, and the other one I brought along klonked [conked] out on me. Sweden, you know, is famous for its crystal, so I went to the special shop that sells it, and sent Bernice[3] and her husband a beautiful, beautiful vase that cost me about $10.00. It was such a good deal though that I couldn't pass it up. The outside is pure white crystal, the darker part a deep blue. It is heavy glass, and must cost 3 or 4 times as much in the U.S. I remember from Peacocks[4] the tremendous cost of such items, so I felt very lucky to get it. What did you send her for the wedding?

We had already made reservations for the ferry ride from Sweden to Germany, and since the boat didn't leave until 11:20, we thought it best to waste as much time as possible. We left Malmo at about 5:30, and I forgot to check at Am. Express (if they had one) for mail. I hope you didn't write there!

We arrived in Trelleborg, the port town from which the ferry left about an hour later, and after Karl went hunting to see about reservations and Rick and I went poster hunting, we found a small restaurant in a hotel that looked fairly cheap, where we had dinner. We had some kind of wiener schnitzel with potatoes and gravy, beer and ice cream for about $1.50, and while there met some very interesting people. Two fellows sitting at another table, one a Swede from Trelleborg and one a West Berliner on vacation, were really characters. They both spoke good English, and we invited them over to the table. The West Berliner had much advice to give about his fair city, and the Swede was becoming more and more obnoxious as he took successive drinks of some mixed drink, slowly getting looped. And to top it off, the captain from the boat he worked on was in the restaurant in a kind of drunken stupor, muttering to us in Swedish, and making a real idiot out of himself. It was another lively production leaving the place, with the combination of trying to pay the old fat waitress the bill and speaking broken English and German simultaneously—everyone yelling.

When we finally got out again in fresh air, we decided it best to see about the ferry, and by this time, we were too tired to do any sightseeing, and since there was nothing to see anyway, sat in the car until 11:00 when they started boarding.

The ferry was mammoth, and since it was going to be a 9 hour trip (all night), upon boarding, we bought tickets for sleeping chairs. So here I am on the boat writing. It is a boat dating back probably to 1920, and the decorations and construction is very much like you would expect one of these things to look—wood paneling, mahogany furniture, partly stained glass windows, etc. Karl and Bill, who were having a beer in the bar, fully expected to see some mysterious looking beautiful Marlene Dietrich type to come slinking in, trench coat, rimmed hat, the works, sipping on a glass of wine, and staring at them. This didn't happen, but it should have. It is rather exciting, crossing the Baltic Sea so late at night.

I'm bushed, and it will be a long day tomorrow, with probably very little sleep in these damned chairs. Until tomorrow night, au viterseine [auf Wiedersehen].

Love, Tom

BERLIN
5
Trouble at Checkpoint Charlie

To the victors went the spoils. Following World War II, the Allies agreed on a negotiated division of Germany. The three major occupation zones—American, British and French—became West Germany; and the Russian or Communist held zone became East Germany. Berlin which lay completely within the Soviet area was also divided.

Tensions ran high between the two German states and in l961 Walter Ulbricht, the East German leader, built the Berlin Wall to prevent East Germans from fleeing into West Germany. The wall prevented almost all emigration to the west for the next twenty-eight years. Over three hundred people lost their lives attempting to cross the wall—another five thousand were captured.

Checkpoint Charlie in the American zone became the best-known entry point between East and West Germany. The five guys got to experience this in a way they will long remember.

§ § §

Berlin—Wednesday, July 10, 1963

Hi–

Well here we are—in Berlin. I had quite a restless night on the ferry, not that the trip was rough, but those damned chairs were so uncomfortable to sleep in. Karl and I were the first ones up at 6:30, and we decided to go to the boat dining room for breakfast. For 3 DM[1] (75 cents), we had a real good meal of all the coffee or tea we could drink (I took tea), bread (both rye and whole wheat), cheese and butter. The bread in Sweden and on this boat was not really comparable to any we serve—it is heavier, and somehow tastier. Rick soon joined us, and we sat there eating, smoking and relaxing until about 8:00 when the boat was nearing the port. We were within a mile of the East German coast for about an hour, and this made us anxious more than ever to get to Berlin as soon as possible. Bill decided to have only coffee for his breakfast, and Freddy was busy writing. We soon piled into the car in the hold of the ship, all of us kind of tired and disagreeable, as well as feeling mungy [grungy]—the way you feel after sleeping in your clothes.

Before we had driven far at all, we found ourselves in Lubeck—the town of the seven steeples. Lubeck was well-known to us for two things only, its cathedrals and its town gate. So the first thing we did here was park the car, where I finished writing my post cards from Copenhagen (slightly late), and then find a rest room, where I could get cleaned up. Incidentally, I had a funny thing happen. I walked into a men's store, asking the clerk if I could use the toilet (toilette in German). Well, he didn't understand what I wanted, and kept bringing out shirts, socks, sweaters, trousers, etc., until I finally managed to explain to him that all I really wanted was a place to relieve myself. When he caught on, he thought it was very funny, and so did I later, but at the time, it was most imperative to take care of the business at hand—business which can't wait. Anyway, after returning to the car, we took a look at the Cathedral, which was very much different from any others we had seen. The exterior was red brick, badly damaged from the war, and very unimpressive. But the inside was quite impressive in its uniqueness. It was very bright and colorful in contrast to many churches which had dark, dingy interiors, and was characterized mostly by its combination of white wash walls with red brick trim. Also many murals had been uncovered, and there was a lot of colorful trim lining some of the Gothic vaulted ceilings, and the tall mammoth pillars. It was not spectacular, but its unusualness made it appealing. Another strange thing about the statues decorating the church was the fact that they had a skeletal appearance. Many of the angels had skeleton heads carved out of stone, and it indeed seemed quite different from most of the statues which decorate European churches and cathedrals. I stayed there only about 15 minutes, and then returned to the car, where we decided to grab a bite to eat, even though it was only about 11:15.

    Bill, Karl and I went hunting for a place to get a sandwich, Rick and Freddy deciding to try the nearest grocery store. I was in no mood to play do-it-yourself-sandwich, so we found a typical German restaurant and ate ham sandwiches and beer. The sandwich left a lot to be desired, but I was beyond the point of caring, so we ate quickly and returned to the car.

    Our next plan of strategy was to check out the old town gate and leave as soon as possible. The old gate was built in 1477 and is now a local museum. It is really an interesting looking old place, and we noticed that there was a sag in the middle—almost as if it were going to collapse any moment. We stayed there for about a half-hour, buying post cards, taking pictures, and standing under a tree to avoid a sudden rainfall. Lubeck is quite an interesting town, and we were sorry not to be able to stay there longer. It was founded in 1143 by Duke Adolf II of Schaumburg, and was an important trading center and cultural exchange for centuries. It is a leading producer of red wine. Its population is 238,000 and is now a tourist and industrial city.

    We left Lubeck about 12:30 and headed for Berlin, following the road signs. After a few miles we stopped to replenish Victoria with gas, and at the station, found out that the East-West border was only 1 kilometer from where we were, so we decided to drive to the border to see what it was like. I was somewhat nervous about the whole thing, but decided that there was really nothing to worry about, so we drove about 5 kilometers, turned left on a small road, and headed for the border. It soon became apparent that we were near the border, for there were many signs giving warning and distance. We parked the car about 100 yards from the border, where we could see a bridge, a West German soldier on guard at the bridge, and a gate painted bright red in front of the bridge preventing entry. We then walked slowly toward the bridge, which we then noticed was a very small old wooden relic with no road at all on the other side. The river was narrow, and there were boats on it and children swimming. The guard on the bridge had binoculars, and was peering through them at an old wooden tower on the other side, about 200 yards from the river. He glanced down at us, nodded, and seemed friendly enough, so we decided to go talk to him. What a blessing Karl speaks German—we are getting quite an insight. He not only talked to us, but led us across the bridge onto E. German soil, so that we could get a better view of the town across the field thru his binoculars. There is, you know, an area of 5000 meters (1 meter slightly longer than a yard) along the border of E. Germany where no E. Germans are allowed unless they are confirmed communists or perhaps Polish or Hungarian foreigners. This area is heavily guarded, mined, and triggered, that is, it has sticks or wires in the fields which set off rocket flares, in case there are any attempted escapes at night. There are, within this 5000 meter strip, five guard houses, none of them at all coordinated, so that there is less chance of someone escaping thru one, without being seen by another. They really make it very difficult for one to escape, and it's a strange feeling, standing on free soil, realizing that on the other side, no one is allowed to leave, or even think about it. Through his binoculars, we could see the two men who manned the tower area across the field, and he then pointed out other towers, one to our left about a quarter mile away, one on the right about the same distance, and one over a hill, directly behind the one nearest. He then explained that the chances of escape here were very slim, and that the best opportunity was still in Berlin, although that was now becoming a bad risk. Another interesting thing was a road they had put in of dust all along the border, which is smoothed down every day, so that footprints can be seen when they check on the following day. We were there about a half-hour, and it was quite an eye-opener. People in the United States, not all but many, like myself, are simply oblivious to things like this. And I'll be the first to admit that I am one of those– until now. One's interest is kindled greatly by seeing these things first-hand, and it is a shame that more people can't witness it. It is sad and pathetic to realize that today, in the modern world, there exists something as ridiculous as a wall between two countries—and especially two countries who desire to be one. It's like brother against brother. I compare it to the childish-sounding medieval dungeons, moats, and walls built 500 years ago. But I haven't lived through a war as you, so I suppose I'm only an idealistic idiot about the whole thing. But, admittedly, it is a horrible, hopeless situation, especially for the East Germans.

We then walked back to the car, piled in and took off for Berlin. We followed the signs that said "Berlin—26k"—but upon reaching the border crossing, found out we didn't have the right visa to cross over there, so were forced to drive to Helmstedt, the only place where we could go across to Berlin, without a special visa. We talked about spending the night there, but as it was only 6:30 by the time we arrived in Helmstedt, and it takes only about two hours to drive to Berlin, we decided to make the trip tonight. Once the decision was made, there was no backing out, and what followed was pure hell! No wonder tourists are discouraged from traveling to Berlin. We first had to show our passports to the West German police, then proceed through E. German customs, which is an inefficient, bothersome, hectic ordeal. We had to park the car and go into a barrack where we could get the tourist's visa. We stood in line for a half-hour waiting only for the right form to fill out, and after receiving those, proceeded on a long drawn-out questionnaire, one asking things about occupation, money, etc. After completing this, we again stood in line at another window for another half-hour to get the visa, which cost about $2.00. After this, we had to go to another window where the questionnaires and passports are checked thoroughly, and finally, we were allowed to go. We wondered if the inefficiency of the whole mess wasn't planned—it seemed obvious. We then drove on to another check of passports and visas, and to aggravate us even more, were told there that we had not the proper pass for the car—so Karl had to walk all the way back to the barracks to get the pass for the car—which cost an additional amount. We then went through another E. German check, and finally a Soviet check. And to top it off, at the Soviet check, they told us we didn't have some other kind of paper we needed, but instead of making us go back they filled it out for us right there—it sort of rekindled my faith in the human race! One of the Russian soldiers was very friendly, but the other had the sourest expression I've seen, giving us a particular going over. Perhaps it was my imagination.

At last, we were on the Autobahn headed for Berlin, and it was a relief to be away from all the red tape. However, that relief was balanced in the opposite side by an anticipation that we acquired simply by being on E. German, Communist soil. Our plan to be in Berlin by 8:30 had certainly backfired, since it was then about 8:30—exactly an hour and 50 minutes since we had started thru customs.

The drive on the Autobahn was interesting however and the countryside extremely beautiful, the road signs in German and Russian. All along the way were bridges crossing the road, and at almost each one, were several people standing by and hanging over the railings, waving to us as we drove by. There were also teenage boys all along the way who stood by the highway begging for cigarettes. It was a disheartening ride in that way—these people knowing that we are free, and they aren't and never will be. It tends to make one acutely aware of the difference.

At about 9:30, it began to get dark, and about 10:00, we saw signs indicating that we were close to Berlin. At one point, we almost made a terrible mistake. One sign said, "Berlin—straight ahead" and the smaller one under it had the names of several other towns, the one on the bottom being "West Berlin—to the right." The great temptation at first sight was to go on straight, but we caught it in time to go right to West Berlin. God knows, we didn't want to go to East Berlin! The East Germans refer to East Berlin as simply "Berlin"—and they make no distinction, except for calling West Berlin by its proper name.

We arrived in Berlin about 10:30, and the first foremost thing on our minds was to find a hotel, which took an hour-and-a half. We drove and drove, asked directions, finally ended up walking all over downtown Berlin looking for a place. There was just no room anywhere. Finally, we found a place on an off-street, and it is a very nice place, although the price is $2.50. The rooms are enormous and there is even a bathroom. It is on Hietzenburger Strasse, which is close to downtown, but we're too tired to really care where the hell it is.

Tomorrow we are going to catch up on sleep, get mail at Am. Express, and try to get orientated to the city—as well as try to find a cheaper place to stay. Berlin already looks beautiful. It reminds me much of Paris—large streets, sidewalk cafés all along Kurfurstendamm, the main street (Berlin's Fifth Avenue) and busy, breathing people. It looks very thriving.

Well, I must sign off. Until tomorrow, good night.

Love, Tom

Berlin—Thursday, July 11, 1963

Hi–

Oh, how wonderful it was to get mail today—I think that I've never been quite as excited over getting mail. We slept late this morning—until about 10:30, and after getting up, we all took baths. It was the best bath I've had in ages—as a matter of fact, it had been ages since I had one, Malmo, to be exact. By the time everyone had bathed, it was noon, and by this time, we were anxious to get down to American Express to pick up mail, see if there were any messages from other U. of I.[2] kids, and get oriented—as well as finding a cheaper place to stay.

We hopped in the car and upon arriving at Am. Express, found that it was closed till 1:30, so on that note, we set out to eat lunch. We crossed the Michigan Avenue of Berlin, Kurfurstendamm, to a place that resembled the New York Automat, where I had a bowl of delicious bean soup, a bratwurst and glass of beer for about 80 cents—very cheap, and very good. The Kurfurstendamm is quite an impressive thoroughfare, and reminded me much of the Champs-Élysées in Paris. The sidewalk cafes with their bright colored awnings, the movie theaters with almost all American movies in German translation, and the elegant shops boasting everything from men's pointed shoes to fine china and silverware. The street is set off by the Kaiser Wilhelm memorial church, a large triple structure including what's left of the original church, plus a new church, very modernistic in looks, and fairly small. There is also a new bell tower, matching the new church, on the other side of the original. The new church and bell tower are called by W. Berliners the "powder box" and the "lipstick," as they do resemble such. The glass used in the new structures were brought from Chartres country, so famous for its beautiful Chartres blue.

Kaiser Wilhelm memorial church in West Berlin—the "powder box and lipstick"

At 1:30 we headed back across the street for Am. Express, and then picked up our letters. American Express here in Berlin is about one third the size of the office in Paris and about half the size of the same in Copenhagen. We hear that many Americans are afraid to come to Berlin, and being here, that sounds ridiculous, but some of the red tape at the border might discourage many, especially those who know no German. But how great it was to get mail—you don't know—I received two letters from you, one from Ann, two from Mary Louise, and two from Mary. We all sat around there laughing while reading, each of us anxious to tell each other news from home.

After we left American Express, we then headed for the Berlin Technical University, which we had heard had a gasthaus for tourists— and very cheap. We traipsed around for about an hour, and finally, after finding out that their gasthaus was on the other side of town, we took refuge in the train station, which then informed us to go to Amerika Haus, directly across the street. Sure enough, the lady there found us a place to stay on Cornerstrasse, called Hotel Pension Schifft. Rick, Freddy and I headed back to pick up the car, while Karl and Bill took off for the hotel. When we tried to find the street, it was impossible, and we drove all over hell's half acre until fed up. I decided we had better go back to Amerika Haus to get fresh directions. At last we found the hotel—we had just gone too far. While at Amerika Haus, there was a

Chinese American from San Francisco there looking for lodging, so it worked out that he stayed with us in a six-man room. Believe me, it is very crowded! The hotel is run by a Jewish fellow who is quite a character. His father had been a millionaire in East Germany before the war, and he rattles on and on about how much he is making, with his American Stock and his small hotel business. He sends 5,000 Deutch [Deutsche] Marks to Israel each year and says he doesn't need a big house or car. He said that he would be in Israel now were it not for his elderly mother, who is too old to travel. He's quite an unusual person.

    After getting settled down, I decided to try to hunt down my sunglasses from Copenhagen, so I walked for blocks and blocks till I came to the Post Office on the slip of paper which American Express had given me. Talk about exasperating—when I finally found the proper window, the man didn't have the package, but filled out another official looking document, and pointed to another address. I felt like an idiot, not being able to communicate at all, and not being able to understand what he kept yelling about. I did finally find a student there who spoke enough English to tell me that I was to pick up the package in another place. It was already 5:15, and there was no time left today to get it—I'll now have to wait. On the way back I stopped at American Express to see if there was any more mail. There was no mail, but there was a message from Betsy Baldwin, a friend from school, that she and the other three girls she was with, were in Berlin, and would appreciate a call before they left in the morning. So when I got back to the hotel, I gave her a ring, and we planned a wine party in their room at 10:30 since I had a lot of writing to do and the others did also. At about 7:30, the five of us headed for a restaurant on Kunststrasse, called the Paris Bar, and supposedly famous as a student professor, arty type place. Sure enough, the food was very good, and the atmosphere was more Parisian than Paris. There were drawings on the walls of the famous Paris attractions, the Métro, the Eiffel Tower, the Seine, etc. I had onion soup, 2 steaks (small), French fries, wine and apples for dessert. It was a delicious meal for only about $1.00. We sat around talking, comparing notes of the afternoon. Karl had bought 5 tickets for the Symphony Saturday night, and Bill and Freddy had walked all the way to Brandenburg Gate. I wasn't very excited, of course, with my wild goose chase after the package, but it was a good meal with good conversation. Afterwards we talked about U. of I, and so much of the silly petty things that seem important there. It's no wonder the Berliners are bright, sophisticated looking people with a half sober look. They have something to worry about.

    After eating we returned to the hotel, and Bill called a fellow by the name of Al Courier, who was and is a friend of John Rice. He is a minister in West Berlin, and one who spends a great deal of time working in East Berlin with the few Christians who are left there. He wasn't at home, but his wife told us that tomorrow he is taking a group of students from Minnesota over—some segment of a Presbyterian workshop for students and church people from the United States. She thought that perhaps we could join them, giving us more of a complete picture of the East German situation. She said that we would have to wait until tomorrow morning, and that she would have him call about 8:00. It sounds very exciting!

    We all wrote until about 10:30, and then Bill, Karl and I headed for the girls' hotel, Rick and Freddy, too tired to go. We stopped on the way and bought a bottle of wine for about 85 cents, and then took about a half-hour in finding the place. The girls were waiting for us, and after much greeting, how are you's, etc. they asked us to go with them down to Check Point Charlie, the place where Americans and British can cross over to E. Berlin, and give the American Officials the time you'll be back as a safeguard, so that if you aren't back, they will go searching. We were there for about 15 minutes, talking and watching the guards, police, and people who were crossing over or coming back. There were very few at that hour, but it was an interesting sight. The wall between the two sections is just as you would imagine—very crudely built, and thoroughly fortified. We drove back to the hotel, where we stayed till about 2:00 AM comparing notes, drinking wine, and having a great time. One of the girls had refused to go with us to Checkpoint Charlie, because she was afraid. That seems silly to me now.

So it is late, and I must close. Until tomorrow, *auf Wiedersehen.*

Love, Tom

P.S. I will use this space to answer questions. No, I have not had time to write Dad and Mary, except for post cards. I know it's a shame, but it takes me ages to write these letters, as you can well imagine, and I simply don't have time. If you want to copy and forward all of the letters, fine, but I would like for you to keep the original copies.

Also, if you are going to forward these letters, be sure to edit them properly, leaving out personal things, and using proper discretion. I have a question: are you getting a letter for every single day? I certainly hope so since I have not missed a day yet. If you aren't getting these letters for each day, let me know as soon as possible, so that I can rewrite them before I forget what we did. And do me another favor and tell me what you think of the letters. I'm losing sleep over them, since they sometimes take several hours to write. I'd give anything for a typewriter. Have you been getting my post cards also? I heard nothing today from Stunt Show or the fraternity—nor from any friends, etc. It was kind of disappointing—although I shouldn't expect anything since I haven't written. Well, I must sign off. Until tomorrow, good night.

Berlin—Friday, July 12, 1963

Hi-

Well, today was the eye-opening day. We spent the entire day over in East Berlin, and it was really fascinating! We got up early, as we were expecting the call from Al Courier, and sure enough, at 8:00 AM, he called. He informed us that he could not meet us in E. Berlin until about 3:00 this afternoon, so the rest of the day would be up to our discretion. So after eating breakfast—2 rolls, coffee and pineapple marmalade—we headed for the Berliner Bank to get some East German Marks, which later turned out to be a terrible mistake. After getting the money, Rick bought some film for his camera, and we proceeded on the U-Bahn (the Berlin Subway) to the nearest station near Check Point [Checkpoint] Charlie. Also, before we left, we took Victoria to nearest VW garage for her checkup and oil change. We had to change subway trains twice, and upon arrival at the right station, we ascended the stairs to find ourselves very close to Check Point Charlie—perhaps within 50 yards. We then strolled toward the checkpoint, each of us anxious as to what the day would bring.

The street leading to Checkpoint Charlie

    Check Point [Checkpoint] Charlie is a British, French and American controlled point where all people of these countries register before crossing into Soviet territory. The friendly soldier at the American window registered us as a group, asking us what time we would be coming back to W. Berlin. Since we weren't sure what time it would be, and what Al Courier had up his sleeve, we told him 12:00 midnight, then changed it to 2:00 AM, just to make sure. Our next step was a passport check by the W. Berlin police, and then we walked through the wall to the Soviet sector. West Berliners are not allowed to go into E. Berlin since the wall went up, so most of those crossing over were Americans, British, and very few Germans who were not from Berlin. The wall at this point is crudely built of concrete blocks, and there is a very narrow opening for pedestrians, and also another opening only wide enough for a bus to pass through. There are still gates for each of these openings, and they are operated by E. German police who carry very foreboding looking machine guns. In fact, all the guards carry their guns, and you feel strange indeed strolling through all of these hostile surroundings! Before we entered the customs barrack, our passports were checked by E. German guards, and they seemed friendly enough—almost as if they wished they too were on the other side—and free.

Behind the wall at this point were several walls, built strattled [straddled] as far as car openings are concerned, and each one manned with a guard. This is to prevent cars from zooming through—just another way to keep E. Germans from escaping. We were told the story of a man who recently took his family through by obtaining a car low enough that it would fit under the steel openings. How he did it I don't know. It must have been a real task!

Signing in at Checkpoint Charlie

Walking toward the East Berlin border

Going thru customs was pure hell—and especially for us. Upon entering the barrack, you stand in line at a window before you present your passport. They take it and give you a number, which you hold while they are checking your passport. Then you wait forever it seems until the check has been made, until one of the clerks calls your number.

While standing in line, I saw one of the most compassionate scenes I ever hope to see. A woman of about 40 came in with two young children, both of whom were dressed exactly alike looking like a picture. They were about 3 and 4, a girl and boy respectfully [respectively]. She talked to the guard at the window, showing him her passport. They kept talking back and forth in German for several minutes, and she suddenly began to weep. She pleaded something hysterically to him and he finally agreed to check on something for her. Karl, who was getting as much as possible out of the conversation, told us that she had come 2000 miles to see her daughter, who lived in E. Berlin, whom she hadn't seen for 15 years. It seemed that she had been a Berliner, had moved to the U.S. or Canada, but was not a citizen there. Therefore the passport was not good for E. Berlin. An American girl who was in line behind her was consoling her in German, and she offered to take the coffee and other things to her daughter as she was not allowed to go across. This girl had obviously been living in Berlin, going to school for the past year, and as she talked to her, the woman began to cry again, which then started the children crying, and it was really horrible. I wanted so much to run over to her and try to help, but knowing no German, there was nothing I could do. But it was such a sad thing that the whole place was quiet, and we were moved emotionally to the point of tears ourselves. I hope I never see anything quite like it again—unforgettable!

But this was not all of our problem there. We waited and waited for about an hour. We had declared all of our money about 45 minutes before, and it did indeed seem strange that people who had been in line behind us were already checked and sent through. You don't realize how insecure you feel, sitting in an E. German checkpoint, especially when they have your passport! All of a sudden, one of the guards called Karl's name, and he was then taken behind the counter by two E. German guards into a room, and they slammed and locked the door. Soon one of the female guards gave me my passport, only to take it back fifteen minutes later. By this time, we were going out of our minds wondering what had happened to Karl, but he soon came out of the room, and they called me in next.

Not knowing what to expect, I was extremely nervous, and I'm sure I showed it a bit more than I wanted to. Upon entering the room, there were two guards, one sitting at a table, one standing. He asked me if I spoke German, upon which I answered no, and he then proceeded to question me. Talk about excited—words can't express exactly how nervous I was. He first asked me what my occupation was—I answered "student." He then wanted to know what I was studying. I told him advertising, and he had no idea what it was. So I tried to explain, mentioning billboards, products, etc. It is no wonder he didn't know. There is no advertising in E. Germany. Everything is owned, run, and operated by the state, thus eliminating the need for advertising. It seems very funny now since advertising is the very symbol of capitalism! He then wanted to know where I got the E. German money, which turned out to be the key question. I told him that I had gotten it at the Berliner Bank in W. Berlin, and then he wanted to know why we had gotten it. It was all beginning to make good sense now—it now fit together. You are never supposed to take E. German Marks in from the West because the rate of exchange is different. In W. Berlin we had received 10 E. Marks for 4.25 W Marks. In E. Berlin, however, you get one for one, meaning that we had exactly doubled the value of the E. Marks we possessed. He never did come out and say this, but he told me that I would have to spend all of my E. Marks while in E. Berlin and to never bring them across again. I left the room somewhat relieved, and they took all five of us in the room, one by one, until we had all been scolded. We finally received our passports, and left the barrack exactly two hours after we had entered, and it was already 11:45. We were extremely happy to hear that they finally did let the woman go into E. Berlin with her two young children—after much weeping, pleading and red tape. It was a great relief to me also!

At last, after a couple more passport checks, one by an E. German soldier and one by a Russian soldier, we were in E. Berlin. The difference between East and West was strikingly noticeable as soon as we were there. One difference was the complete lack of commercialism, except for government posters and propaganda. Another difference was the dirty, shabby appearance of not only all the buildings, but the people as well. They looked very poor, and also depressed. We walked along the wall, which was heavily guarded and took note of the many ruins—obviously untouched since the war. They hadn't even bothered to clean up piles of bricks and rubble, and it was strange indeed. We then headed for Brandenburg Gate, long the symbol of Berlin. It is really a beautiful structure, but seems so strange, surrounded by guards, gates, steel fence, etc. It is part of the Soviet section, and even on top is a plastic dome where sits a Russian soldier with a machine gun. The streets,

This currency exchange note was the cause of all the fuss!

the trees, the sidewalks, and buildings are very unkept [unkempt], and look grimy and dirty. We then walked from the gate down Linder Allee, a wide boulevard leading into E. Berlin. The sidewalks were simply dusty, dirty gravel paved paths, and the street had the look of one that had at one time been very beautiful. The boulevard where we walked was extremely wide, and lined with trees down the center, reminiscent of the Champs-Élysées in character, but not at all in the surroundings. The boulevard was not concrete, but dirt and fine gravel. We crossed over onto the sidewalk, and checked out the shops. The prices were high, but the quality of the merchandise seemed second rate and none of the windows were well-decorated, and of course there were no product displays, which seemed strange to us who are used to so much advertising.

We stopped in the first restaurant we came to—one that seemed little different from those anywhere, except the clientele. The curtains were dirty looking, and the people were not like most people in a restaurant of that type. There was no laughter, no happy groups of people talking. They were subdued and serious. The place seemed to have been at one time very nice, but it had a contrast that was noticeable to me right away. The floors were concrete, and from the appearance of the rest of the room, they should have at least been tiled, if not carpeted. The reason the contrast was obvious was because there were tablecloths on each table and there was a large beautiful chandelier hanging in the middle of the room.

A lone horse and wagon on a deserted East Berlin street

We had real good food, and the prices were low—especially since our money was cheaper. For 50 cents, we had wiener schnitzel, potatoes and sauerkraut as the main course, beer to drink and ice cream with whipped cream and fruit for dessert. The whole time we were there, we kept getting hungry looks from people nearby. It was either curiosity or envy—probably a combination of the two, but as soon as they hear us speaking English, they kept watching us until we left. I couldn't help but wonder what they were thinking, what their life is like. We found out later.

We left the restaurant and headed toward the old government and city center which is found in and around Marx-Engels Platz. By the time we were there, we were truly amazed at the atmosphere of the city. It was like a ghost town. There were no cars and no people. And the buildings were like deserted ruins that could only be found in some ancient city that had been excavated. They were obviously damaged by the war—and looked as if they had been untouched since Marx-Engels Platz is a wide—very wide-open boulevard parkway area, surrounded by large massive government buildings, churches and cathedrals. They were architecturally very beautiful, many of them in Greek and Roman style, with pillars, etc. The odd thing was that many of them were dirty and others were falling to ruin. One old man stopped us on a street corner and asked about Kennedy and the United States. He was quite a character and we joked and talked with him for several minutes, he always whispering when we mentioned Abreight [Ulbricht][3] or E. German government. Karl, of course, had to do the translating, and it was interesting. He even made a few sick jokes about the wall, but I imagine that deep down, he didn't think it was funny. Imagine living in a city from which you could never leave!

"Tell me about President Kennedy and the United States," said the old man

Granted, there were a few people and cars, but so few in such a large, majestic place that it was downright weird. After talking to the old man and giving him a cigarette which he asked for, we crossed the street and entered an old cathedral called The Dome, but before the war was referred to as St. Hedwig's Cathedral. It was particularly damaged by the war, and when we stepped inside, we were really amazed. It was almost untouched since the war, and amid beautiful statues and paintings were heaps of stone and rubble. There was no furniture at all, and the dome had been hastily repaired with wooden beams and boards. The floor itself looked as if it had been purposely chopped up, as it was one mass of small pieces of rock. It was a sad sight to see, as it had obviously been at one time a magnificent place. The exterior of the church was not as destroyed as the inside, but at close look, the bullet marks and the bombed out statues and towers were apparent. This was such a shock to us because every cathedral we've seen thus far in Europe has been almost completely restored—and all are being used, restored or not!

Amid all the ruin of this place was one new structure—a massive bleacher stand used by Obreight [Ulbricht] when he makes speeches—also used by Nikita K.[4] It stood out like a sore thumb. To the left of the area was a grove of trees which resembled the park area near Champs-Élysées, but there was not a soul in sight, and a contrast to Paris, with its hustling, bustling crowds.

We then walked on down Lindenstrasse, the wide street we were on before. We passed the Berlin Opera, and decided to go inside. It had previously been the main opera house for all of Berlin, and was completely restored in 1955. It was really a beautiful place, and just as grand as it had probably been before the war. John Rice and Ginny had gone there often and spoke highly of it. We next passed the Russian War Memorial and stepped inside. It was guarded by 2 Russian soldiers, and was an impressive place. There was a large stone in the center and two columns of stone on each side. The guards at attention in front did not move a muscle, but Bill caught him looking at us as we left. Since it was now about 2:00 and we were to meet Al Courier and the group at 3:00, our task was to find the right place. We accidentally ran into St. Mary's church, the one so famous for Bishop Dibelius'[5] rash sermons. He was kicked out of E. Berlin when the wall went up in '61, but the church seemed thriving. We stepped inside, and sat for about 15 minutes listening to probably the best organ church music I've ever heard. The church was red brick on the outside, and not real large inside. Many of the paintings and statues which flanked the interior seemed out of place, so we assumed they had been confiscated from other churches and cathedrals which had either been destroyed or put out of use. Our time spent there was good enough time to make you think about the significance of such a place in E. Berlin.

After asking directions of how to get to the church we were seeking, we had to give up, since the fellow we asked seem to know nothing of it—and seemed to think that it didn't even exist. So we headed toward Alexander Platz—one of the main shopping areas of E. Berlin. After getting there, we were surprised to find that even this section was sparse of people. We walked into an indoor market place which as Karl said, seemed to be a combination of Woolworths, Montgomery Ward and the Chicago Stock Market. It was a filthy, smelly place—and the people seemed about the same. The floor was of cinders and the building itself was like a huge warehouse. Bill and I left this place and walked down to another corner, where we got some information on the city at a tourist bureau and the other three were in the Post Office, buying stamps.

Great organ music at Bishop Dibelius' St. Mary's Church

At about 2:30, we located the street we wanted—Georgenkirchstrasse, and started walking—looking for either a church or mission—we weren't sure. We did find the place—a massive but modest red brick building across the street from St. Bartholomew's Church. We entered, told a lady why we were there, and she led us to another room and told us to sit there and wait. Soon she led us to the study of the fellow who was in charge—a very personable young man of about 30. We soon found out that he was a student of Theology and did this work on the side. He took us upstairs to a meeting and banquet room, and we sat around talking for a while—as Al Courier's people weren't to be there for a half-hour or so. There was a piano there in the room and I played for a while, glad to get my hands back on a keyboard, even if it was E. Berlin. Soon Al arrived with 10 other Americans, as did about 7 others who were E. German students. We all introduced ourselves and went down to the basement for coffee and rolls. We small talked for about 45 minutes. The American group of ten was in Berlin on a work mission for the Presbyterian Church, cleaning and fixing up apartments in W. Berlin for the underprivileged. They were in Berlin for six weeks, working during the week and using weekends for things like today. They were quite a diversified group of all ages and occupations. One girl I talked to was just entering her freshman year in college, and seemed a bit immature to be on such a trip. Others ranged from college students to people who were working. Basically, they were an uninteresting group, but they at least were doing some good. One girl I spoke to, a Junior next year at some small school in Minnesota, was a music major and very nice. She, however, was the only lily in the pond. The leader of the group was head of the McKinley Foundation at U. of Minnesota, and he struck me as a real do-do [dodo], but I shouldn't judge people on first impressions.

I talked to Al Courier for quite a while, and he made a very striking impression. A liberal theologist, he wears a beard, speaks German impeccably and is to be admired for the wonderful work he's doing in E. Berlin. He got a real laugh about our bringing over the E. German Marks, and so did the E. Germans who were there. He said it was amazing we got by with it, but said that only our innocence saved us. If they had caught us smuggling the money, we would have had a 5 hour interrogation—which certainly wouldn't have been very pleasant.

After coffee, we went back to the 2nd floor, where everyone sat around the banquet tables and introduced themselves, telling where they were from, what they did as an occupation, and what they were doing in Berlin. The E. Germans were, of course, the most interesting. They were all students, except one girl who had been one before the wall. The majors ranged from agriculture, theology and physics to literature and engineering. The agricultural majors were required to split their college time, spending 2 years in school, 1 year on a collective farm, and then back to school again, rotating for several years.

I talked to the girl who had been an English and German literature major at the Free University in W. Berlin before 1961. She was home on vacation when the wall went up, thus preventing her from returning to W. Berlin, even to finish school. She said that she could have continued in E. Berlin, but didn't want to because of the extreme communist, socialist interpretation of the literature as studied there. So she had gone to work for a firm that needed an English speaking secretary. I felt sorry for her, but she didn't want sympathy. I guess there is a point reached by most of these people when sympathy and self pity are futile—and she had obviously reached it long ago.

By this time it was 6:00 and Al told everyone to go downstairs and talk until the meal was ready—at about 6:30. I spent that time playing the piano, and at about 6:30, Al came upstairs, informing us that dinner was ready.

The meal consisted of bread, butter, cold cuts, tomatoes and tea, and tasted pretty awful for the 5 marks we each had paid. However, we realized that it was for a good cause, and it didn't really matter. I sat by an American girl at dinner, and the conversation wasn't much more than sympathy and facts about E. Berlin—facts of which we both were not sure. The E. German boy who sat across from us knew no English, so communication at that source was impossible.

After the meal, we all went back upstairs, and we were invited to stay for the wine party. To show you how liberal Mr. Courier is, he had smuggled 8 bottles of wine across the border, for it is a rare occasion when E. Germans are able to afford wine. We decided not to stay, however, since we were tired, and there was still quite a bit which we hadn't seen in E. Berlin.

Leaving the mission, we headed for Karl Mark Allee, a street which was completely rebuilt by the Russians after the war. It is a wide, beautiful boulevard, lined with trees and new buildings. The architecture is definitely Russian, resembling pictures you see of Moskow [Moscow] University. There is a large square with a beautiful fountain in the center of this area, and it is surrounded with shops, hotels, etc. One very noticeable thing about this area and buildings was their veneer look. Almost every building was coated with a white enameled brick, which is actually very attractive, but the catch was that in places, the veneer had fallen off, leaving crude brick or concrete block beneath. It reminded me of a Goldblatt's basement furniture sale!

Near deserted streets and the "new" Soviet architecture

    Just for kicks, we decided to have a beer at the fancy restaurant on top of the Berlin Haus, a hotel there on the square. Before we could go to the top, we first had to check our coats with a fat old lady in the cloakroom. The price was 30 finig [pfennig] or .30 Marks and she took either E. or W. money. She also whispered to us that if you gave her a W. German cigarette that we wouldn't have to pay. It was a pitiful gesture, and we all felt sorry for her. We understood later why they want West cigarettes, for Bill bought a pack of E. cigarettes, and they were absolutely rotten. In fact, they are so bad that every restaurant, bus, or place where people smoke has a sickening, repulsive stench.
    The restaurant upstairs was a riot! It was not real large, but had a small orchestra playing typical Viennese type music, the real corny, whimsy type. It was decorated well, but still seemed kind of tinny, and again, there were no carpets at all on the floor. The service was fine and the wine wasn't expensive and very good. We had heard that this was one of the finest places to come in E. Berlin, but it certainly suffered by comparison to any nice restaurant we are used to. After finishing our wine, we

went back downstairs to Karl Mark Allee, where we began our trek back to W. Berlin. Again I must mention that this street was completely dead. It is supposed to be the main part of "fashionable" E. Berlin, but there was not a soul in sight, except for a few pigeons flying around the fountain, and a few cars buzzing by. It is an eerie feeling strolling down a street that in the U.S. or Western Europe would be swarming with people. You feel almost as if you are in a dream.

We walked from there to Checkpoint Charlie, and all the way back, it became more and more desolate. We passed many war ruins that had been untouched since the war, apartment buildings, half of which were destroyed. Some of these old ruins were inhabited by poor souls who were hanging out their glassless windows, being entertained by not much more than the cooing of pigeons and five Americans (us) who strolled by. We walked again through the area where we had been that morning, and at night E. Berlin was even more ghostly than in the day. One old man stopped us and talked about Kennedy[6] when he had been in W. Berlin. He had seen it on TV (privately) and then told us how it had been when the Big K was in E. Berlin several days later. Everyone was required to go out to see Khrushchev and there was hardly any cheering at all, as compared to the screaming mobs that greeted Kennedy in the West. Surprisingly enough, the E. Germans know what is going on, even though the state does its best to prevent it.

It took about an hour to walk back, and we went through E. German customs very quickly, as it was late at night, and very few will stay in E. Berlin after dark, let alone go over on their own. It only took about 15 min. as compared with the two hours this morning.

Upon arriving back in West, the feeling we had was close to ecstatic. And believe it or not, it was great to see good old colorful commercialism again. We jumped on the subway, arriving at the Kurfurstendamm in less than 15 minutes. Rick and Freddy returned to the hotel, while Bill, Karl and I decided to sit on the wonderful, colorful, crowded street in a sidewalk café to try the Berliner Weise, a drink found only in Berlin and consisting of beer with a small amount of raspberry juice. Needless to say, it was bad, but we drank every drop while discussing today and all its very sad and serious implications. Well, it, as usual, is late, and I must sign off.

Until tomorrow—good night—and thank God I'm free and American!

Love, Tom

Berlin—Saturday, July 13, 1963

Hi–

Well, today was not nearly as interesting as yesterday, but I approached it in a different way. We were aroused at 10:00 by Karl who informed us that if we weren't in the dining room in 10 minutes, that we would not get breakfast—so that, being enough incentive for even a lazybones like me, influenced my tired body to arouse itself from bed. Since we had not as yet really seen much of W. Berlin, we decided that a bus tour might be the quickest way to do it, even though we were not too anxious to do it this way. We bought a ticket from the old Jewish fellow right here in the hotel, and it didn't depart until 1:30, which gave me time to take care of some essentials which I had been neglecting. The breakfast was the same—coffee, rolls, butter and marmalade, and right afterwards, Karl and I went down to the VW garage to get trusty "Vickie." After that, we set out to find my package, and it took about a half-hour to locate the post office—and upon arriving there, it was closed. This was extremely frustrating, and with time as precious as it was, we had not wanted to waste it. Needless to say, I had to wait till Monday to get the glasses!

We then returned to the hotel, and after writing several post cards, it was time to find the place where the tour started. So four of us left, Karl choosing not to go, since he wanted to get a haircut, write a letter, etc. The tour, 2½ hours in length, turned out to be very worthwhile. What made it so pleasant, I think, was the gorgeous creature who acted as guide. It left from the Kaiser-Wilhelm church, and the next 2½ hours were filled with sights and facts which just made us sorry that we couldn't stay longer in Berlin. We saw the Free University, the various court houses of W. Berlin, streets, buildings, memorials, etc. that were too numerous to mention. Impressive particularly were the convention hall (Ann got a postcard), the eternal flame which is supposed to burn until Germany is reunited, the parks, the universities, Brandenburg Gate (from this side), the Russian Memorial, the Gashtat [Gestalt] (former building heading Nazi Government), the Victory Statue and a palace which was copied from the palace at Versailles. One interesting fact about the Russian Memorial is that since the riot there several years ago, when the two Russian guards were almost killed, there are now 2 British soldiers who guard the Russian soldiers who guard the monument. The W. Berliners get a big kick out of this! We also saw many of the former embassies which are now consulates and—oh yes!—the group of apartment buildings which were designed by different architects from various countries. They were modern, unusual and very beautiful. One which was designed by the famous architect who planned the city Brasilia, was known for the boo-boo he had made in its design. He forgot to put in elevators—and when one was finally added, it only had stops at the 3rd and 7th floors, making it imperative and necessary for those living on the other floors to simply walk. Our beautiful guide had many funny things to say about some of the things we saw. Also, we saw the spot where Kennedy had been while in Berlin, a large square near one of the main court houses. We passed all of the military headquarters and residences and drove out to the stadium where the Olympics were held in Hitler's time. It was a mammoth place, and now only used for "football" (soccer) games. There was a statue of a nude man which we passed, and our guide told us that this was a man who had been hit hard by taxes. She made several comments about taxes—evidently, Berliners are very conscious of them. Of course, we hear that they are heavily taxed for almost everything they own. Sounds familiar, eh? I got into a short conversation with the guide, found out that she had been an art student (commercial art) until her parents refused to give her more money on the grounds that they didn't like the atmosphere of an art school. So she is now working her way through school, not only studying art, but language. By the way, her English was almost perfect!

At 4:00, we departed from the bus, glad we had gone both for the sights and the guide. She looked somewhat like Sophia Loren. Since we were right near the Kaiser-Wilhelm church, we decided to go in and look around. As I told you before, it is a modern structure, built near the ruin of the old one. Inside it was really beautiful. The stained glass came from Chartres and there was a modern gold statue of Christ hanging over the altar. It was good to see that modern structure of churches can be as appealing as the ancient versions—and this was an excellent example. We sat there for about 15 minutes, listening to the organ and thinking.

After looking at the old part of the church, Bill and I crossed the street to a Berliner Kindl snack restaurant and each had a shish kabob on a stick and a beer. We then returned to the hotel.

Prices in Berlin are relatively cheap, so we decided that this was the night to have a good meal—and this we did! Everyone adorned suits, and we headed (with Vicki) back to the Kurfurstendamm, where we parked and walked to the French Consulate building, whose 4th floor houses a restaurant "Maison de France" known for its good food. Since it didn't open till 6:30, we sat in the bar and had a drink. I had scotch and soda for the first time this summer, and it was a welcome change from all the beer and wine we seem to be living on. It was an elegant well-decorated place, and I couldn't help but compare it to the place in E. Berlin where we were last night. This was so much nicer, and any kind of comparison was too much. There was a beautiful grand piano there which I started to play, but was stopped very quickly by the head waiter who mumbled something in German which I didn't understand. Our dinner was five-course no less, the first being a consommé soup. It didn't compare to Luxembourg's version, but was good just the same. The next course was French fried filet (fresh) and it was by far the best part of the meal—really delicious. The main course was veal, cauliflower and potatoes with gravy, and was really tops. We were already getting stuffed, but no sooner had we finished this course, when the waiter wheeled a whole cart of cheeses over to the table. One looked real good to me, but turned out to be so strong and smelly that I couldn't eat a bite. When the waiter came back, we asked him what it was. Get this: he said that it was a special German cheese called "limburger." We all roared and said that we have it in America too, but I'm sure he wondered why no one touched it. We're just not connoisseurs of cheese. The last course was a dish of vanilla and chocolate ice cream with whipped cream. Need I say more—we were all stuffed, and the meal, with service and even the drink was only $2.50. We've never had it so good!

It was now 8:15 and we were already 15 minutes late for the concert for which we had tickets. So we went back to the car, spent the next half-hour looking for the place where the concert was to be, and finally got there about 9:00. It was located on the outskirts of W. Berlin in a beautiful park and no sooner had we arrived, when the concert ended. We only saw about 20 minutes of it.

We got back in "Vicki" and headed for town, suddenly changing our plan from going to a jazz spot to driving along the wall. This turned out to be one of the most interesting things we did all day—if not the most! The wall is not perfectly straight, but zig zags in some sections. One section, perhaps 5 blocks, is right along a street in N. Berlin, and it is here that the whole problem becomes so very obvious. This particular street was like any other street in a residential section of a city except that the side the wall was on was completely fortified. Where there were buildings, the windows, doors, cracks, were completely sealed. Instead of curtains behind these windows were walls of concrete block. Some of these apartment buildings were four stories high, but not one window was missed. Where there weren't buildings, there was a wall, ranging in height from 7 feet to 12 or 13. Along the top of the wall was a layer of cement on which rested entombed in that mortar, jagged cut glass. There was also barbed wire at a slant as added insurance. Even on top of the buildings were barbed wire fences (as if someone would jump four floors.) The greatest impact of all, however, came from seeing the memorials to those who had died in trying to escape: Each of these memorials consisted of three wooden poles placed triangularly, surrounded with barbed wire. There was a board across each with the name of the person who had died and the date. They were placed all along the wall at the exact spot where they died, and they were a shocking sight.

Blocked windows and a make-shift memorial at the Berlin Wall

    On each of these memorials hung a withered wreath, and beneath lay small vases of flowers. Try to imagine these shrines along the wall—it's repulsive. One memorial lay right beneath a four-story building and it seemed obvious that he must have jumped—and died. I remember only his first name—Rolph—and the date was 1961—probably right after the wall went up. There were W. Germans on duty all along the wall, so we decided to talk to one. He told us that there had been no escapes there recently, but several had tried, only to be shot before they made it over the wall. Of course, he had no control over what happens on the other side of the wall—but he did say that if someone gets over the wall and the E. German guard (whom we could see watching us with his binoculars within 30 ft.) tries to shoot the escapee once he is over the wall, that it is his (the W. German guard) duty to shoot at the E. German guard. The street here was almost deserted except for a bus now and then and a few people. I imagine that most tourists and even Berliners don't want to be near it at night. We noticed that the other side of the wall was completely lit with spots, and the guard told us that over the wall were several high barbed wire fences and in some spots, even another wall. He told us to go a few blocks north and we could climb a stairway and look over, only as long as we stayed near a guard. So we drove up there and sure enough there was a guard with binoculars on a stairway-type ramp looking over the wall. It was very quiet here, and no one said a word. But he motioned to us to come up and look for ourselves. This we did and saw what the first guard had described. There were 2 barbed wire fences and within 20 ft. a booth where two Russian guards with machine guns were staring us right in the face. For some reason I didn't feel at home up there, but it was fascinating! In a few minutes we saw three Russian guards stomp past laughing. They were beyond the 2nd barbed wire fence, I presumed making some kind of routine search. One of the guards so close had disappeared, and the other seemed to be trying to avoid our looks, although I imagine he wondered what in the hell we were doing, 5 innocent looking idiots, peering over the wall. I suppose they can't trust anyone, however, and even we could have been trying to help someone escape—which is one of the things they guard against. We descended the ramp and spent the next 15 minutes just walking along the wall, reaching up to feel the jagged glass, and looking at the memorials. At one point I jumped up to see if I could see anything, and to my surprise, saw a guard staring me right in the face. The glass was really treacherous along there though! What impressed me most was the difference between the two sides of the street, the West side very normal, people living in the buildings, some with their heads out of windows, and then the East side, so dark and dead. And the concrete blocks in the windows made it so much worse—and realistic.

We returned to the hotel at 11:30, and it's late. Until tomorrow, good night—and again, thank God for America. I believe you really don't appreciate it until you see what it could be like without it.

Love, Tom

Berlin—Sunday, July 14, 1963

Hi–

Today was another good day, although somewhat less active than the two previous. I slept till noon because I was so dead tired. I sometimes wonder how long I can keep up the writing—but I'll be thankful later on because it's surprising how much you forget after a couple weeks. By sleeping this morning I missed out on going to E. Berlin to lunch with Karl and Rick, and on going to church with Bill here in W. Berlin (an English speaking service for tourists). I only regretted the E. Berlin jaunt, since they went to St. Mary's, the church I mentioned in my letter of Friday, where Bishop Dibelius had been so rash in his sermons before they kicked him out. Karl said later that the sermon this morning was the same kind that must have caused Dibelius' expulsion, and he was amazed that they actually got by with it. Bill went to the church where Al Courier was assistant minister, and said that it was an interesting sermon, but not phenomenal.

Freddy and I both missed all this—but I think at that point the sleep was just as beneficial—and I felt a lot better when I got up. So Freddy and I got dressed and headed down to the Kurfurstendamm to find some lunch before meeting Bill at the Dahlem[7] Museum at 2:30. We went to the Automat (Quickie) for some bean soup and bratwurst, and believe it or not, ran into Karl and Rick there, who had just returned from E. Berlin. They told us that they had had very little trouble at the border and that customs only took a half-hour going over and about 5 minutes coming back. Of course there were few people making the crossing on a Sunday. They told about how different it was on Sunday. There were more people taking Sunday strolls, and to spice things up, about 1000 Russian soldiers who had just arrived in town were running all over the place, taking pictures, shouting, and raising about as much hell as any army would on leave for a sight-seeing day. Rick said it was very funny the way that they would pose for pictures. They would stand at attention, put their right hand inside of their coats over their hearts, and be very sober and serious about the whole production. Rick got a picture of this, which I hope turns out.

After eating bean soup, bratwurst and a Coke, I changed my mind about going out to the museum, and instead, Freddy and I decided to take the car down by Brandenburg Gate and then drive along the wall, where we had been last night. So we walked back to the hotel, jumped in the car, and took off. Our gas tank and been on empty for quite a while so we thought it best to at first find somewhere to give "Vicki" a drink. We drove for about 20 minutes pulling into closed stations, praying that she wouldn't go dry, and trying again. We did finally find one open, and after putting in $2.00 worth, we took off for Brandenburg Gate.

As I said before, it is a beautiful structure, and is even nicer on the West side, since there is a huge park flanking either side for several blocks approaching it. We parked the car and walked through the park up to the gate, or as close as we can get since the wall runs right in front of it. Incidentally, the wall is a crudely built pile of concrete blocks in front of the gate, and the contrast seems almost ironic. Directly adjacent to the Gate is the Russian War Memorial, which takes a hunk out of the West territory. Sure enough, there were the two British soldiers in front, guarding the two Russian soldiers who guarded the memorial. It's really a ridiculous situation. There was a platform right in front of Brandenburg Gate which had been specially built for Kennedy when he was in Berlin, so that he could see over to the Soviet zone. But on the day he was there, the Soviets draped huge red flags in front of the gate, so that he couldn't see over. Sounds stupid, yes? That seems to be a typical gesture, however. You also know that they closed E. Berlin to Americans when he was there so that he couldn't go over. Very petty!

After getting our fill here, we walked back to the car and headed for the section of the wall where we were last night. Today was beautiful, about 70 degrees and sun shining brightly. It hardly seemed like the right atmosphere for the sights we were seeing. We drove again past the Raschtach [Reichstag], the former Nazi central government building, and finally arrived at the wall. We parked the car, and I shot a picture of a deserted church which was right behind the wall, a strange sight. There were flowers and wreaths lining the wall here, and it seemed to be a special memorial or symbol all its own. We walked on down the street, taking pictures of some of the memorials I mentioned last night until I stumbled on a scene I'll never forget. An old lady, probably 60 or 70 was standing on the corner across the street from the wall. She wore a black dress and black stockings and her eyes were red and tearstained. In her hand was a wrinkled handkerchief. I stood there for a while, wondering what she was doing. I followed the direction of her gaze, and then, suddenly, I saw what she was looking at. Over the wall, and perpendicular to it was an apartment building, and from its windows could be seen several people, an old couple, a young girl and a child, their heads leaning from those windows, their gaze toward the West and this woman. She just stood there on the corner for several minutes, her hands nervously fondling the handkerchief. She raised the handkerchief slowly and waved it two or three times, and before long, the old woman across the wall returned her symbol by waving a gray cloth. The girl and her little boy waved their hands. I stood there transfixed at the pathetic sight. After the waving, there was no motion at all. But the four over the wall never turned away their glance. The woman on the corner was now holding her handkerchief behind her, her hands trembling. She stood there for about five minutes, just looking. At last she again waved the handkerchief, but there was no return of waves, and I think it was my fault. She did not see me watching, as I was directly behind her, but those across the wall did, and when they didn't wave back, she turned around toward me. Feeling too guilty to even face her, I turned my head, pretending I hadn't seen. She stood there for a couple more minutes, and when she finally did turn and I had a chance to catch a glimpse of her face, I was almost sorry I had, it was so sad. Her handkerchief was now drying tears, and she walked a few steps, weeping silently. Wiping her eyes, she again turned toward the four, and lifted her hand in one final gesture. She seemed to be trying to prevent herself from crying, and her wrinkled frown was tear-stained and only like something seen in pictures. The whole sequence now seems like it should have been unreal, but it wasn't. It was the pathetic and horrible kind of scene that only belongs to dreams and movies. And what this kind of experience can do to your imagination! This was a woman who felt compassion of some kind for people she had known. She had known them, perhaps as relatives, perhaps as friends, perhaps as neighbors. This was a woman, who at least within an immediate future, would never see or talk to these people again. This was a woman to be pitied. This is a woman to weep for. This is a woman who knows what real unhappiness is—and she also knows frustration—and helplessness. But who the hell can help her? Certainly not I—nor East Germany—they were the ones preventing her from going across. And W. Germany, they could not help her either. Can even God help her? I doubt it, but perhaps. She is only an isolated example of what hate in the world produces—simply an isolated victim of this cold, cold war. Pardon my getting carried away, but reflecting on the sight has riled me up. I'll stop before I make a fool of myself, but I'm sincere in thinking that this situation can't continue. It will break someday! If this old woman makes you want to cry, it should, for I am. Perhaps these things have to be seen to really be felt and appreciated. But I here give emotion as a footnote.

    We got back in the car and went back to the hotel. Karl, Freddy and I had tickets for *My Fair Lady*[8] for tonight, and after eating a stand-up dinner of potato salad, bratwurst and beer, we went to the theater. The theater, on Kunststrasse, was much like Kiel Auditorium in St. Louis—large, majestic, although not quite as elegant. This version of *Fair Lady* was completely in German, and even though I understood not a word, I knew what was happening most of the time, and it was a unique and enjoyable experience. Some of the song translations sounded very funny, particularly "Loverly" and "Little Bit of Luck." The sets and costumes were just as the American version, and there also was an enormous revolving stage, carrying the beautiful scenery sailing away after each scene. By the way, my ticket was only 90 cents, and very good at that, although in the balcony. If you are wondering how the English and cockney accents were translated, they used regular German for the English, Berliners dialect for the cockney—and from audience reaction, it was just as successful in German as in English. One interesting audience reaction was a rhythmic clapping after "Little Bit of Luck" in tempo with that song. It really livened things up.

    We returned after the show to the hotel, and when Bill and Rick came in, we heard about their most interesting and worthwhile evening. They went over to E. Berlin to visit a friend of John and Ginny Rice. She is a schoolteacher of about 35, who has lived in Berlin all of her life. She speaks excellent English and loves to get the practice. The things she told them are fascinating and I must relate some of them.

    She lives in a modest apartment with her parents, and they are friendly, intelligent people. Her father is also a teacher, and her mother a housewife, although now in the hospital. She told them that teachers are allowed to travel, although only 20 out of 400 in her school are allowed a vacation each year. They have only 3 spots to choose from, and they are very expensive, unless they choose another place where prices are lower, but where there are virtually no modern conveniences. Also, out of the 20 that are allowed to go, this is only for one person, not for a family. Ergo, they do not vacation. This woman is one who is intellectually alive and so interested in the world and travel. But she cannot leave E. Germany. This was particularly sad in her case since she had been in the same situation all her life. Before E. Germany, there had been the war. And before that, no money. It is frustrating. She also told that they are not free to say anything at all about the government, and had better not, for those who do disappear. Luckily, there are no communists in her apt. building, except one, who is deaf. So she tunes in West radio and television stations, able to see what is going on. They must be careful however. A friend of hers, a young man of 21, made a careless statement about how bad the wall was in his own apartment, but was overheard by someone on the balcony above his apartment, and was sent to a concentration camp for a year and a half. When he returned, he would not say a word about it to anyone. By the way, from her classroom she can see this concentration camp, located right in E. Berlin.

She also spoke about goods. Clothes, good ones that is, are too expensive for even consideration, and coffee, for example, costs $10.00 per pound. Rick and Bill smuggled a pound over to her. Also, she cannot buy any magazines or newspapers printed in the West, and she cannot buy books about any Western country, unless they are good negative propaganda. Bill and Rick had a wonderful time. They drank about five bottles of wine, and she insisted on paying a cab to take them back to Check Point [Checkpoint] Charlie. She has a friend in West Berlin who has some kind of passport which permits her to come visit, and who smuggles books and food to her. This friend also brings all her mail to her, since any mail sent to or mailed from E. Berlin is censored. They have to be very careful as you can see. This is just another example of what kind of situation it is. I regretted very much not being able to go, and cursed *My Fair Lady* several times, but that's life.

Well, we're leaving Berlin I'm sorry to say early tomorrow—so must get to bed.

Until tomorrow—good night—and give this letter some thought, then count your blessings. We've known no hell—and let's hope we never do.

Love, Tom

SOUTHERN GERMANY
6

From Storybook Bavaria to the Horrors of Dachau

Nestled among the rolling Bavarian hills along the Autobahn to Munich stands Dachau. One of the largest German concentration camps, it represents an appalling chapter in human history. It was liberated by the Americans on April 29, 1945. There are no words to describe the misery and depravity of those who were sentenced to a bare existence here—nor for the many who died and the untold horrors they endured.

One can only hope: "Never Again." (A Memorial at the Dachau Concentration Camp.)

> "In spite of everything, I still believe that people are really good at heart."
> —Anne Frank

§ § §

Weisstadt, Germany—Monday, July 15, 1963

Hi–

We arose today at 8:00, everyone eager to get on the road as soon as possible. But we didn't actually leave Berlin until 11:30. First on the agenda, after breakfast, was American Express, where we made a final mail check and left forwarding addresses. I had none. Karl and I then took off for the post office to get my package, the others returning to the hotel to get final organization of luggage, junk, etc.

It took Karl and I a half-hour to get the package, as there were all kinds of papers to sign, money to pay, etc. I made the mistake of saying that the glasses were unused, and then had to pay a customs tax which could have been avoided with just a white lie. But good old stupid honest Tom told the truth and then had to pay the paper-signing, money-paying price. But I did get the sunglasses, and they are great, certainly worth much more than $7.00.

We drove back to the hotel, loaded the car, bought some groceries at a nearby delicatessen, and left Berlin in a very over-loaded puff of smoke. It took us 45 minutes to find the right Autobahn out of Berlin, but at last we were on the road and at about 12:00 noon we hit the border into E. Germany. This was a miserable time for the border, and there were hoards [hordes] of pushing, screaming tourists and travelers crammed in the E. German barrack. It took at least an hour to go thru a very simple procedure, and again we were completely disgusted at the whole operation. There was one window where forms were passed out, to be filled out by each traveler. The forms then had to be turned in after being filled out at the same window, which was an obvious example of gross inefficiency. There were throngs of people swarmed around the window, and no one knew what anyone was doing. One fat American businessman in sunglasses and Bermuda shorts was shouting and cursing. After paying $10.00 to travel south on the Autobahn (which required a special visa) we took off for Munich.

 We stopped several miles out of Berlin to eat lunch, and the five of us sat there munching on bread, cheese and bananas, as well as sipping out of a bottle of apple cider. While we were eating a car drove up, stopped, and a family of three, father, mother and son got out. Rather than do anything special they just sat around, as though they were waiting for someone. Sure enough, about 15 minutes later, another car pulled in, and it was another family who seemed to know the first family. They started unloading food and setting up a picnic lunch right there on the Autobahn Rastplatz[1]. It seems quite normal, until we got a close look at their license plates. One car had E. German plates, the other W. German. It then hit us that this (the Autobahn) was the perfect place for them to meet. Just another example of how painful a split nation must be to these people!

 We finished eating and took off down the road, following the signs to Leipzig. But we had a problem. There was an E. German control station ahead, and we were stopped by a big stupid E. German cop who told us we would have to turn around and go back through Helmstedt, which would have taken us 175 miles out of our way. Karl proceeded to tell him that we had a special visa that allows us to go south, but instead of being civil, the nut started yelling at us in German, so loud that even Karl didn't understand. And we looked up to see another guard approaching with a machine gun, so without further ado, turned around and started driving the other direction. Trying to decide what to do next, Karl fished through a pile of papers till he came up with the paper the girl had given us in Berlin. "Turn around," he said, and so I wheeled the car around and we headed straight back toward the cop. We were all kind of nervous as to what he would do, but when we showed him the right paper, he said to go on toward Leipzig—and that was quite a relief.

 The Autobahn south from Berlin is in much better shape than the one west, although it was completely E. German traffic. At about 3:00 we stopped at a roadside restaurant and gas station, and it was a real interesting place. The people there were dirty looking, their clothes plain and sloppy. The whole appearance of the place was unkempt, extremely dirty and old. It was dark and dingy inside and had a sickening stench of those E. German cigarettes. We had a drink there and several ice cream sticks and went on our way. Even the gas station was old and dingy looking—no bright colors, no sign, only the sign T which is found on every gas station in E. Germany. These places are by no means comparable to the Howard Johnson type oases found on our toll or freeways. An interesting contrast!

 The countryside in East Germany is truly beautiful. The land varies from mile to mile, ranging from flat areas cultivated in wheat and other grain to hilly country, used for grazing. Much of this hilly land was cultivated, and all along the way we could see their collective farms in full swing, groups of 20 or more, both men and women, working in the fields. Farm machinery was rare, and the sight of these people working in the fields was refreshing in a way. Believe it or not they looked like many of the pictures you see of typical peasants slaving for their sustenance. We kept making jokes all along the way about these scenes, which perhaps wasn't right, but at the time seemed very funny. The women wore their bonnet type headdresses, their long dresses to their ankles, whereas the men wore overalls much like our own farmers. But tell me, how often do you see groups of men and women dressed in quaint clothes, working together in the fields. Admittedly you can't help laughing.

 We took a bypass around Leipzig, but were able to see that E. Germans not only have quaint collective farms, but quite prosperous looking industry. The area around Leipzig was filled with factories pouring smoke in great amounts in the

Leipzig skyline, and this scene seemed little different from one that could be seen in or around Gary, Indiana. It looked thriving. We drove past Leipzig on an enormous 8-lane highway, which stretched straight like a ribbon through the plane. Leaving this area, we took the Autobahn marked Munchen (Munich) and again got into the farm country similar to that we had just been through. We saw approaching signs of the border about 4:15, and 10 minutes later stopped at the first control station. The E. German policeman was very friendly, and after checking our passports, looking in the trunk and luggage space behind the back seat, he opened the gate, allowing us to pass into the *sperrgebiet*[2], the 5000 meter area along the border which is essentially a no-man's land, there being no E. German inhabitants in that area, only confirmed communists who can be trusted not to attempt escape. We were soon at the border, and after 2 passport checks, which took only about 20 minutes, we were again in West Germany. For some reason, we breathed a sigh of relief, not that we had been really worried, but there was something about being back in free country that was most refreshing.

    We stopped at a gas station and restaurant right over the border, a modern, clean, bright colored place which re-emphasized the contrasting counterpart in E. Germany. There we met an American family from Pennsylvania who had come from the direction we were heading, and they were eager to talk and gave all sorts of advice on what to do, where to stay, etc. We listened with a grain of salt, and after eating a mediocre meal of hot broth, potatoes, sauerkraut and Coke, we headed for Weisstadt, a small out of the way town where we are spending the night. We were now off the Autobahn, driving on ordinary Southern Illinois type roads. This town required a turn off the main road, and we stumbled on it by accident.

    It is set in a valley between a series of large hills, and is typically picturesque and of the red-roofed-set-in-the-valley type places—you know, the kind you see in travel posters and tourist propaganda. Being out of the way, however, a group of Americans are a rare sight here, and it's one of the best places we've been. We got a room in the hotel overlooking the square (complete with cobblestones, flowers, and fountain), and from our room we can see the church across the square, and the old church (built in the 12th Century) down the road, farther into the valley. This town belongs only to books and make-believe, but here we are. The room is a good size, on the 3rd floor, and complete with running water and large beds. In Germany, the beds are not one mattress, but 3 pillow mattresses, one which is slightly raised for the head. The pillows are large square feather-filled fluffy things, and there is always a comforter covered with a sheet as complete covers. These beds are extremely comfortable, allowing one to sort of disappear for the night.

Postcard: Our delightful hotel in Weisstadt, West Germany

Downstairs is a wood-paneled restaurant and bar, and I saw the piano as soon as I walked in the room. The German girl who was acting as waitress was really wonderful. About 21, she has a lovely smile, a motherly disposition, and is not a raving beauty, being slightly chunky and having hairy legs. By the way, it seems that European women don't make a habit of shaving their legs. But there was an attractiveness about this girl, a freshness seldom seen in American girls. It was a sweet, innocent, intelligent, but not bashful impression that makes me wonder how American girls can be so worried about pseudo-sophisticated nonsense so much of the time, giving little thought to things which would make life so much more interesting. This girl, although I could not talk to her, spoke with her eyes, and there was a maturity and wholesome sparkle there that communicated without need of words. Karl and I asked her for a beer, and Karl then told her that I played the clavier, and asked if it would be o.k. for me to play. She said it would, and so I sat down. The piano was in surprisingly good tune, and I started out with "Alexander's Rag Time Band." Before long, there were all kinds of people in there sitting around listening, seemingly enjoying it quite a bit. All the time, there had been a group of old town codgers sitting at a nearby table getting smashed. Someone asked me if I knew any German songs, and so I tried to pick out a couple that Karl had been teaching us in the car. All of a sudden, an elderly man (one of the old codgers), probably 60, came to the piano, and started yelling at me in German. Thank God Karl was nearby, for the guy was obviously drunk, but what a character! He was wanting me to play "Hofbräuhaus," the famous German drinking song which originated in Munich at the Hofbräuhaus. So, he thought that I was a fine musician, but no, I'll never be a true musician until I learn to play "Hofbräuhaus." So, he gritted his teeth, decided to teach me the song himself. He got a wild gleam in his eye, stared across the room, puffed out his chest, and with great gusto, belted out the song, stopping after each line yelling at me, still not realizing I could understand nothing. But Karl was busy translating and so I learned the song line for line perfect, and he had me play it over and over until I had mastered it. Karl said he was pretending to be my piano teacher, and the whole sequence was hysterical. He would grab my hands from the keyboard if I hit one wrong note, making me start the damn song again. Believe me, I got my fill of that song tonight, but it was a truly wonderful experience. There was another old man who soon joined him, and after the ordeal was over, they insisted on passing the hat around the room, as the old character thought it was worth at least 6 marks 50. I refused the money, but I shouldn't have. I did get a free beer however which I couldn't finish. A glass of beer in Germany is more like a quart. Impossible! The evening was well spent, however, and I did get a little practice in.

We left the bar at 10:45, and here I am in the room, smelling the fresh country air, writing.

As to schedule, we'll leave Vienna on July 26, arrive Venice the same day, only spending one day there. We'll arrive Florence on 28, probably spend only a couple days there. We'll probably leave Rome on the 5th of August. Write lots and lots, as I'm anxious as to your reactions to things I've written as well as more of the home front.

Until tomorrow, good night.

Love, Tom

Feuchtwangen, Germany Tuesday, July 16, 1963

Hi–

We got up this morning around 7:15, went downstairs to a good b'fast of hot milk and rolls. The girl I mentioned was there to serve us the food, and she seemed very interested in talking to Karl about where we were going, where we had been, what we were studying, etc. We packed and left Weisstadt at 8:15, and even did our "big switch" for the girl—she thought it was funny, but we weren't around to hear her reaction, as we were barreling down the road in a puff of smoke. There was a light haze on the town, and the sun looked like it wanted to shine through. It had seemed like almost the perfect place, both in price and in value. Everything including breakfast was only $1.25.

Endless haystacks on the way to Bavaria

The countryside is very beautiful here with its rolling hills, fields laid out like labyrinths, and small red-roofed towns, only recognizable from a distance by their church steeples. We pulled into Nuremberg about 10:00 and went right to the railroad station to see if we could get some kind of brief guide to the city. This we did, and spent the next 2 hours on our own walking tour of Nuremberg.

This town is really fascinating! The old part of the city is still surrounded by massive walls, stout round towers, forbidding defense ways and deep moats. Towering above the town is a castle where centuries ago the Emperors of the Holy Roman Empire used to pray in the chapel. In 1500, the city was the focal point of all trade in Europe, and the most celebrated German artists of that period made their home here. There were so many things about the town that impressed me, but briefly what I enjoyed most was just the atmosphere of the place—so old and traditional and well-preserved that you actually felt like you were in some long-ago other world. The architecture is really indescribable, but characterized by 3 or 4 story houses, small windows and shutters, steep roofs, sometimes housing 3 or 4 more floors (indicated by many rows of small dormers), red-tiled roofs and wide overhangs. All this is set in tiny winding cobblestone streets, and of course the stone walls, castles and towers which surrounded the old city. I can't omit the churches and cathedrals which added much to the total atmosphere. There were also canals, across which small covered wooden bridges stretched, and also a fountain on a square in front of the Church of Our Lady. This fountain dates from the late 14th Century, has 40 stone figures, stands 60 feet in a narrow pyramid form, and is probably the most beautiful we've seen. I'm constantly amazed at the beautiful artwork found everywhere in Europe. This town is full of it. One interesting thing we're noticing about these towns recently are the drinking devices used on their fountains. They are like huge tilting spouts, which by lowering, bring a gush of water from the fountain. There was one on this particular fountain, and I got soaked trying to wash my hands. We didn't know—you were supposed to tilt the damn things slowly.

After walking on most of the tour, we stopped at noon to buy some groceries. I've caught a terrible cold, so bought all fruit, 2 oranges, a peach and a banana. This I polished off with a Coke. We walked past the old castle, around the moat, which was now a sunken park, to a grassy clearing, where we sat down to eat. It was a pleasant spot, and in about an hour, we thought it best to hit the road, as we had a lot of ground to cover.

Sights along The Romantic Road

    Leaving Nuremberg, we found ourselves on what is called The Romantic Road, a road which passes through some of the most beautiful German landscape. It didn't quite live up to our expectations, but nonetheless, it was quite a beautiful drive. It was similar to what we had seen before, rolling hills, villages, etc. The hills, however, were turning into foothills to the Alps, and the further we drove, the more attractive it became.

    We stopped about 3:00 in the town Rothenberg [Rothenburg], and this town is the epitome of what you imagine a medieval town should look like. In fact, it is famous for just this, so there were many tourists here, and this sort of thing has become a source of irritation. But the charm of this place is overwhelming. It is preserved perfectly. The signs for all the shops were just as they were 500 years ago; the streets and the buildings were seemingly unchanged. It was a very well-kept place, however, and I'm sure they have capitalized highly on their tourist trade. I sent Ann a card of one spot typical to this town, and I stood there myself. Believe me, it is much more impressive in 3-dimension. Rick and I walked around the town for a while, then returned to the square where our car was parked, where we sat down in a small sidewalk café for a glass of beer, which, by the way, cost only about 20 cents. Beer in Germany, delicious beer (much better than anything the U.S. produces) is very cheap.

Postcard: Rothenburg—picturesque medieval town in Southern Germany

    We left Rothenburg at 5:45, by this time looking for a place to spend the night. We passed thru several more towns, all similar in character to Rothenburg, finally settling down in Feuchtwangen, a small ancient looking town, complete with village square, fountain and a courthouse from which periodically, four young lads clad in bright red uniforms, step out through the door and play a bugle call (they each had bugles). We're staying in an equally quaint hotel, and we even have a bath in our room. At 7:30 we went downstairs into their oaken-paneled dining room for a delicious meal of steak, French fries, salad and beer for only about $1.50. We were periodically diverted by the 4 bright-colored buglers across the street, which we soon found out were announcing some kind of dance.

My cold is much worse. So I'm playing the hermit tonight and staying in. We picked up the German equivalent to Coricidin, which I've taken, and I've got to feel better. Until tomorrow, good night.

Love, Tom

Munich, Germany—Wednesday, July 17, 1963

Hi–
We got up at 8:00 this morning after a real comfortable sleep. It felt so good to be clean again! We went to a bakery, where we bought some fresh pastry and Bill and I found a coffee shop where we had coffee while eating our rolls. It was a great breakfast, and so inexpensive—only about 40 cents. We packed the car and left there about 9:00. We washed the car last night by the fountain, so we had not only clean bodies, but a clean car!

The Bavarian country is extremely quaint, with a story-book quality. And especially the towns and architecture convey this feeling. We stopped for a while in Dinkelsbühl, a medieval town famous for its well-preserved houses, churches, etc. There were bright colored flags waving from the Bavarian houses, and we found out later that their festival was approaching. Story has it that each year the mayor of the town has to chug a gallon of beer in celebration of the saving of Dinkelsbühl from Augustus IV centuries ago. It seems that Augustus was going to sack the town, which involved raping all the women, burning the whole village, and killing the children. However, the children of Dinkelsbühl went as a group to Augustus presenting him a bouquet of flowers and begging him not to purge the town. Augustus was so moved by the children of Dinkelsbühl that he changed his mind, causing such a celebration that the mayor chugged a whole gallon of beer. Well, in honor of all this nonsense, the mayor has been doing the same thing ever since. We thought the whole idea hilarious—and wondered what would happen if the mayor was a teetotaler. I suppose he wouldn't run!

Taking a break to do the "big switch"

    We continued our journey through similar towns and countryside, stopping at noon to buy groceries for lunch. I had the usual: salami, cheese, bananas and Coke. We stopped at a quiet spot near the Autobahn to Munich, where we rested and ate. It was an unusual spot in that there were two identical trees there overlooking a field, perhaps 3 feet apart. Between the two trees was situated a crucifix, and it seemed so strange, being in such a relatively isolated spot. But it had a restful beauty all its own.

We then proceeded on the Autobahn to Munich, stopping first at Dachau, located right outside of Munich. If you recall, Dachau was the largest German concentration camp, the spot where millions of Jews and war prisoners were exterminated. I was amazed at the horror of this place. It has been turned into a memorial area, and there is a museum there with pictures and documents concerning operation of Dachau. We were all astounded. First we saw the crematorium where the dead bodies were burned. They were like big ovens, shaped like caskets, and there was a storage bin underneath where ashes were kept before they were carted to the ash box (a storage box for them before they were taken to be used as fertilizer.) The museum was in the same barrack that had been used as the gas exterminator as well as crematorium. Here there were pictures taken during the camp's existence, and they were enough to horrify anyone. There were pictures of things like piles of bodies, all naked, being dumped into a truck. There were also pictures of some of the prisoners who were being led to the gas-room. They were stark naked, their bodies looking like walking skeletons, but their faces full enough to show the misery and agony of what they were experiencing. What seemed most horrible, however, were the pictures of these people in groups, live or dead. They must have literally starved them, for they were like walking dead men. And the piles of dead bodies, stacked like wood piles, was unbelievable. We walked into the gas chambers, where they had murdered them en masse, and noticed how they had the appearance of showers. You remember that they gave them bars of soap, making them believe that they were taking showers, and instead would push them in this room, turn on the gas, and kill them. Written on one of the walls in English was "God Forgive Them." The next room was a huge crematorium, where these bodies were then taken to be burned. There were series of ropes from which the bodies were hung before they were burned in the ovens. (Check the post card for a picture of this room.)

Postcard: The crematorium at Dachau

We spent about 2 hours there, being more and more horrified of such inhumane ideas—and only 20 years ago. This only proves man's basic evil is not a thing of the past—that we can trust no one of avoiding such cruelty, and that a modern world cannot think of itself as immune to anything so horrible happening again. There was a guest book for impressions and signatures as we left Dachau, and glancing through, there was a comment that seemed fitting—and that was: "You German Bastards!"

Leaving here, we were kind of dazed, and talked for about an hour of the implications the place brought to mind. It was so hard to believe that it all hadn't taken place in the Middle Ages—but no, it happened in the 20th Century. We have to be very careful!

So here we are in Munich, the capital of Bavaria! We pulled into town about 4:30 and looked all over hell for a hotel. Finally got one at train station, but it wasn't what we wanted pricewise, about $2.50 including breakfast. It is in the center of town, however, and after getting settled and unpacked, we left the place at 7:30.

Munich is a large city, probably well over a million. But the tallest structures in town are the cathedrals, and it has its share of squares, fountains and impressive spots. We ate dinner in the basement of the Rothaus, which is actually city hall. It's a real interesting building... very massive and richly ornamented with statues and intricate stonework. The restaurant was large, old and plain, and it seemed to have a regular clientele. Our meal of pork, potato dumpling, beer and apple strudel with whipped cream was only about $1.50, and was made most enjoyable by an Englishman who sat with us at the table and joined in our conversation, giving out with dry, humorous and interesting comments through the entire meal. He was a schoolteacher in Toronto, Canada, where he had been for several years, and was in Europe not only on vacation, but to see his homeland, England.

After eating, we took off for Munich's famous Hofbräuhaus, the world-renowned beer hall. And what a place it is! The first floor is a beer hall and huge beer garden with a German band tooting away on numbers which touch off singing, joining arms and swinging back and forth. It's a rude place, old waitresses carrying the famous Hofbräuhaus mugs overflowing with foam from the beer, old men busy pinching the ugly waitresses, and everyone having a grand time! The second floor is a restaurant, the 3rd a restaurant with floor show. We stayed in the garden sipping on beer out of their leder [liter] mug, and had a great time watching the goings-on. A fellow from San Francisco joined us and left a generally bad impression, but was interesting. He was one of those Americans with the show-me attitude, something I can no longer stand. Europe offers so much in such a different way than the United States, and one has to be willing to accept the differences and enjoy them. That is most of the fun anyway!

Postcard: Mugs of beer and arm-in-arm singing at Munich's Hofbräuhaus

    Rick and I decided to leave about 10:30 as we were both tired and wanted to go to bed early. We walked back through the inside section, and saw a ferocious argument between two Germans. One had been socked in the nose, and there was blood all over the place, the table, the floor and his face. He looked stunned with his face covered with blood, and the fellow across the table was still boiling mad.

    We walked back to the hotel, stopping to look at some of the beautiful fountains and watching some of the people on the huge square adjacent to our hotel.

    Since we're leaving tomorrow evening, tomorrow will be a big day, so I must sign off.

    Until then, goodnight.

    Love, Tom

Weissbach, Germany—Thursday, July 18, 1963

Hi–

Well, it's been quite an eventful day, busy in Munich and trouble with Freddy. We arose around 8:15, packed our bags, and went to the breakfast room for breakfast. It was continental breakfast, as usual, and there was an American lady and her daughter at the next table who engaged us in conversation. She had lived in the United States since she was sixteen, and had come back to her native Germany to see relatives. The catch was that she had been born in what is now E. Germany, but was allowed to spend a month there visiting. She had been given quite the royal treatment there, wined and dined by government officials, interviewed on the radio, etc., and she had quite an interesting slant on the whole situation. She didn't impress me as anyone very original, but what she said did make sense. In E. Germany the only people who are unhappy are the educated and professional, for they are not able to obtain all they want. The commoners, however, are better off now than they ever were before, in that socialism has given them a better living. These are the kind of people with whom she stayed, and they were also the kind that weren't at all bothered by the things which bother professional people. It was an interesting and worthwhile idea, although still making little sense to me as long as there are those who are extremely dissatisfied. At least in socialistic government, few starve!

After paying our bill to the old hag who runs the hotel, packing our bags and loading them in the car, we set out on foot to see Munich. We first went to the top of the cathedral Frauenkirche, where one can see all over the city and even the foothills of the Bavarian Alps. It was a hazy day, though, so our view was limited to just the town. After descending, we separated, Rick and I heading for the Modern Art Museum, Karl, Freddy and Bill for the Science and Industry Museum. Almost forgot to mention something we saw before going to the cathedral. In the rothause [Rothaus] (city hall), there is a famous mechanical clock which goes off every day at 11:00 AM. This mechanized clock, however, is not an ordinary one, but it does everything but turn somersaults and stand on its head! Situated near the top of the tower on the rothaus [Rothaus], at 11:00, a stone statue and a mallet begins to strike a bell, which it does, 11 times. Then the production begins. There are two levels, the top one flanked with a king and queen in the center, surrounded by subjects, including pages, knights on horses, ladies in waiting, and even two comic jesters. To the tune of twinkling bells, all of these figures parade in front of the king and queen several times, and the knight on their horses seem to be jousting. Sure enough, second time around, one knight is stabbed by the other's joust, and he falls off his horse. When this is finished, the lower level begins its production. It consists of a group of court dancers, who whirl around while doing a circular dance around a center figure who is directing them with his arms. After this is finished, the whole thing is polished off by a huge gold eagle who flaps his wings. The whole procedure takes 8 minutes, and quite amazing it is, at that. The clock was made in the 15th Century to represent the marriage ceremony of the king who was ruling at the time.

So after this we went to the top of the cathedral and there Rick and I left for the Modern Art Museum. On the way, we came across a small out-of-the-way restaurant which looked very good, so decided to try it. We were right. It was a great place to eat and not terribly expensive. I had ground beef, fried potatoes, cream of celery soup and milk for less than a dollar, and it really filled me up. After eating we headed for the Museum, passing through several interesting areas of town on the way. We found ourselves on Odeonsplatz, a square surrounded by huge structures and buildings. We crossed this and walked through the Hofgarten, a beautiful garden laid out in formal style and surrounded by an enormous palace on one side, reminiscent in some ways of Versailles, and a war ruin on another side. This ruin had been a magnificent Military Museum before the war, but was now only half there, and looking strange with its empty windows and jagged walls and tumbled columns overlooking this park. There was grass and greenery growing all over the building, and it seemed untouched since the war. We later found out that it was left there in that form on purpose to remind the people of Munich of the war.

We then walked to the Haus der Kunst (Museum of Modern Art) and spent about an hour there, looking at their unusual exhibition. It was an excellent museum and after seeing only part of it, we went out onto a veranda, sat down with a Coke, and looked out over the park. This particular park, called the Englischer Garten, is Munich's largest and most beautiful. We spent about an hour just walking through this place, and were impressed by the beautiful landscaping and two structures, an enormous Chinese pagoda and a white marble pavilion which towered high above the tree level. After leaving the park, we stepped into the National Museum located close by. Here we managed to finagle a couple of posters from the old man who worked there, and leaving here, we headed back to the Hofgarten, stopping first in the American Consulate building to see what it was like. A beautiful modern structure it is, and we found out here that we could have had mail sent to them or Embassy, and it would even be forwarded free. American Express charges a dollar to forward from each city.

On the way back to the car, we stopped in the Hofbräuhaus, where I bought some gifts and souvenirs. We arrived at the car at 4:45, and while waiting for the others to return, stepped in an ice cream shop which served delicious ice-cream and sherbet, very cheap, only 2½ cents per scoop. Believe me, most Americans don't realize how cheap food and living can be over here. You only have to be willing to give up a few of the luxuries we have at home, but you get other benefits however without paying the price.

The others finally arrived at 5:00 and we zoomed away at about 5:15, the delay caused only because the others saw the ice cream and decided they must have some. While waiting, some German boy struck up a conversation with us, telling us of his cousin who attended the University of Illinois. Naturally, we didn't know her, but it was interesting just the same. It took us about 20 minutes to drive thru Munich, but we at last were on the Autobahn, headed for the Alps of Bavaria. It didn't take long, for in less than 45 min. we drove over a hill, and lo-and-behold, before us was a splendid panorama of mountains, looking like pictures, and arousing our curious and adventurous spirit. We kept driving on the Autobahn for another half-hour or so, looking at the beautiful country, until we could stand it no longer, and decided to leave the Autobahn and take the German Alpine Road toward Berthesgarten [Berchtesgaden], a road which winds thru the most beautiful mountain region in Bavarian Germany. Once on this road, we found ourselves winding up, down and around through the mountains, valleys and charming Bavarian villages, mountain towns simply too interesting both architecturally and culturally, to adequately describe. But if you have been impressed with my description of quaint towns with red-roofed cottages and beautiful church spires nestled in valleys, these towns were 100% more beautiful and picturesque. So fascinated by the scenery, we didn't even want to stop, so kept driving, constantly surprised by things like the sound of mountain brooks, the beauty of a crystal clear ice blue mountain lake, and the peacefulness of the near-deserted Alpine Road. But, we came around a bend in the road, to see the sign of the town Weissbach, and beyond the town was a Bavarian hotel, not too large, and not too small, complete with an outdoor eating porch with bright colored umbrellas, and a beautiful view of the mountains. Unable to resist, we pulled in, so here we are. The price: $2.50 per night, including breakfast, and the surroundings peaceful and calm. At last—a vacation away from the vacation!

Medieval village along the Alpine Road

But alas! Too good to be true that such perfection could stay perfect, two mishaps spoiled the day. Upon arriving, Rick has found that his camera is gone. He fears leaving it in the Hofbräuhaus in Munich; of all God-awful places to leave a camera. We called the Hofbräuhaus and they know nothing of it. And we have looked everywhere.

Second mishap of the evening: Karl, Freddy and I were seated downstairs in the restaurant waiting to get some food to feed our weary, hungry stomachs. Conversation as follows.

Freddy: "Well, Tom, I guess you'll have to buy me a new pen."

Tom: "What do you mean. I put your pen on your side of the dresser in Copenhagen."

Freddy: "But I haven't seen it since, and you were the last one to use it."

Tom: "Freddy, where we unloaded our junk in the small room behind the Bruzilius' garage, I saw it there on the table."

Freddy: "But I didn't see it, my room was in the house. That was your room."

Tom: "As I see it, it was your responsibility to keep track of your own pen. And I can't see buying you a new one. I swear I returned it to you in Copenhagen."

Freddy: "Well, it was your responsibility to return the pen, and I haven't seen it since there."

Tom: (Getting madder and more irritated) "Let's don't talk about it. It's so ridiculous."

Freddy (louder): "Well, you don't want to talk about it! If that's the way you want...."

Tom: (Shouting and slamming an ash tray on the table before getting up and running out of the room.): "Shut up, God damn it!"

That's what happened, and I was so furious, I spent the next hour and a half walking around outside in the rain, while the others were inside eating. I realize it was ridiculous, but I just had to argue, even though it was such a petty thing. Freddy's irritation to me had reached its ultimatum, and I couldn't avoid getting boiling mad. I waited until Freddy had finished eating and gone upstairs, and went inside to eat. By this time, there was no hot food left, so I had a ham sandwich and a glass of wine. Soon Karl and Rick joined us, and we spent the next hour or so playing hearts, and after Bill and Karl retired, Rick and I played double solitaire until the place closed at midnight. By this time I was over my terrible fury, and they said that Freddy had sat through the whole meal, not saying a word. I imagine I hurt his feelings quite a bit, so when I went upstairs (he was in the other room), his light was on, and Rick said he was writing. So I martered [martyred] up, deciding that such a petty thing shouldn't ruin the trip, and stepped in the room to apologize. It was awkward business, but he was very humble saying it was probably just as much his fault, and I said that I shouldn't get so carried away! I hope that things turn out. But at least the patch-up work has begun.

So it is late as you can imagine, and I'm going back to Munich tomorrow with Rick to help him look for his camera. So our stay in the mountains has sort of flopped.

Until tomorrow, good night. Tune in for more exciting adventures then. Ho, ho!

Love, Tom

Weissbach, Germany—Friday, July 19, 1963

Hi–

Rick and I got up early this morning so as to get back to Munich as soon as possible in search of his camera. For some reason I had no trouble at all getting out of bed at 7:15, and after eating a typical continental breakfast of rolls, butter, jam and coffee, we headed for Munich. It only took about an hour to get there, as we took the Autobahn rather than the mountain road we drove on last night. The morning was bright, just the right temperature, sun shining, and made even better by the mountain scenery, which was almost as impressive on the Autobahn as it was on the mountain road.

We arrived in Munich at 9:30, heading first for the Hofbräuhaus. Upon arrival there, the woman who had worked there yesterday wasn't to be coming in until 10:00, and the manager upstairs said that no camera was found. So we sat by the souvenir window until 10:20, and still no woman. The manager appeared on the scene several times, and kept muttering about her being late, which didn't liven our spirits at all. At 10:30 when she still hadn't shown up, we proceeded to the police station where the central lost and found department was located. Alas! There was no camera there either, but they filled out a form with all necessary information, promising that if the camera was turned in, the American consulate would be more than happy to send it to his home. So we proceeded back to the Hofbräuhaus, and there found the old lady who had been there yesterday when Rick lost the camera. Alas! She hadn't seen it, and had no idea where it could be. So we likewise filled out a form here, now almost sure that the camera was gone forever. There was one more possibility: the ice-cream shop where we had bought cones yesterday before leaving. So we drove there, and as we suspected, they had seen nothing of it. So there was nothing left to do but return—having exhausted all possibilities. It was now about noon, but we decided to wait and eat in one of the villages on the road we had taken last night. So we got back on the Autobahn, turning off at the same point, toward Bernau, and found ourselves again on that same picturesque drive, which seemed even more so in bright daylight.

We stopped for lunch in a typical Bavarian town, probably the quaintest of the bunch. Our meal of Bavarian white sausage, mashed potatoes, sauerkraut and beer cost only 50 cents, and seemed like a wonderful deal, in that the outdoor restaurant with bright-colored umbrellas and loaded with tourists, appeared to be a more expensive place. However, we've found that this road is almost completely German or European tourists, very few, if any, Americans. This is what makes the trip most enjoyable, for me, anyway. The more I see of Americans over here, the less I like them!

We arrived at our hotel at 2:30, and not only had the other fellows slept late before climbing a mountain, but they had found Rick's camera! All that trip for nothing! But Rick was so relieved to get it back, and we had enjoyed the drive so much, that it made no difference.

I'm now sitting outside on the porch under an umbrella sipping a Bock beer. The others have gone swimming in one of the glacial lakes, I thinking that I'd better not since I still have the cold.

They returned at 6:00, and at 7:30, Karl, Freddy, Bill and I went down to the village to get something to eat. Stopping in a fairly new place, our greasy meal consisted of pork, potatoes, beets, potato salad and wine, and it wasn't an especially good meal. We drove back past some kind of festival, a field all lit up with different colored Japanese lanterns, but we were all too dead to stop. Upon arrival back at the hotel, we were surprised to see all kinds of cars and people, swarming the place. It turned out to be a typical Bavarian brawl, and we spent the next hour and a half watching the proceedings. They had been drinking all day, and there was a typical German band playing the folksy kind of stuff which made anyone want to jump up and polka around the room. There was even a traveling group of Bavarian dancers, dressed fit to kill in their authentic Bavarian lederhosen and the girls in their best mountainish dresses. The people were joining arms, singing, after standing on their chairs in some heart-throbbing toast or national song. One old codger was drunk as can be, bragging about the 15 leeders [liters] of beer he had drunk that day, and embarrassing all of the women he was trying to dance with. He would pick them up, throw them in the air, and pinch the waitresses as they went by. It was quite an affair—and certainly not designed for tourists!

I pulled myself away from all this at about 11:30, and I can still hear the singing and the music up here. So until tomorrow, good night.

Love, Tom

P.S. An interesting point I forgot to mention was a group of men and women dressed in black who had been drinking and getting high all day. We later found out they were mourners from a funeral. Quite an unusual way to mourn, etc!

AUSTRIA
7
Minnesota Girls and Magnificent Music

This land-locked country was annexed by its native son Adolf Hitler in 1938. It became part of the German Third Reich. Following the defeat of Nazi Germany in 1945 and a period of allied occupation, Austria re-established itself as a self-governing democratic nation.

Of course, when one thinks of Austria, the sound of music fills the air. This nation boasts such famous composers as: Joseph Haydn, Franz Liszt and Johann Strauss Sr. and Jr. Perhaps the greatest of them all, Wolfgang Amadeus Mozart, was born in Salzburg. No other country in all of Europe can claim the crown for such outstanding musical contributions to the world. Vienna, the capital, is both the heart and soul of this heritage. What better place to experience beautiful music?

§ § §

Salzburg, Austria—Saturday, July 20, 1963

Hi–

Here we are in Salzburg, home of Mozart and a beautiful town located in the Bavarian (now Austrian) Alps.

We got up this morning around 8:30, went down to breakfast, and spent most of it talking about what we would be doing today. After eating, I finished some writing and took a walk to the post office, and what an enjoyable walk it was! This place is so peaceful and scenic, we're completely surrounded by mountains, and the way to the post office led me down some narrow roads, over an old wooden bridge, and thru part of the village. Even the new homes in this country are built in a Bavarian style, and they have a distinct character of their own. Most are two stories, a fruitwood, heavily carved balcony surrounding the entire second floor, and adorned with shutters also of fruitwood. Oftentimes there are paintings on the sides of the white stucco walls, or decorative painted frame-like paintings over or around the windows. And no building is an exception. Even the post office was in this style, only truly described by pictures. After walking back, it was about 11:00, and we decided it was time to get packed and on the road. After packing the car, we stopped in a nearby grocery store to buy some food for lunch. I had the usual salami, cheese, grapes and Coke. We then hit the road, stopping at 12:00 on a high bluff overlooking one of the glacial lakes to eat. After eating, we roared off for Salzburg. The ride this afternoon was made interesting by not only the continuing gorgeous mountain scenery, but also by a stop at Berchtesgaden, the place where Hitler had his mountain hideaway during the war. We decided not to spare the time to go up and see it, but rode on through, stopping only to buy some postcards and medicine for the colds. (Incidentally, Karl and Freddy have both caught it!)

We finally got back on the Autobahn when we hit the Austrian border, and arrived here in Salzburg about 4:00. Being so anxious to see Kay Olson[1] (the girl I sat next to on the plane) who is studying voice and German here, the first thing I did was get cleaned up and go to the place where she lives. A woman of about 50 answered the door, and she spoke no English, but even so, I managed to convey to her who I wanted to see. She immediately called another girl to the door, an interesting creature who turned out to be from Tours, France and also studying in Salzburg. She spoke English well, but had a hard time understanding me, constantly asking me to slow down. So when I would come to a phrase I knew in French, I would use it, so there we were, talking back and forth in two languages. It was fun! Anyway, she told me that Kay was at the swimming pool, and wouldn't be back until 6:00. Also, that tonight was the birthday of a Swiss girl who was also living there, and they had planned a small party for that evening. But she said to come back at 7:00 and she would tell Kay I was here.

I then jumped in the car and headed back to the pension where we are staying to see if I could catch the others before they left for dinner, thinking that perhaps they might be able to also have dates with the other girls. But when I arrived they had gone, so I put on a sport coat, and went back near Kay's apartment, where I parked the car and started hunting for a place to eat. I ended up on top of Europa Hotel, a modern structure obviously designed for wealthy American tourists. But for only $2.00, I had a delicious steak, French fries, salad and beer—plus a beautiful view of the city. It was really no fun eating alone, and I realized that touring Europe alone would never be as much fun.

At 7:00, I made my way back to Kay's place, and after a royal greeting scene, we talked for a while about what we had been doing, etc. Mrs. Kurg then invited me to stay for the birthday party, and it was very interesting. The Kurg family had adopted one girl, and living with them for the summer besides Kay were a Swedish girl, the French girl, Claude and the Swiss girl, Christine. The language situation was very funny, as Mrs. Kurg only spoke German, Christine spoke only French, Claude spoke French, German and English, and the Swedish girl spoke not only Swedish, but German and English. And Kay and I spoke only English plus a small bit of French. The party sounded like United Nations must sound, with constant translating, starting sentences in one language and finishing in another, and much confusion. But it was fun, using all the French I could think of plus the German phrases I've picked up this summer. They even had a piano, which of course meant performance, so Kay and I spent about 15 minutes playing and singing. Kay, you remember, was the cute blonde who played the teenage role in *Bye Bye Birdie*[2]. We left about 8:00 and began driving around Salzburg.

Salzburg is a town, much like Heidelberg, steeped in the traditions of music, castles and the like, and loaded with all kinds of churches, fortification walls and cathedrals. It is situated between two mountains and the castle is located high on a plateau, overlooking the city. As soon as we saw this castle (supposedly one of the best preserved in Europe) all lit up, and "beckoning," we decided to go up. We parked the car on Kapitel Platz where is located an ornate and elaborate fountain, and proceeded to climb up toward Hohensalzburg Fortress (the castle). The higher we climbed, the more beautiful the view became, the lights of the city gradually blurring together, the silhouettes of the church steeples are the only structures blotting out the lights.

At the summit, the city below looked like a "dream," and we walked all around the dark inner court of the castle, finally stepping out onto a veranda which not only overlooked all the city, but was covered with small tables on which were candle lamps. So we sat down, Kay ordering a meal, and I just a beer. We talked for several hours, and really had a tremendous time!

We left at 11:00, both of us being tired, and I drove her back home. By this time, my stomach was killing me, and I felt like I was coming down with something. So, I should get to bed. Bill I found out, came in at 8:30 with the same trouble, so it could have been something we ate. So, until tomorrow, good night.

Love, Tom

Vienna, Austria—Sunday, July 21, 1963

Hi–

The stomach bug has got me, but I can't think of a better town than Vienna in which to have diarrhea!

I woke up this morning at 7:00 in Salzburg with stomach cramps which improved after relieving myself and after taking some of Karl's medicine, I felt much better and went back to bed, sleeping until 11:00. I hated to miss seeing more of the town, but in this condition, sleep was much more valuable. After getting up, dressing and packing we paid our bill which was only $1.40, and took off for Wien (Vienna). It had been probably the worst hotel we had stayed in, the bed so hard and full of bumps that sleep was impossible. I didn't feel like eating breakfast, so instead drank two Cokes, which I thought would help settle that stomach. Bill was feeling worse than I, and we thought it might have been the pork we ate in the small mountain town two nights ago. It was real greasy stuff, and I guess our gallbladders just couldn't take it!

We got on the Autobahn for Wien (Vienna), which was great while it lasted. But it isn't completed all the way from Salzburg to Wien, so half our time was spent on detours and lousy narrow roads. The car was very quiet, Bill and I with our trouble, Freddy and Karl with colds. (I still have mine too—double trouble!) We stopped for lunch at a small restaurant, and not feeling like really eating much, I had bouillon soup and lemon soda. We asked the waiter what a good thing for upset stomach is, and he pulls out this bottle of Austrian natural herb juice, so Bill and I tried some. It was a sweet, strong liquor and tasted much like crème de cocoa or similar after dinner drinks. But he said it did wonders for the stomach, which is the kind of statement you can easily believe but not help wonder just what kind of wonders it works. Since the difference between constipation and what I have is close to the difference between the devil and the deep blue sea, I just hoped that it wasn't a home brew for constipation. (We later figured out it was probably a hangover tonic.)

We pulled into Vienna at 7:00, stopping first at some places recommended in "Europe on $5 a Day," but having no luck there, finally went to the Westbahnhof (Railroad Station). They found us a place which is a student dormitory during winter, hostel in the summer. Our room for 4 nights will be only about $3.00, a great saving—and we even have showers! It's called the Studentenheim, and our room is wonderful—one of the best yet, very modern, desk, plenty of storage space and lots of room. We have really hit it lucky!

After unpacking, I've been only relaxing and writing as I still don't feel great and it will be a busy 3 days ahead. Bill went straight to bed, feeling very badly.

So until tomorrow, good night.

Love, Tom

P.S. As you probably have guessed I'm behind in writing as I've been sick and can't write every night. But I still write as though I'm writing each day. Bear with me. I'll try to catch up. Write me in Rome and Nice, France; please write; I want mail so badly. I checked today in Venice; no mail.

Vienna, Austria—Monday; July 22, 1963

Hi–

We arose this morning about 8:00, and after eating breakfast at the small café around the corner from the Studentenheim, we headed for American Express to check on mail. We got there about 9:30 and it was mobbed with people waiting to get mail, so we decided to come back later. The Grand Imperial Hotel, located right next door, we found out was being host to Richard Nixon[3] on his stay in Vienna. There was an enormous Cadillac parked in front with chauffeur, and we learned that Nixon would be leaving at noon—so having not the patience to wait, we went back to American Express to get mail. We later found out that we probably could have talked to Nixon, as there aren't just swarms of people around him over here as there would be in the United States. One lady we met had had quite a lengthy conversation with him. We should have waited!

At American Express we waited about an hour and a half for the mail, and it was a hot, exasperating experience; but it was a joy getting letters. I not only got two from you, but one from Mary L.[4] While waiting in line we got into a conversation with some fairly sharp American girls. One pair were expounding on their experiences, and they were very funny. They had been throwing away their dirty clothes rather than trying to have them cleaned. In one hotel, the maid had run after them, with a suit in her hand. But the girl told her to keep the darn thing; that it was too dirty for her to fool with; they were funny to listen to, but I got plenty tired after a while. There were also some girls there from Minnesota who were nice, nice enough in fact, that I had a date with one tonight.

After getting our mail, we were all sitting outside on the pavement, reading, when the girls from Minnesota came out. So after some preliminary conversation, we all decided to go somewhere to eat together, and we ended up in a Civil Service cafeteria which served a lunch for only 30 cents consisting of beef and noodles, soup, a cookie and all the water we could drink. We were all ecstatic about the place—even though it was far from luxury, the prices couldn't be beaten!

After lunch, we took a walk down along the Danube Canal, then strolling south toward the inner part of the Ring to St. Stevens [Stephen's] Cathedral, a beautiful place famous mostly for its Gothic detailed steeple. This whole time I was with Marilyn Dawson, a cute number from Minneapolis. After touring the church together, we left the rest of the group and headed for a sidewalk café, where we spent the next hour drinking Coke and talking.

Vienna's St. Stephen's Cathedral with its ornate tiled roof

Since our date for tonight was set at 8:30, and it was then about 4:30, we headed back for the Ring, she going North and I—West.

The Ring in Vienna is a fantastic Avenue which completely encloses most of the old palaces, parks and government buildings. It is Vienna's version of the Champs-Élysées, but not quite as spectacular, the pace being much slower. It has a wide center traffic lane for the heavy traffic, two boulevards on either side of this, and then two more traffic lanes for parking and slow traffic going either way. It is a huge octangle [octagon], one side which follows the Danube Canal.

On the way back, while enjoying all the splendid buildings and parks, I ran into the rest of the group, who were admiring the Natural History and the Art Museum, two identical buildings which face each other over a park and statue of some mammoth goddess sitting on a throne.

Then all eight of us headed back toward our place, passing three statues of the men who founded the Austrian Republic and turning left in front of the impressive Parliament Building. We all stopped in a café for a Coke before Rick and Karl took the other three girls back to their hotel.

Bill received his slides from Paris today and it was fun looking through them and recalling those great times in Paris. I still think that that is my favorite spot!

I spent the next couple of hours cleaning up (they have wonderful showers here!), shining shoes and writing. Rick and I took off at 8:15 to get the girls (he got a date too) and we spotted them just in the place where we had planned to meet. It was amazing what showers and clothes can do to people. We were, I swear, a completely different group. We then drove to a place called the Volksgarten (Garden for the Folks) where we had a terrific time! It was located right across from the Parliament Building in a beautiful garden. There were thousands of tables with red candles making them more appealing; and the trees were lit with blue and green lights. There was a huge dance pavilion in marble and the best dance band I've heard in ages. It was a huge outfit with all kinds of soloists, groups, etc. They did everything from the Twist to the Cha-cha and Samba. We ate wiener schnitzel, salad, drank gin fizz. The band was perfect to dance to—and we spent the entire evening there eating, talking and dancing. And the meal, service, cover charge, etc. amounted to only about $12.00 for the four of us. What a deal!

Another day gone—and time to say good night. (By the way, it costs 24 shillings to get in this place after 12:00 midnight, and we lacked it by 10 groschen. The drunks at the door laughed, and we ended up having to beg the money—very embarrassing!)

Love, Tom.

Vienna, Austria—Tuesday, July 23, 1963

Hi–

Today has been another interesting day, and I'm beginning to get more of a feel for Vienna. I slept till 9:00 this morning, and upon arising, I found everyone gone—and I had no idea where. So after getting dressed I went over to the café for breakfast. The little old lady who worked in there I'll never forget—she speaks German with a Brooklyn accent (if that is possible) and scurries around saying "*Bitte*" constantly (Germany's expression for "please" or "may I help you"). But she was quite a comical figure, almost as entertaining as any of the sights I had thus far seen in Vienna!

After eating, I went back to the room, gathered some of my dirty clothes, and proceeded downstairs to the washroom, where I did my laundry—very crudely, but done. After this, I finished some writing and went back to the café for lunch, which consisted of a ham sandwich and lemonade.

I then headed for downtown, where I first went to American Express hoping for some mail. There was no more, so I purchased a ticket for the tour of the city which left at 2:30. While waiting to buy the ticket, there was an obnoxious American man of about 50 talking to one of the American Express people about reservations in Venice. He wanted some impossible type of arrangement made about picking up tickets for a train at some airport in Venice, and he was loud, stupid and maddening to watch. I can't understand how some of these Americans can expect so much. They are really obnoxious. Of all the people from other countries I've observed over here, the Americans are by far the most obnoxious of the group: it makes you wonder just what is wrong with our manners and tact.

It has been a terribly hot day, and the tour was the same, although interesting. We passed the Fountain of the Divine Province, the fountain across from which Marilyn and I had sat yesterday. Our guide led us then down below a cathedral into the Imperial Vaults, the tombs of more than 250 persons of royalty and their families. It was merely a series of rooms containing elaborate coffins, of varying degrees. Franz-Joseph's coffin was there, it being the last of a series which started centuries ago. It was a fascinating place. We then passed all kinds of statues and monuments, most of which I can't remember now, but including things like the Palace of Justice, The Spanish Riding School, the Imperial Stables (400 horses), and Vienna University.

We then took a tour of Shönbrunn [Schönbrunn] Castle, actually a palace located on the outskirts of Vienna where the royal families lived for a couple hundred years. Although not as impressive as Versailles, it came very close, and some of the rooms equaled it, although in a different way. We went through 41 rooms, the Royal Apartments, and they were well worth seeing, even on a hot day!

On the tour bus I sat next to some gal from New York, and she was amazed at the low prices we're paying for things. Of course she and her husband were paying $12.00 a night for room alone, and I was aghast myself, since we have consistently been doing it for $2.00 and less. She was nice but a character.

The tour ended in front of the Opera House, a huge monstrosity still under construction from the war. Our guide told us that the bombers mistaked [mistook] the Opera House for a Railroad station, and completely demolished it. After stepping out of that oven of a bus, I headed back to American Express where I was supposed to meet the four from Minnesota and Rick at 5:30. The girls arrived on time, but at 5:45, there was still no Rick—so not knowing how I was going to get my ticket for the concert if I stayed with the girls, I bid them adieu, heading back for the hotel. It is about a 45 minute walk from there to the Studentenheim and I arrived about 6:30. Rick had decided that he didn't want to wait until 5:30 which I wondered about, courtesy-wise, and Bill had not returned yet from his date. He was out with a girl he had met in Berlin by the name of Irmtrout Vodka. (Can you believe that name?—her friends call her Irmy for short!)

After a shower, change and cleaning up, Karl, Rick, Freddy and I went over to the café for dinner of wiener schnitzel, salad, potatoes and lemonade. By the way, my stomach trouble has completely disappeared, which is quite a relief to my food-loving soul.

After eating, we headed to the Rothaus for the concert, and entered an inner courtyard, completely surrounded by massive walls 6 floors high, and an ideal place for a concert. We saw the girls from Minnesota there, and sat in seats right next to them.

The concert was terrific—Mozart, Steffani and finally Dvořák's New World Symphony, which was the best on the program. The Vienna Symphony Orchestra lived up to all our expectations, playing every note to perfection.

After the concert, we took the girls to a small café for drinks—but everyone was too tired to try much of anything else afterwards. It seemed kind of anticlimactic to the wonderful evening before, but we all said our awkward goodbyes, realizing that we'd never see them again—and not really caring. It was strange.

So, it is late—and I must get to bed. Tune in again tomorrow for more exciting adventures. Good night.

Love, Tom

P.S. Enclosed is program from concert.

WIENER SYMPHONIKER

mit Unterstützung des
Kulturamtes der Stadt Wien

July 23

KONZERT IM ARKADENHOF
des Wiener Rathauses
Dienstag, den 23. Juli 1963, um 20 Uhr

PROGRAMM:

Wolfgang Amadeus Mozart . . . . Dorfmusikanten-Sextett,
1756—1791   („Ein musikalischer Spaß") K. V. 522
  Allegro
  Menuett
  Adagio e cantabile
  Presto

Jan Stefani (Bearb. G. Fitelberg) . . Suite aus der Oper „Krakowiacy
1746—1829   i Górale"
  Ouverture
  Polonaise
  Krakowiak
  Oberek

— PAUSE —

Antonin Dvořák . . . . 5. Symphonie, e-moll, op. 95
1841—1904   („Aus der Neuen Welt")
  Adagio, Allegro molto
  Largo
  Scherzo (molto vivace)
  Finale: Allegro con fuoco

WIENER SYMPHONIKER
Dirigent:
WITOLD ROWICKI

In den Sitzreihen ist das Rauchen verboten!

Programmpreis: 50 Groschen

Program—Vienna Symphony performing Mozart, Steffani and Dvořák

Vienna, Austria—Wednesday, July 24, 1963

Hi-

Good evening, ladies and gentlemen. Are you all ready for another exciting episode in the adventures of Tom and the Idiots abroad? If so, sit back, relax, light up a Lucky, and get ready for more fascinating anecdotes. Seriously, I'm beginning to wonder if that isn't the way these crazy letters are beginning to sound. I hope not!

We got up around eight o'clock, and after a breakfast downstairs in their own cafeteria, went our separate directions. After writing for a while, Rick and I set out in the car looking for a place which could develop our film. I now have ten rolls finished and it will soon be eleven. We were directed to a place on the other side of Vienna, near the Danube River; after arriving there, we found that they could not do it and send it to me in Rome since they didn't know what would turn out and what to charge us for. So we gave up on that idea, deciding to take a walk to the river. After standing on the bridge for a while and taking a few pictures, we walked down by the bank over to some kind of boat station, where we bought a Coke and some ice cream, which we used to make Coke floats—the first one I'd had in months. We then headed back for the car, passing a huge church located right there on the bank.

We then drove out to Belvedere Palace, a huge castle also used at one time by Austrian Royalty, now used as a museum. It was a beautiful place and was flanked by very large and impressive formal gardens in the French style. We spent about an hour there, looking at some of the paintings and walking through part of the garden.

We then jumped back in the car, heading for the Prince Eugene Hotel, where, if you haven't heard, King Saud of Arabia is putting up some of his wives and relatives while they are staying in Vienna. It seems that King Saud fears [for] his life and has escaped the country, bringing with him not only his 80 or so wives, but also his several hundred children and servants for all. Rick and I walked into the lobby, but sure enough, here comes some dark-skinned Arab slinking down the red-carpeted steps, completely wrapped in some white gown, with headdress and earrings, trailing behind him was one of the children, a little girl dressed in a very Western style, and a comical contrast to her elder. King Saud himself was not staying here but in some private villa in the mountains with only his select wives and concubines. We heard that the eligible sons are wooing the Vienna girls with all sorts of jewels and gifts. We also heard that one of the servants is following them around town in a Chevrolet; and his only purpose is to throw them gold coins whenever they need them on their nighttime tours of the city. It's a riot.

Rick and I then headed back toward our hotel, him letting me out near the Art Museum. It was then only about 2:30, so I had the entire afternoon to do as I pleased. I made the mistake of spending about an hour looking for film, which I never did find, but the excursion took me to interesting parts of the city which I had not previously seen. There was a beautiful park right inside the Ring which I strolled through, amazed at the countless people just sitting around there enjoying the surroundings; there were young mothers with their children, old men and women and American tourists (can't get away from them). But it is by far one of the nicest parks I've seen—perhaps because of the beautiful buildings which loom through the trees or the good upkeep of the grounds. I also spent some time just looking at some of the fountains which flanked the exterior of the Palace located in the Ring. Some of the craftsmanship and skill displayed in the sculpture is unbelievable!

At about 4:00, I was checking on film in another shop when I heard a feminine voice call my name, and I looked up to see Freelen Arbeiter and Sue Small, two girls from the U. of I. that I had last run into by accident on top of the Eiffel

Tower. So we spent the next hour in The Mozart Café talking about what we had been doing thus far etc. They had just come from Italy and told us to expect a dirtier, more conning place—so we shall see. But it was a real enjoyable time, even though I can hardly stand to make small talk anymore about silly things—which seemed to be the mode of the conversation most of the time. I then headed back toward home after bidding them a lengthy, sappy goodbye.

I walked past the Rothaus on my way, passing through a garden with a beautiful fountain on the way. I made it back about 6:00. Almost immediately after returning, I left again with Rick and Karl for dinner, which kind of irritated me since I had not had a chance to get cleaned up, but they had been ready, so I figured that I shouldn't say anything and make things unpleasant.

I developed a terrible cough today, and the cigarette I had after eating in a small outdoor café (roast beef, green beans and wine) really did me in. So instead of going with them nightclubbing, I decided to stroll over to that park near the Rathaus and sit by the fountain watching the people.

This I did, and it turned out to be a real interesting time. Before I had been there 20 minutes, some old lady sat down beside me, mumbling something to me in German. I told her I spoke no German (in German) and she proceeded to go on talking. Well, we had about an hour and a half conversation in German, most of which was a German lesson for me. I have picked up quite a few German phrases, which I was able to use in finding out how to say other things; and it is surprising how similar the two languages really are. After hearing German for over three weeks, you really begin to understand quite a few things; my vocabulary consists of only a few verbs and nouns and very common things that we have needed. But tonight I learned to count as well as the words for flower, lamp, fountain, finger, etc. She was quite a funny old gal, and to top off the whole situation, the man and woman next to her (also an old couple) were offering their two cents worth throughout the whole thing. It was a refreshing experience. And they seemed real impressed that I was an American.

When she left, my cough seemed to get worse, and all of a sudden I felt a chill. I put my coat on which seemed ridiculous since it was such a hot night, and after a few minutes, I felt much worse, and my cough was sounding chronic. So I got up and started walking back to the hotel which is actually quite a ways from the park. I had to stop periodically to rest; and it was now quite apparent that I had a fever; I was freezing and my head was swimming. I finally stumbled into the café, ordering a hot lemonade hoping that this would help break the fever. Bill and Freddy walked in, and I didn't even feel like talking. A few minutes later I made my way to the room, stripping and getting in bed. Bill came in, gave me two pills and some Ben Gay, which I rubbed on my throat and chest. As you have guessed, I am writing this much later than today (figure that one out) but I went to sleep tonight worrying about not only being sick but spoiling the plans to leave tomorrow; no I won't tell you what happens. Find out for yourself in tomorrow's letter. Ha, ha!

Love, Tom

P.S. I did get better!

ITALY
8

Getting Lost in Venice, Finding Art in Florence

A breezy summer afternoon…an outdoor café in the Piazza Something-or-Other. Church bells are ringing from the centuries-old parish church just footsteps away on the cobblestone street. The young Americans sit at a table covered in a starched white cloth. A gentle breeze moves in concert with the flow of water from a nearby fountain. A rather plump waiter, wearing a matching white apron, eagerly awaits their order. Will it be espresso? Or perhaps a bottle of local wine… resting in a straw holder? Time stands still. Stay at your leisure. Life here is well-lived…whether in 1963, today or maybe even forever.

§ § §

Somewhere on N. Italian Border—Thursday, July 25, 1963

Hi–

We got up this morning around 7:30, and thank goodness, the fever was gone, even though the cough was still here. But I think that the Coricidin and the 11 hours of sleep made all the difference in the world as to how I felt. About 9:00, after packing and getting dressed, Bill, Rick and Freddy took off for American Express, Karl and I for the University of Vienna Health Clinic, in hopes to see a doctor. We spent the next hour or so going from building to building, and finally ended up buying some medicine in a drug store.

By the time we got back to the car, it was 11:30, and after drinking a Coke to replenish our spirits, we took off for our journey to Italy.

Getting directions—a necessity in the days before GPS

We soon were in mountains again, very similar to the ones before we got to Salzburg. We stopped in a small grocery store along the way to buy lunch, consisting for me of ice cream, a banana and a Coke. I still didn't feel great, and the cough was terrible. The mountains were now getting higher and higher, and the country was even more beautiful than it had been in the Bavarian Alps. Some of the mountains even had small patches of snow, a sight we had not previously seen.

We crossed the Italian border at approximately 7:30, and granted, it has been a long day. We were then anxious to find a place to stay, as we were all bushed, and ready to plop!

We inquired in the first Italian town we came to, but there was "no room at the inn," so to speak, as we proceeded up the road to the next village. We stopped in a gasthaus which was filled, but some old man in there said that his sister ran a wonderful pension up the road and to follow him. Granted, it sounded fishy, but at this point, we were too desperate to care. Upon arriving at his sister's pension, we were immediately shown two rooms on the third floor, and they seemed fairly decent, and the price was very low, so we figured we had not a thing to lose. His sister was a woman of about 55, and not only quite a character, but fluent in two languages, German and Italian. She looked very German to me, as did half of the people in this part of Italy, and I suppose she in a way is half German!

After a meal of soup (some kind of delicious minestrone brew), wine and cheese, I was feeling pretty badly, and went up to bed. So, that is all for today. Goodbye Germany and Austria, hello Italy. What are we going to do to communicate? Until tomorrow—good night.

Love, Tom

Venice, Italy—Friday July 26, 1963

Hi–

We got up this morning after one of the most miserable nights I've spent in ages. I coughed all night, a condition which is certainly not conducive to sleep, and to top it off, there were trucks and heavy traffic passing by our window on the highway all night. This wouldn't have been so bad, but there was another building directly across the street, and each time one of these monstrous trucks would pass the window, it would then set the two buildings playing some kind of exchange the vibration game, and there were continual reverberations all night from those damned trucks. And if it wasn't the traffic, it was the cough. So today I'm dead. Another thing I forgot to mention. The beds were made out of straw; need I say more? Needless to say, we felt that for once we didn't get such a wonderful deal, and that the dollar we paid for the room was too much. Before leaving, we had breakfast at the hotel, and it too was miserable—the coffee was half curdled milk and half black stuff they call coffee—it's actually more like mud. There were two Italian women in the breakfast room who kept asking us questions—Karl, Rick and I were the only ones down. We finally figured out that they wanted a ride to Venice—this became apparent when they quickly gave up the idea upon seeing our other two comrades. But to us this kind of custom seems strange.

I'm mute today—after that whole night of coughing, I can't say a thing—just have to whisper—and as you can probably tell from the tone of this letter so far, I'm not in the greatest mood. It's a terrible handicap not being able to sing while driving—I've found this one of the best ways to pass the time. However, I may become much more popular with the group after losing my vocal abilities.

The mountains in this part of Italy are truly beautiful, much more majestic than anything previous. The Italian countryside also has a distinct flavor all of its own. We're beginning to see more of the characteristic Italian architecture and landscape. The villages still have their red roofs, but they have taken on a Southern look, the type of look typical to Spanish architecture, but not that severe. The landscape is more bare and seems typical to a hotter area. The characteristic cypress and pine trees dot the roads and countryside; and the interwoven vineyards and forests on the mountainsides combine to make this country distinctly different looking than Germany.

We stopped in Udine to get some Italian money and to take a rest around 10:30, and then proceeded on toward Venice. The Italian drivers lived up to our expectations; racing like mad and passing at impossible places; we saw some close calls, but everyone seems to make it.

We arrived in Venice around 1:00, and received a very poor introduction to a city which later turned out to be fascinating. As there are no cars allowed at all in Venice (the city of canals), you must park your car on the outskirts of the city and take a canal bus. There were two distinct parking areas: one nearer the city, and one a few hundred meters further away. So we tried first of all to find a place in the lot near the city, and spent about an hour driving around looking for a place to park, unsuccessfully pulling into spots where we weren't supposed to be, and simply goofing away time. We finally ended up in the other parking lot, and it was a simple matter parking there, and the price only about 25 cents. We had a riot talking to the Italian man who ran the parking lot. The Italians are so completely different from the Germans and Austrians, that it is amazing, being that they are so close together.

It was terribly hot, and we were all feeling muggy and sticky. We unloaded only the essentials from the car to lug all the way into the city, and after locking it up, took off on foot back to the other parking lot, where there is a boat-bus station. On the way, we met some other fellows who had been in Venice for a couple days, and were willing to show us the way into the city and point out several good hotels.

We hopped on the boat, luggage and all, and then watched the city of Venice unfold. It was one of the most fascinating experiences so far; this city is unlike anything I've ever seen: The buildings along the canals look extremely ancient, probably 14th Century, and they have a distinct Eastern flavor in their design. They are mostly of stone or stucco, and they are painted different shades of yellows, greens, reds, and browns—these colors faded by the years and weather. And yes—there are thousands of gondolas gliding through the canals; their colorful gondoliers in blue-striped shirts and straw hats with ribbons yelling at each other each time they reach an intersection and skillfully maneuvering their gondolas with one oar. We got off the boat at station 7, heading down a narrow alley-like street, all the time pushing through crowds of people and climbing the small bridges which span the canals. All the streets, except a few in Venice are narrow, possibly because of the lack of cars. Being in this city seems truly like being in Venice must have seemed several hundred years ago.

Upon arriving at the hotel, we immediately made a deal, and for 15,000 lire, we have an antique sweet [suite] of four rooms, the price including two meals a day, lunch or dinner and breakfast. The proprietor's son led us through a labyrinth of very tiny pathways and streets over a small bridge to a door with a gold plate and huge knocker in the center. We knocked, and soon from a window on the third floor, a little old lady appeared and unlocked the door, after which we were led up two flights of narrow marble stairs to our "suite." It was not complete luxury, but we did have four rooms, a small sitting room, two bedrooms for two each and one small bedroom for one (I was immediately designated that room because of my cough.)

After getting settled, we made our way back to the restaurant and sat down to a delicious lunch of spaghetti, roast chicken, lettuce and tomato salad and peaches for dessert. The place is very nice—tablecloths, waiter who speaks English and good service.

After lunch, we went to St. Mark's Square, probably one of the most unusual places I've ever seen. A huge thing, it is swarmed with pigeons, formerly fed at the expense of the Republic. All around the square, covered galleries shelter famous cafés and luxury shops. In front of the basilica three flagpoles with bases carved in the 16th century carry banners symbolizing the Venetian Kingdom of Cyprus.

Pigeons and people in *Piazza San Marco*

The square opens onto the Grand Canal through the Piazzetta, formerly called Intrigue because from 10:00 to noon only the nobles were allowed to meet there to traffic in appointments and to discuss their plans. The two granite columns surmounted by the Lion of St. Mark and the statues of St. Theodore were brought from Constantinople.

Pictures are really the only near adequate expression of this place, but it is overloaded with grandeur, and seems so very old—and somehow more convincing than many of the other old things we've seen.

The romantic Bridge of Sighs

Venice is built on 117 islands, has 150 canals and 400 bridges. Many of the brick bridges, with white stone trimmings, are pitched high to allow barges to pass under them. The hub of Venice public life is found on St. Mark's Square, where tourists and citizens sit on the terraces of the famous Florin cafés to listen to the music played by the small orchestras which line the square and watch the thousands of pigeons being fed. Venice was founded in A.D. 81 by inhabitants of Malamocco, near the Lido, fleeing from the Franks. It has been a famous artistic, cultural and trade center of the world for over a thousand years—also a meeting city of the East and West.

After looking at the sights on St. Mark's for a while, I went to American Express to see if there would be any mail, was surprised to find none. Either you're not writing everywhere or something is happening to the mail. After that disappointment, I headed through the narrow streets, window shopping and preoccupied by the interesting sights that I was seeing. I headed for the Rialto Canal and spent about an hour just walking along it and back eventually to our hotel, where I rested from about 5:00 to 9:00. My cough had been getting worse, and the rest was very much needed. The others soon returned, and I had missed the ride on the gondola, which was disappointing, but I'm sure the world won't end.

I took off again at 9:00 on my own, wandering back to St. Mark's Square, where I ran into by accident a special treat. The University of California Glee Club was doing a concert right there in the middle of the place, and I stood there for about an hour watching and listening. They were a good singing group, and had many unusual and interesting numbers. It seemed like old home week, and made me anxious to get back in a way. You do get that kind of feeling every once in a while.

After the concert, a group of the Glee Club was still singing away at some drinking and school songs, which were loyally greeted by a group of American girls who were obviously from the same school. They seemed to be having a lot of fun—and the Italians were having almost as much fun watching them.

On the way back I ran into the rest of the group, and we spent the rest of the evening strolling around the square, drinking lemonade and Coke, and observing all the sights.

Before the concert, I had been walking in the direction toward a dock, where a boat left that I wanted to take. Well I got lost, and wandered through the streets and narrow passages for about an hour before I finally found out how to get back. I kept walking through more and more desolate areas, and the swarming crowds were now a few Italian sailors and local Venetians. I finally stumbled into a dark square near an old church, and standing there bewildered for a moment, wondering what to do, I spotted a couple of nuns who were scurrying out of the church. I ran over to them, asking them if they spoke English. They didn't, but they did speak French, so I asked them in my atrocious French where St. Mark's Square was, and they shook their heads, smiled and said to follow them. So here I am in Venice, scurrying after two nuns down narrow and dark passageways. We had a minimal conversation in French, accomplishing not much more than who I was with and how long I would be here. But I did finally find my way, and that is when I ran into the concert.

At around midnight, we returned, and as usual, it is late. So until tomorrow—good night.

Love, Tom

P.S. The whole episode with the nuns now strikes me very funny—what do you think?

Florence, Italy—Saturday, July 27, 1963

Hi–

I arose early this morning, and after eating a terrible breakfast at the hotel, decided to walk down to St. Mark's Square with Rick and Karl. My coughing during the night has enabled me not to be able to talk, and it's a frustrating experience.

St. Mark's Square as I said before is unlike anywhere else we've seen. The pigeons are swarming all over the place—all over the street as well as the people—to the point of irritation. This square is huge, surrounded on 3 sides by this immense columned building and on the other side by St. Mark's Cathedral, a monstrous church with a very Eastern look, made so by the oriental domes, gold inscriptions and strange structure. Karl and I went inside the place after walking around the square a while, Rick staying outside since this old man with a sword and napoleon's hat wouldn't let him in with Bermuda shorts on. Inside, we saw a very ancient looking place, and different too from any other church we've seen. There were red-robed priests saying mass like mad back behind the altar, and we were quite amused at the combination of this with tourists swarming all over the place. It somehow seemed very unreligious—as does much of the ecclesiastical area when visited by many tourists. We ran into Bill and Freddy then, and after leaving the church, turned left toward the Grand Canal. The area between the church and canal is also very magnificent, adorned with huge white columned buildings and two massive pillars in the middle of the square. It all seems like it should belong in India, not Venice. Even at this hour the gondoliers were trying to get customers, and one practically has to fight them off. Some of the gondolas are very plush—beautiful red velvet chairs with gold tassels. Others not quite as plush. And they are expensive.

Gondolas—the only way to get around in Venice

We turned left, walking up the canal. What a beautiful place this is. And the lack of any motor vehicles makes it seem like it shouldn't exist. We passed the Bridge of Sighs, walking up the island. The colorful Venetian buildings plus the wide walks and the white bridges crossing each side canal add up to give Venice a charm no other city in the world could possibly possess. There are absolutely no new structures here. They seem to have been standing just this way, patiently watching the tides creep up around their sides for hundreds of years. Perhaps you can understand more what I mean about the atmosphere of Venice from the post cards. It actually looks just like that. We walked all the way up the waterfront to a small park, where there were old couples, young children and cats sitting soaking up the shade of the Venetian trees. From this end of the city, one turns back to see a panoramic view of all of the Venice waterfront and the division into two islands. It's really an amazing sight.

Here we boarded a boat which headed back toward the city, and this perhaps, is the best way to see a city like Venice. The canals are full of these bus boats, plus private yachts, gondolas and transportation barges, which I assume deliver the food and goods to all the shops each day. We passed the fire house, and sure enough, there were the fire-boats. We rode past St. Mark's Square, around the Grand Canal toward Station 7, which was the one closest to our hotel. It was a fascinating trip. We departed from the boat and made our way to the hotel, pushing our way thru the mobs of people on the streets, thru the narrow alley-like passages, over several bridges, and finally to the hotel. We paid for our suite of rooms, for five amounting to about 15,000 lira [$24.19], and took off. In Italy, you feel like you really have a lot of money, especially when throwing around 5000 lira bills. There are 620 lira to one dollar. Translating can get confusing at times.

Before leaving, Rick and I wanted to get some posters, so we went back to St. Mark's Square, where Rick got a couple of posters, and I went to American Express to check on mail. It was closed, so we headed toward Pier No. 7 where we were to meet the others. There we grabbed a sandwich and a drink, sitting outside right on the canal, around this very small table, with all of our luggage plus the people and the pigeons. We were even serenaded by two old beggars, who were playing Italian songs on a mandolin right there on the canal. The boat arrived soon, and we gathered everything together, lugged ourselves plus luggage on the boat and headed up the canal for the end of the island, where the car was parked. Getting off the boat we flipped to see who would get the car, and good old lucky Tom won (or lost, whatever), so Bill (feeling martyrish) went with me to the lot. The attendant had to move about 5 cars to get ours out, and also tried to charge us another day, which I refused to pay, since we hadn't been there 24 hours. He got a sheepish grin on his face, upon which I was certain I was right and, not listening to any more of his garbling in Italian, I drove off, yelling a repeated "*Gratsie* [*grazie*]," which in turn, drowned out his yelling. And it sounded great in a hoarse voice—very funny.

We therefore left Venice at 12:30—exactly 23 hours after arrival, and it had been plenty long enough. There is really not much more to see in Venice than the city itself—but that is certainly well worth seeing. We were now headed toward Florence—the art capital of Italy outside of Rome, the home of Michelangelo and other famous artists. We stopped about 3:00 for a Coke and continued on without stopping. The Italians are senseless drivers, stemming probably from the fact that they had motorcycles until a few years ago, and when they began driving autos, a lot still think they're on a cycle—believe me, a situation that doesn't breed a cautious driver.

The Italian countryside is very different. The tall cypress pines, the barren hills, the rock walled vineyards and the warm weather makes Italy so different from Germany. We hit an Autostradda [autostrada] about 5:00, and also the mountains. From there on, all the way to Florence, we were on a road which weaved thru the mountains—and a very beautiful one at that. We must have gone thru countless tunnels, and it was a truly spectacular drive.

We arrived in Florence at 6:00, and the first thing we did was call a Student place recommended by Frommer in "*$5* *a Day."* It was filled however, so we then made our way to the Railroad station for hotel reservations. Since no one knows any Italian, we had a terrible time trying to ask directions to the place. After finally finding out the name of the station, Rick and Bill got out of the car, and by our own radar system, we made our way slowly, but surely, to the station. They would stop at every street corner, asking the direction. Upon the point of a finger, we would go in that direction, Rick and Bill running along the street, the rest of us following in the car. There were swarms of people on the streets, and we were a strange processional, roof racked piled high, trying to get to the stupid station. We did finally arrive there, and soon found a place to stay. It's called Hotel Alexandra and is located on one of these small curved streets (alleys). It's on the 3rd floor, and we later found out it was a palace at one time. After unpacking, getting settled and cleaned up, Bill and I took a walk. We're very close to the famous shopping bridge, a bridge built over the river just crammed with shops several stories high. Florence is a town famous also for its low prices on linen and leather goods, so we priced some linen in a shop—all hand-made stuff and very beautiful.

Bargains on the bridge—shopping in Florence

Since dinner was served at 8:00, we went back to the hotel, where we ate a mediocre meal of soup, roast beef and fruit. There was a whole crew of kids from London staying here also, so Bill and I got into a conversation with a couple of the girls afterwards. I love to hear the English accent, and we had a good time chatting away with her and Eve. Eve loved the American accent, which surprised me, and they were fairly impressive girls. I'm looking forward a great deal to England.

We returned at 10:30, and it's fairly late, so must go to bed. So, until tomorrow, good night.

Love, Tom

P.S. I'm really behind in my writing. It's now the 8th of August, and we were in Nice yesterday, where I got your message to call. Since I thought you were worried about my health, and it takes so long to call (about 7 hours from here), I decided to send the telegram. So sorry I haven't written, but I have been kind of sick. However, I feel fine now, and hope it continues. Please don't worry. If you received back-dated letters and they are about me being sick, remember that now it is all over, and I'm only doing it for purposes of this diary, which I want to be very complete. Write me if you still want me to call in Edinburgh, Scotland—and I'll call from there. Hope nothing serious.

Love, Tom

Florence, Italy—Sunday, July 28, 1963

Hi–

Arose this morning around 9:00, feeling dirty enough to pay for a hot bath, which was the most wonderful thing in the world. It's amazing how things like baths can become such luxuries over here. Karl, Rick and Freddy had already left by the time I finished splashing around in that hot water, but Bill was still in the room. We decided to go to an English-speaking church, which turned out to be the Church of England, no less, and also one of the funniest experiences of the whole trip.

Before church we had a couple of rolls and some hot tea in a small bar nearby. The church itself was very inconspicuous on the outside, looking no different than a small office or store. However, upon entering, it took on quite a church-like air, and actually was quite elaborate. Not really knowing what to expect, we sat in pews near the front. Soon we saw that everyone was kneeling during part of the service, and some "sweet old lady" was kind enough to point out where we were in the prayer book. Even though the Church of England is Protestant, it had many similarities it seems to a Catholic service. The young priest, very, very English and adorned in long elaborate robes, we soon learned was substituting for the regular priest who was home in England curing some ills.

Today was communion Sunday, so his sermon was all about the blood that was shed by Christ for our sins. It was truly a ridiculous sermon, and the young priest's extreme English accent added to the preposterousness of the whole situation. It was obvious from his stage fright that he had had little experience in the pulpit, and the whole presentation consisted of one boo-boo after another. When he stepped up onto the pulpit, he laid down a Bible which proceeded to fall to the floor. This wouldn't have been so bad, but it was filled with tons of papers which in the falling, flew all over the room. Someone picked them up for him, and after a few embarrassing comments, he proceeded into the sermon. The subject being bloodshed, he began with an analogy of the early Jewish temples where little white lambs were brought to be slaughtered in sacrifice, and their blood trickled over the white marble floor into a golden chalice. He then told of how Christ was the true sacrifice for all our sins and of the blood shed on the cross, etc. In one violent gesture, his hand went flying up, and alas, hitting an enormous gold carved crucifix near the pulpit, it went flying through the air and crashing on the pew, finally to the floor. I was at first stunned, then amused. But he continued as though it hadn't happened, which made matters worse, because laughter was almost impossible to contain. I actually dug holes in my hands to keep from laughing, even though I felt sorry for the poor chap at the same time. His sermon didn't help either, for his next example was a personal experience— when he was a student in Australia and had to give blood to save a bushman's life. Bill and I should have received a medal for self-control. To top it off, after the sermon and a few songs, he adorned two long lacy robes in which to serve communion, and while walking up the steps to the altar, he tripped twice on the robes, a sight so funny, that Bill and I had to get up and leave. It's strange how much funnier things are when you're not supposed to laugh.

After church we walked back to the hotel, there running into Freddy and Rick who had been out exploring. The four of us decided to leave, not knowing where Karl was, and we did so, stopping in a small restaurant for lunch. We had spaghetti, veal cacciatore, spinach, Coke and peaches, and it was extremely mediocre, the grease on the veal giving the whole meal a bad taste to me.

We then headed toward Piazza Della Signora, a huge square where is located ancient buildings, the large fountain and statues and monuments. The fountain, noted mostly for its huge statue of Neptune by Ammannati is beautiful. There is also a huge copy of the statue of David by Michelangelo there as well as the Uffizzi [Uffizi] Palace and Galleries—one of the most famous museums in the world for great masterpieces of art from the 14th, 15th and 16th centuries. After walking in the courtyard of the palace, we went into the museum, which unfortunately closed at 2:00. We did, however, get to see such things as Lippi's "Madonna and Child," Fabriano's "Adoration of the Magi," and my favorite: Botticelli's "Birth of Venus." These paintings you've seen thousands of times in reproduction and in books, but they are quite different in person.

When the museum closed, Bill and I decided to see The Cathedral of Florence, a gorgeous and huge structure built entirely of white and deep green marble, and looking as clean and new as the year it was built, 1369, to be exact. The Papistry, right adjacent to the Cathedral, and built of the same marble, is the oldest structure in Florence. It was used as the cathedral of Florence until 1128, and even Dante was baptized here. It's octagonal in shape, dedicated to St. John the Baptist, and is an example of Tuscan Romanesque architecture. The doors of the church are cast in solid gold, and the East Door is the most famous— containing panels representing biblical scenes, carved by Ghiberti in 1452. The door is really an amazing piece of art—even Michelangelo called it the Door of Paradise. The interior of the Papistry is also the white and green marble, but the ceiling (cupola) is a Venetian mosaic of the 13th century—most of it in gold. These mosaics are truly beautiful works— unlike anything one could ever see in the U.S.

The Florence Cathedral—with its marble panels of various shades of green, pink and white

We then walked inside the cathedral, which was not nearly as impressive as the outside, but noteworthy for some of the art found there. Most mentionable is Michelangelo's "Pieta," a statue by him done at the age of 75. It is an unfinished work, but very beautiful—and unlike pictures of it. We sat there for about a half hour, just looking at the work, and impressed by the smoothness and naturalness of the lines. Michelangelo was evidently an artist who knew how to make his subjects appear human—an added touch which many artists seem to lack.

We left there about three, stopping in a sidewalk café for a lemonade on the way back to the hotel. There we met Karl, and the 3 of us decided to walk up to Michelangelo's Piazza, a huge square located on the side of one of the mountains overlooking Florence. We took off across the bridge and left along the riverbank for several blocks, turning right, and beginning the climb up the side of the mountain. It's a beautiful area, surrounded by trees, and made more beautiful by the breathtaking view of Florence. We kept climbing until we reached Michelangelo's Piazza, the square overlooking Florence and flanked by a huge reproduction of "David" in the center. After watching the sunset over the city for a while we climbed even higher, toward the Church of San Miniato Al Monte, a building, again of white and green marble, begun in the 11th century and finished in the 13th. We sat up there for a while watching the nuns scurrying around and the city below, and then took a road down toward the city, which took us through a section of the old city wall. I must say that the view of Florence was completely refreshing, the tallest structures being the cathedrals, and the sun setting over the buildings, shining its reflection into the waters of the river. The old bridges looking then like they must have looked 500 years ago. The lack of skyscrapers is a distinct thing about European cities which makes them so very different from ours.

On the way back we watched the fisherman by the river, lazily passing the evening hours away with pole in hand, wife and family by his side.

It's been a wonderful day—and I like Florence very much. The Italians seem to have a no-care attitude, and are also very disorganized. You have to always count your change, as they must think it some sort of prestige symbol to shortchange tourists, but they are an interesting lot. I must at least give them credit for producing so many masterpieces of Renaissance art.

So until tomorrow, good night.
Love, Tom

Florence, Italy—Monday, July 29, 1963

Hi-

Another interesting day in Florence! I got up this morning around 8:30, and our goal for the morning was to see the Pitti Palace, an old palace now used for a museum. The Uffizi museum was closed on Mondays, so this was our only alternative. Rick and Freddy had already been here, so Karl, Bill and I left the hotel around 9:15 for the place, which was located across the river, to the right of the bridge. We stopped at a small coffee bar on the bridge for breakfast, which consisted of a couple of rolls and tea, and I then mailed some post cards and a letter.

Upon arrival at Pitti Palace, we decided to first take a walking tour of the gardens, since at the time there were busloads of people trying to get into the museum, and we didn't feel like fighting the crowds. The gardens were impressive, but after places like Versailles and Schönbrunn, they seemed like second fiddle. Karl and I found a bar in the garden, where we had a Coke and got into a conversation with an interesting fellow from New Jersey, and then headed back for the palace. On the way back, I ran into a girl from home I'd met in American Express in Vienna and then seen again in Venice. It's truly a small world!

The Pitti Palace museum is a wonderful collection of art—both paintings and sculpture. We spent about 3 hours there, impressed not only by the famous paintings by artists like Raphael and Van Dyke, but also by the magnificent interior of the palace itself, built in the 15th century. The Medici family was responsible for so much of the artwork in Florence, and the world is now thankful to their extreme enthusiasm for art. We left there about 2:00. We stopped on the bridge at the same place for lunch which consisted of a cheese sandwich and ice cream. Ice cream in Italy, by the way, is delicious—and I find myself stopping all the time for some.

We then headed for the Medici Palace, which houses the famous Medici Chapel, but it was closed at the time, so we walked over to Piazza Santissima Annunziata, a square which supposedly contains the harmony of the Renaissance spirit. Opposite the square is the Church of the Santissima Annunziata, built in 1250 by the founders of the Order of the Servi di Maria. The inside is richly decorated in the Baroque style, the ceiling of inlaid stuccoes, the decorations of statues and paintings very beautiful. After about a half-hour here, we returned to the Medici Palace, where we ascended a flight of stairs into a small chapel, where is located the famous painting "Voyage of the Three Kings" by Gozzoli, painted in 1459. We sat in the room for about 20 minutes just looking at this work, which covered 3 walls in a mural style, and were amazed at how different it looked from the reproductions we had seen.

Leaving here, we headed toward the cathedral, splitting up. I proceeded to American Express where I stood in a line from 4:30 to 6:00 for mail, and after all that, there was none. I was very disappointed, but figured you had not received my card saying I would look for mail here. It matters not. I then headed back for the hotel, and while crossing the bridge, ran into Bill who was with some fellow from Minneapolis who goes to Stanford. The three of us went to a small sidewalk café for a Coke, Bill telling of the beautiful linens he just bought, I of the horrible ordeal at American Express. The fellow from Stanford was very interesting and gave us some wonderful tips on what to expect in Rome. We're leaving tomorrow for there, and any added information was helpful.

After this, I stopped in the linen shop and bought some beautiful place mats and napkins, which you should receive soon. They are all hand-made, and were so inexpensive that I couldn't pass up the deal. The beige set is for Leslie DuBoe's[1] wedding present, the green ones for you.

Bill and I then headed for the university, where is located a cafeteria serving meals to students very cheap. On the way I ran into Kathy Hanson, a girl from the U. of I. whom I had no idea was in Europe—again, small world! We arrived there at 8:30, and the meal of spaghetti, beefsteak and tomatoes, beer and fruit was delicious for only about 50 cents. These are the kind of places we should find more often.

We walked back to the hotel, and here I am on the nightly grind. By the way, at the restaurant, we ran into Bob, the fellow from Stanford, as well as Karl, Rick and Freddy. I suppose we all go to the same places!—but it seems strange always running into someone when you're not expecting it. So, until tomorrow, good night.

Love, Tom

P.S. Also bought Ann an umbrella on way back to Hotel. To open it, you must give it a sudden jerk, or else it won't open. Should receive it soon.

ROME
9

*The Forum, the Fountains
and a Surprise on the Appian Way*

Located in the heart of Italy, Rome is known as the "Eternal City." It remains to this day a cultural, political and religious capital. Where else can you experience such wonders as the Coliseum, the Roman Forum and Trevi Fountain, to name a few. Rome has for centuries been the home of the central Italian government. Within its boundaries is the physical seat of the Roman Catholic Church: Vatican City, the only existing example of an independent country within a city.

Italy under Mussolini fought against the Allies in World War II. After its defeat and liberation, Rome and Italy's post-war development proceeded at a quick pace. Lots to see, do and "experience" in this glorious city.

§ § §

Rome, Italy—Tuesday, July 30, 1963

Hi-

Well, here we are in Rome! Believe it or not. Unfortunately I don't feel much a part of the city since we've not had a chance to do anything yet.

We got up early this morning in Florence—around 7:30. After cleaning up and getting packed, I ran out to mail some letters and see about having Ann's umbrella sent. In the post office I ran into Marsha, the lady we met in the Louvre in Paris who knew so much about art and was so informative. She has been in Florence since then soaking up all the art, getting to know the artists, etc. She was also headed for Rome, so I assured her that we would probably meet again there. She was spending the rest of the summer there before returning to San Francisco.

When I arrived back at the car, everyone was waiting, and the first thing on the agenda was The Gallery of the Academy, which was closed yesterday, and houses Michelangelo's "David," which we had to see before leaving Florence. Upon arrival there, there were mobs of buses and people trying to get in, but after a patient wait in line, we did make it—a wait that was worth every minute. "David" is a huge sculptured figure of a nude young man, carved when Michelangelo was 25 years old (1501–4). What is so impressive about the statue is its extreme life-like quality. Michelangelo was a great student of anatomy, it is said, and in order to find out how all the human muscles work, he would dig up fresh corpses, cut them up and examine their muscular structure—only for the purposes of his art. That is the sign of a true perfectionist—a quality necessary for the very fine artist. Located also at the Academy were unfinished sculptures also by Michelangelo, and they were interesting too, although not nearly as much so as "David." We left there around 9:30.

On our way out of Florence, we stopped at the Automobile Club of Italy to buy some gas coupons, enabling us to make a great savings on gas money while traveling thru that country. Karl and Rick went to take care of this, which took about 45 minutes—a lag which made it already about 11:00 when we finally pulled out of Florence headed for Rome.

The drive from Florence took us through the mountains, and a most scenic route it was. The poplar trees, the distinctly Italian umbrella pines, the rocky terrain all made the drive interesting. About 1:00, we stopped in a small Italian village, where we bought some wine and fruit to keep us nourished until reaching Rome. It was a small place right in the mountains, and while there, I took a walk into the old part of the town, strictly medieval, and complete with narrow winding streets, and in this town, very few people. The drive through the ancient city gate of the old town wall and of the mountains was amazing. The wine we bought must have been the local brew, for it was really fowl [foul] tasting stuff. I couldn't down a drop, so to quench my thirst, I bought a Coke—that wonderful international drink!

The fork in the road that leads to Rome

The rest of the drive to Rome was long, beautiful and tiresome. We wound around and up and down thru the mountainous roads, sometimes wondering if we weren't going backwards—but we finally saw road signs that proved Rome was nearby, and about 3 miles from Rome, we stopped at an information center, which turned out to be a place to make hotel reservations. We asked the gentleman there about a Student Place since we had had such good luck with the like in Vienna, and he told us where it was, but could not call them for me. So after getting a few city maps of Rome, we headed for the place.

The student place we found was in the university area, and was a series of beautiful, modern dormitories. Rick and I went into the main desk to see if there was room and found out unfortunately that they were all filled. By the way, I had to use my French here as the fellow at the desk spoke no English. It's amazing how French has come in handy. Upon leaving, we drove by a huge open area, surrounded by statues of Roman design, and found out later that it was the Olympic Stadium.

So now our only alternative was to drive to the railroad station, to see if they could find us a place. This drive was quite an ordeal, but while being pushed thru Rome almost like a helpless beetle caught in a rainstorm, we did manage to see the Colosseum, old ruins we presumed to be The Forum and numerous fountains and churches, many of which seemed to strike a bell from pictures from high school Latin texts. I swear that the Roman drivers don't know what they're doing. There are several streets meeting in one square, with no stop signs or traffic lights. You merely close your eyes and dare the other drivers to go before you—and surprisingly enough—it seems to work out. We did overhear one very disconcerting comment, and that is that one person is killed every 23 hours in Rome traffic accidents—and the accidents are too numerous to mention. Another interesting fact—the traffic commissioner of Rome recently resigned after spending three years crusading to improve traffic conditions. He resigned after finding out some statistics which are: in 1960, when he started, one person was killed in Rome every 25 hours, and someone injured every 30 minutes; now, there's one killed every 23 hours, one injured every 20 minutes. I guess I would have resigned too!

We finally made it to the "Termini," and Karl and I went inside to make the reservations, the others staying in the car. At the information booth, the Italian there was so rude that we were furious. He could only give me a room at $5.00 per day including 2 meals, and we knew that we could find a place cheaper than that. He gave us no courtesy or satisfaction at all, spending most of the time flirting with the American girl who was behind me in line. So Karl decided to go hunting, while I waited for the others, who had to come there in order to tell us where the car was parked. I stood there for about 20 minutes when Freddy and Rick came bouncing up. When I told them the situation, they headed for one of the Airline offices, in hopes that they could give us more help.

When they returned, Karl showed up also, and he told of finding a place for $1.50 per night. About this time, an old gentleman hobbled up to us, asking in broken English if we needed a hotel. We said yes, and he then said he could fix us up for $2.00 per night. We said that we had found a cheaper place—one for 900 lira ($1.50), and after a short hesitation, he said that we could have the same price in his hotel, if all 5 of us slept in the same room. He then said to follow him, and this we did. He had a shabby sport coat on, baggy pants, and a funny little hat with hotel printed down the rim, and he walked as if he owned the city, leading us across streets, stopping traffic, and winding through mobs of Italians, fruit and vegetable stands, finally into a huge doorway into an ancient looking flat—dirty, but reminiscent of finer days, with its marble floors and staircase and its high vault-like ceilings. We boarded a huge ancient black elevator and ascended to the third floor, where turning left, we found ourselves in Hotel Comer, a small pension that looked halfway clean, and certainly good enough for our purposes. The room was immense, and from the window was a view of the huge modern railroad station, as well as the surrounding tenements. So we declared it a wonderful deal, and told him we would take it—for five nights. Since buses to any part of the city could be caught at the station, we actually had a wonderful location, and even though not luxury, it was adequate.

We then made our way back to the car, which was parked a couple blocks away, and even the old man followed us—determined to help with the baggage. I'm sure he wouldn't have been so free with his services if he had known how much baggage we had. After reaching the car, where Bill had been waiting, the old man wanted to lead us back to the hotel, and so we went, he with Karl and I walking through the streets, the rest of the lot in the car following. We made a strange procession I'm sure, Karl and I both in Bermuda shorts, a manner of dress just not seen in Rome. We finally made it to the hotel, got unpacked, found a place to park the car, and unloaded our junk in the room—a task which was harder than it sounds, being that the total of our luggage plus us takes an amazing amount of space. I've seen people frequently amused by our packing or unpacking the car. As Karl says, it is truly a "Keystone Cop Scene."

By this time it was 8:00, and we were starved. We went to a small bar-like snack shop across from the station, and what to our wondering eyes should appear on the menu but hamburgers and milkshakes. Not having seen or heard of hamburger since leaving the States, we went wild, ordering ten hamburgers to start with, and milkshakes too. The hamburgers were delicious, made with a lot of meat plus onions, tomato, lettuce, and topped with loads of ketchup. We couldn't have been or looked anything but American, all of us literally cramming them down. But, admittedly, it was one of the best meals of the trip!

After eating we went into the railroad station to buy some magazines. Here I got into another minor hassle with Freddy who thought I should buy a *Time* magazine, since I hadn't yet bought one, and he thought I should, since I had been reading everyone else's. He was right, but could have said it in a nicer way. I was infuriated, but refrained from blowing up, remembering the last terrible incident. After this I found a camera shop in the station that would develop some film for me. So I returned to the hotel to get the film, taking it back over to the station.

So that's our first day in Rome, but there is so much to see that is going to be interesting. So, until tomorrow, *arrivederci*.

Love, Tom

Rome, Italy—Wednesday, July 31, 1963

Hi–

This has been by far one of my favorite days of the entire trip. Rome is a fascinating city, made so by its wonderful history and relics of that history.

We all got up early this morning, all anxious to get to American Express for mail as early as possible and then to explore parts of Rome which we have heard so much about. So at 7:00 we were out of bed, and on our way to American Express by 8:30, after getting dressed and grabbing a quick breakfast at a coffee bar across from the termini. We boarded a bus at the termini, and rattled along the Roman streets, up and down some of Rome's seven hills, until we found ourselves at American Express after about a 20 minute ride. It wasn't open yet, but the line was already about 300 feet long, wrapped all the way around the building, but we gritted our teeth, hoping that we could make patience the virtue it is supposed to be. So when the doors opened at 9:15, all the Americans went charging in, us included, most everyone clamoring up the stairs to the mail room. The line was divided into 5 lines, 4 for receiving mail by alphabet division, one for leaving forwarding addresses. But did they have 5 people to take care of the 5 lines? NO! One gentleman handled 2 lines plus the mail forwarding line, and two girls took care of the rest. Such inefficiency is worse than getting into East Germany. We've found that American Express is so poorly handled in some of these cities that something should be done. The line moved very slowly, but after about an hour I finally received my mail—and it was well worth the wait.

Not only did I get the two letters from you, but two about Stunt Show, one from Mark Juergensmeyer and one from Vicki Grometer.[1] They gave me nothing at all to go on, but Mark's letter was full of wonderful witticism so typical of him, and I thoroughly enjoyed reading his letter. By this time it was about 10:15, so we really had to hustle if we were going to accomplish anything at all today. On the way out I bought a guide book to Rome and a map of the city, two things which are essential it seems to really benefit from a visit to a city. Rick had already received his mail and was gone, so the four of us set out to get orientated. We first headed for the American Embassy, in hopes that we could buy some cigarettes there cheap. Following the map, we wound thru traffic and narrow streets in search of the place. We ascended the Spanish Steps, a beautiful wide staircase about 200 feet high, and leading to the section of Rome we were looking for. The square there is called Piazza di Spagna, and was the most important square and the heart of Papal Rome. The fountain at the bottom of The Steps of Trinità dei Monti is designed by Bernini, and is said to commemorate the great flood of 1598 and to mark the spot where a boat was left by the retreating waters. The staircase was built at the private expense of the French Ambassador Gouffier.[2] It was competed in 1725. On the right of the staircase is the Memorial House of Shelley and Keats, where the latter poet lived during his residence in Rome, and where he died on February 24 in 1824.

After climbing these steps, which was quite a feat in itself we headed toward Via Vittoria Veneto, one of the smartest and most exclusive streets in Rome, where is located the American Embassy, actually an old palace built in 1886. It is considered one of the finest palaces of modern Rome, built from a design by the architect Koch for Prince Boncompagni who, later on, sold it to the first queen of Italy, Margherita de Savoy. It has belonged to the American Embassy since 1944. When we arrived there we found that the commissary was closed for repairs, and even if it had been open, we would not have been able to buy anything there without some official type card. So even though Karl had worked for the Army and Air Force Exchange Service last summer and had an official looking card, this alas, did us no good whatsoever.

So after a cold drink of water at a water cooler there, a device almost unseen anywhere in Europe, we headed toward the old center of Rome, where is located things like various forums, monuments, the Colosseum, etc. We stopped on the way in a small coffee bar for lunch, where we stood up while munching on tuna fish sandwiches and Coke. These coffee bars, by the way, have two different prices for everything, the price if you sit at a table, one if you stand. Since the stand-up price is lower, we naturally have made it a habit of doing that.

All along the way, we kept seeing old ruins of buildings and walls, some of them I'm sure dating from ancient Roman times. We soon arrived at Piazza Venezia, the heart and most important center of city traffic. It's a beautiful square surrounded by buildings of great artistic and historic interest, most impressive of which is the Monument to Victor Emmanuel II, an enormous white building adorned with statues and fountains. Begun in 1885, it wasn't completed till 1911, and at that time was dedicated to the Unity of Italy. To the left of this building runs the Via Del Fori Imperiali, a huge wide boulevard opened in 1932 in order to bring light to the remains of the Imperial forums, hidden for centuries under the medieval sections of the city. It is one of the most important archaeological promenades in the world. Along this avenue there is an uninterrupted succession of temples, forums, basilicas, triumphal arches, towers, and churches representing every period of the history of

Rome. The splendid monument to King Victor Emmanuel opens the avenue, while on the left is seen the imposing column of Trojan towering over the remains of the basilica Veia. Farther on is the slope of the Quirinal with the market of Trojan surmounted by the balcony of the Knights of Rhodes. Farther on the left is the forum of Augustus and on the right the large ruins of the Forum and Palatine hill, one of the most beautiful panoramas I've ever seen. There are many more impressive churches, forums and old ruins along this street, and as a background to this certainly unique enough view is the majestic ruin of one of the seven wonders of the world—the Colosseum.

The first thing we did was wander into the old Trojan Market, imposing ruins uncovered in 1932. The market was at one time a beautiful circular structure, and today remains still beautiful, but in ruin. The front of the Market was formed by three stories of shops one above the other which could be entered from five different parts. It begins on the ground floor with a series of eleven shops running around the Forum. On each side of the semicircular edifice is a flight of steps leading up to another series of 21 shops while a third series is still higher, on another level. This market being in the center of the city must have been the aristocratic shopping district of ancient Rome and the best and most adapted for the commerce of precious products from Egypt, Arabia and India. Here also must have been the shops where pepper was sold, at that time so rare and precious. We spent about 45 minutes just roaming about in these old ruins, most of which were in an extremely good state of preservation. It gives you a funny feeling indeed to stroll along streets and through old buildings where Caesar himself probably strolled 2000 years ago.

We then passed by the Forum of Augustus and the Forum of Julius Caesar on our way to the Roman Forum. All of these ruins are set down from street level about 20 feet, a strange situation in itself. I suppose that the constant building over the centuries kept raising the level, thus causing these ruins to now appear so far below street level. We reached the entrance to the Roman Forum, and upon entering found that we had to pay a price. Hooray for the student ID's which got Bill and me in for free. Karl and Freddy didn't bring theirs, so they left us then to return to the hotel to get theirs.

And so I spent the rest of the day in the Forum, one of the most fascinating places imaginable. This historical place saw the origin, the development and gigantic increase of the powers of early Rome and of the Kings of the Republic. It was the scene of the greatest events of history, where the fate of humanity was discussed and decided by the men who for centuries directed the destinies of the world. This valley witnessed later on the slow decline and final ruin of that great people and of its wonderful monuments. Even though mostly in ruins, the Forum still shows traces of its ancient architectural splendor, and like an immense book of marble, the leading events of the history of Rome are still chronicled in monumental structures.

Upon entering the Forum the first thing we saw were the ruins of The Temple of Julius Caesar, a temple built by Augustus in 29 B.C. in honor of Julius Caesar and built on the spot where Caesar was cremated and where Mark Antony delivered his famous oration "Friends, Romans, Countrymen, lend me your ears," etc. etc. Across from the temple is The Basilica Aemilia, erected in 179 B.C. and one of the oldest basilicas in Rome, mentioned by Cicero for the magnificence of its decorations and for the money lavished on it. It is now simply a flat area, with many broken marble columns left, a reminder of its ancient splendor.

The endlessly fascinating Roman Forum

    To the Northwest of this is The Curia or Senate House, built in 670 B.C. and later rebuilt in 80 B.C. We stepped inside this ancient place, amazed at the wonderful state of its preservation. The only reason it was preserved was because of a Pope in the 7th century who converted it into a Christian church. It was in this building that the Roman Senate assembled for so many centuries and the fate of the Roman world discussed and decided. Inside can be seen the step-like seats for the Roman Senators, some of them still preserving their original marble decoration. At the end of the hall facing the entrance on a platform, stood the so-called "curules," the chair of the two consuls who presided and directed the assembly. Between these, during the Empire, stood the throne for the emperor and the praetor. It has been assumed that there were 300 members of the senate, as this many chairs have been found during recent excavations. You can't imagine the reflective feeling you get standing in such a place—it's the kind of awed feeling you get when you think of how very important this place was to the world—decisions made here have affected even us—and they were made so long ago. And now all that's left is a deserted ruin—chills in the spine are easy to come by.

We then walked back along the Via Sacra, the most celebrated street of the Forum and of ancient Rome. Here passed the most important triumphal and religious processions. We then turned right past the Temple of Julius Caesar and passed by the Temple of Vesta, the famous shrine where was kept the ever burning fire, symbol of the power of Rome. The temple, with its sacred fire was for so many centuries considered the power of Rome, but had to yield to Christianity and be closed together with all the other temples. In 394 A.D., Theodosius I ordered the closing of all pagan temples, and it was then that the sacred order of the virgin priestesses were suppressed and the fire extinguished forever, after having burnt without interruption for almost eleven centuries. This eternal fire grew out of ancient customs of fire worship, and in Rome, a group of girls was appointed to guard the fire, later becoming the Vestel [Vestal] Virgins. These girls were originally chosen from the most noble families in Rome, and their chief duty was to watch the fire, in turn, both day and night. They took a vow of chastity, which if broken, was punished by stoning and other horrible forms. Later on, it became difficult to secure girls whose families were willing to let them go, so the Vestals were from the Plebian classes. We next passed into the ruins of the House of the Vestals, which now is most impressive for its small garden and pools in the center, surrounded by statues of some of the more outstanding Vestals. Here we ran into Rick who had been exploring the other end of the Forum, so the three of us continued our exploration together. The most refreshing thing about the Forum today was the lack of tourists. The place was almost completely empty except for us, and it made it much more enjoyable; to be able to walk around these fascinating ruins in a quiet atmosphere was wonderful.

We then decided to walk to the top of Palatine hill, one of the hills overlooking the valley of the Forum, and now a quiet place loaded with ruins and ancient memories held only by the many ruins which lie there. The Palatine is supposedly the cradle of Roman civilization and the place where Romulus built the first walls of Rome. We spent about a half-hour wandering about among the old ruins of the houses of the early Roman patricians, and stopped to get a Coke in a small bar on top of the hill. We then took a flight of steps down toward the Forum, taking us through the ruins of some very ancient palaces which were built on the side of the hill, overlooking the Forum. These ruins were really fascinating, and it was a mysterious feeling being the only people there. We found traces of old mosaic floors, small patches serving only as reminders of how splendid this part of Rome had been at one time. Rick and I, feeling in an adventuresome mood, crawled under some fences where we weren't supposed to go, and wandered about the old interiors of the palaces, coming upon all sorts of interesting relics of the past—statues, patches of the ancient mosaic floors, and of their stuccoed walls. Bill left us here, heading for the Colosseum.

We finally descended again into the Forum, passing The Temple of Castor and Pollux, a ruin of three huge columns, originally built in 498 B. C. We then headed toward the Via Sacra, turning left toward the Curia. In front of the Curia is The Tomb of Romulus, a place held in controversy by archaeologists. At the end of the Via Sacra is The Arch of Septimus Severus, erected in 203 A.D. in honor of that emperor, and a huge arch covered with carvings representing ancient military victories. Behind this arch and covered by a wooden shed is The Vulcanal, the first meeting place of the Roman Senators, where they gathered in the very early days of Rome before the Curia. Nearby is the Umbilicus Urbis Romae, a brick construction which marked the exact center of the ancient city. Rising to the left are three Corinthian columns, The Temple of Vespasian, built in 81 A.D. Nearby is The Temple of Concord, built in 367 B.C. and a place where Cicero delivered one of his famous orations.

On the south side of the Arch of Septimius Severus is The Rostra, the platform where orators used to address the people, including Cicero. We took turns standing on this old ruin, and felt almost like orating. Nearby is the Column of

Phocas, pictures of which you've surely seen, and erected in 608 A.D. Behind the Rostra is The Miliarium Aureum, or golden milestone, a monument on which were inscribed the names and distances from Rome to the most important towns of the Roman Empire. Right next to this is The Temple of Saturn, the most ancient temple in the Forum, dating from 497 B.C. It has quite a few columns left, and is one of the most impressive structures in the Forum. In front of the Rostra is the Comitum, the place where people gathered to listen to the political speeches, and to the left of this is The Basilica Julia, once used as a court of justice, begun by Julius Caesar and finished by Augustus.

Rick and I then headed back down the Via Sacra, leaving the forum by way of the Via del Fori Imperiale [Via dei Fori Imperiali], turning left, and walking toward Capitaline [Capitoline] Hill. We climbed the steps where the author of "The Decline and Fall of the Roman Empire" supposedly stood when inspired to write the book, and found ourselves on Piazza del Campidoglio, designed by Michelangelo under Pope Paul III. There is a huge statue in the center of the square, and it is surrounded by three grand looking palaces. Spending only a short time here, we walked then toward the Forum, out onto a ledge overlooking it. The view from here is truly breathtaking and wonderful for getting the full flavor of The Forum. We then descended the hill and walked over to The Forum of Augustus, where we stood meditating for a while, before walking to the Forum of Trojan, most noted for the huge column protruding from its floor. We then returned to The Forum, where we climbed up between the columns of The Temples of Vespasian, and sat for about an hour and a half, watching the sun set over the Forum. This is one of my favorite moments of the entire trip. After spending the afternoon investigating the Forum, the view was made so much more awe-inspiring, and we were able to get the full effect of the place. In the distance we could see the ruin of the Colosseum, towering over the ancient ruins, and it was one of those undescribable [indescribable] moments, the once-in-a-lifetime type experiences. The shadows of those ancient buildings kept getting longer and longer, and we wondered if Cicero, Caesar and Mark Antony had too sat between these columns centuries ago, watching the day end, and thinking of the problems they faced. It was a wonderful experience.

Around 7:00 we started walking back to the hotel, passing by the Colosseum on our way. We stopped for dinner in a small restaurant on one of the side streets, and enjoyed a very good meal of ravioli, beef, Coke and lemonaid [lemonade], which we made ourselves from the lemon they gave us for the beef. I'm sure they thought we were nuts. Rick asked the waiter there where he could buy cigarettes, and he led Rick all the way up the street to a tobacco shop. This was fine, but all through the meal, the fellow kept begging for a cigarette, which after three times, became very irritating. When we got the check, we were infuriated by a linen charge, which we hadn't known about before stopping. But it only costs about $1.50 for the entire works, so we had no real reason to complain. We arrived back at the hotel about 9:00.

We had tickets for the 10:30 performance of "The Spectacle of Sound and Light," given right in the Forum itself. At 10:00, we returned to The Forum. There we saw Karl, Freddy and Bill who had also decided to get tickets. The "Spectacle" turned out to be a beautiful and entertaining thing. We sat in bleachers on the side of Palatine Hill, and the show was a production in narration, music and light, giving the history of the Forum and Rome. It's a show that shouldn't be missed by anyone going to Rome, as it very dramatically and emotionally presents the history. You feel almost as if you are traveling back in history, as the voices and lights paint the picture. It was most impressive. Words could never describe it, unfortunately.

We then returned to the hotel, and as usual, it is late, and I must get to bed. Tomorrow we will spend the day at The Vatican City, which should be very interesting. Until then, good night.

Love, Tom

Rome, Italy—Thursday, August 1, 1963

Hi–

Well, today has been another interesting day in Rome, but nothing to compare with yesterday. I got up around 7:30, and after a free cold shower, which seemed like the coldest shower I've ever had, Bill and I took off on a bus for Vatican City, which lies on the opposite side of Rome. The buses in Rome are ridiculously crowded, and when you step out of one, after being pushed and scrunched by the mad screaming Italians, you feel almost like a sardine that secured its freedom from some overly tight can. Descending from the bus, we found ourselves near the Vatican City, in front of St. Peter's Basilica. The square in front of St. Peters is called Piazza St. Pietro, and is a huge area surrounded by colossal porticos, which form the semicircle around the square. It was designed by Bernini and in the center are two beautiful fountains built in 1620 and 1685 under the Pope's order.

The church and the square of St. Peters occupy the actual historical spot of the circus of Nero where many Christians, accused and convicted of having burnt Rome, suffered martyrdom. The church itself is enormous, but even in its enormity has a pleasantness of architectural design. Since we were anxious to see the Sistine Chapel, we headed for the Vatican museum, located quite a distance around the church, on the other side. As usual at such museums, there were crowds of people trying to get in, but we decided to go in anyway, and to buck the crowds.

The entrance to the museum is made interesting by a double ramp or staircase, one for ascending and the other for descending. The staircase is very ornately decorated, and the optical illusion of the two staircases is quite amazing. Upon reaching the main part of the museum, we followed signs to the Sistine Chapel, and after climbing and descending countless stairways and trudging thru many corridors we arrived in the chapel, which was swarmed with tourists, but nevertheless just as interesting as we imagined. The ceiling of the chapel, you know, was painted by Michelangelo, and is world famous for its beauty. The nine panels of paintings represent events taken from the Old Testament, the creation and preparation of the world for the coming of the Messiah. He divided the ceiling into nine compartments: in the first three, he represented the creation of the World; in the other three, the creation and history of Adam and Eve; in the last three, the punishment of Humanity and its regeneration. Most impressive of the nine panels to me are two, the one where God gives light to the Sun and the Moon, and the Creation of Man, a very famous painting of God, with outstretched hand, giving life to Adam, by touching his hand. The painting truly casts some kind of spell, and especially after staring at it for a while. We stayed here for about 45 minutes, our heads upturned toward the ceiling. Leaving here with sore necks, we returned to an open terrace, where we ran into Karl, Freddy and Rick, who had been in St. Peter's church and touring that part of the Vatican. We then decided to see the rest of the museum, no easy task because of its enormity, and then did so, spending the next several hours there. The museum has a truly fantastic collection of art and documents, from ancient Egyptian mummies to statues and early books and written documents. Most interesting to me in the collection was the Vatican library, a huge section of ornately and beautifully decorated galleries, one of which, called Sistine Hall, housed some extremely interesting old documents. There, under glass, are things like Gutenberg's first printed Bible, love letters from Henry VIII to Anne Boleyn, the first recipe book and very early musical notation of Gregorian chants, the early hymns of the Catholic church. Also there were letters written by Martin Luther and Michelangelo.

After seeing countless things of this sort, Bill and I left the museum about 2:00, heading for St. Peter's. We stopped in a coffee bar to eat a hamburger and drink a soda, and continued around the wall of the city. While stopping at a melon stand, near a street corner, all of a sudden we heard a blare of horns and screech of brakes. Looking up, we saw a carload of girls, obviously American, and a carload of Italian men, involved in what looked like a minor collision. Well, we stood there watching the proceedings for a while, and the whole thing was very much like a comic opera. Everyone was yelling in Italian, and the American girls were looking like lost sheep in a rainstorm. So Bill and I strolled up to see if we could be of some help. By this time there was a huge crowd gathered around the scene, and such confusion was hilarious. The girls refused to do a thing until the police came, so we all stood there waiting for them to show up. Well, we waited and waited, the crowd kept getting bigger and louder, and still no police. The four Italians in the other car finally left, deciding that it would do no good to wait, and none of our pleas could persuade them to wait for the police. All this time, one of the American girls kept holding a cat they had found in Rome and named Michelangelo, petting it, and telling it not to get excited. The whole mess was completely ridiculous, and even when the police arrived, they told the girls to forget the whole thing since there are so many accidents in Rome every day, and they would never be able to collect insurance from the Italians anyway. This the girls couldn't understand, and they were bound and determined to go to the central police headquarters. They thanked us and took our names down as witnesses, and went zooming off. I did truly feel sorry for them since any small dent in the car would make their insurance policy nondeductible, and necessitate a loss of $50 for them. I'll always wonder what happened.

After this exciting flurry, Bill and I walked on to St. Peter's, thinking that the day was certainly made complete by being able to get in on such a crazy mixed up affair. We arrived at the Square, and ascended the stairway into St. Peter's, probably the most elaborate and beautiful church I've ever seen. The church is enormous inside, and at the present time it is set up in plush seats and beautiful red velvet tapestries for the Ecumenical Council, which resumes its meetings in September. I'm sure you've seen pictures of this church, the place where the council meets. We then turned right and found a small chapel where is located another "Pieta" by Michelangelo, carved when he was 24 years old. It's really a beautiful statue, and one of his best-known works.

We then spent about an hour walking around inside the church, looking at all the magnificent artwork and elaborate decorations. The huge murals on the wall are mosaics of marble, but can hardly be distinguished from paintings, so detailed are they in design and color. The hugeness and plushness of this church is indescribable, so amazing is it. We then took an elevator up to the roof, from there a staircase which wound around the dome to the very top. From the top of the dome, there is a magnificent view of the city, and from there, one can see almost all of Rome. While up there I met a couple of college kids from Murfreesboro, Tennessee, who were camping through Europe, and seemed not to be enjoying the trip nearly as much as we. We descended from there about 6:00, heading back for home base. The dome of the church, I must mention, was designed by Michelangelo, and is supposedly a miracle of human achievement. He devoted the last sixteen years of his life to the construction of this dome, and it seems like his work was well spent. The interior of the dome is adorned in beautiful paintings or murals, and around the dome is an inscription in gold letters, each letter 5 feet high. From the floor of the church, the letters don't appear nearly this large, an illusion common to the whole church, whose size is deceiving. It's actually much larger than it looks.

The bus ride back to the termini was just as sardine-like as the earlier ride, but we made it in one piece at about 6:30. At the station, I checked on my film which wasn't ready as of yet, so I walked back to the hotel. We ate dinner in the restaurant next to the hotel, and had a delicious meal of lazania [lasagna], ravioli, Coke and fruit cocktail. I had two bowls of the fruit, which tasted wonderful to me, I suppose because of the lack of fruit in our diet recently, or because it had been so long since I had eaten anything quite like it.

Rick had bought tickets to the opera "Toska" [Tosca] for tonight, so after dinner, we headed to the theater. The theater is set outdoors at the ruins of The Baths of Caracalla, ancient baths built in 216 A.D. and at the time of their use, able to accommodate 1600 bathers at one time. I was so tired by this time that I slept through most of the 1st act, and so when it was over decided to leave. The rest of the group, feeling similarly, left also. We took a bus back to the termini, and instead of going back to the hotel, I headed for Piazza Exedra, a huge square near the hotel, surrounded by two large semicircular buildings, and flanked by an enormous fountain in the center, the Fountain of the Naiads, which at night is really gorgeous. The reason for this trip was a lead I had on a piano in one of the hotels overlooking the fountain. Rick had met some girls who were staying here, and they told him of the piano. So I ascended the staircase to Hotel Terminus, and upon arrival, found that it was too late to play. But the fellow at the desk said to return tomorrow anytime, and it would be all right to play. So I went downstairs, sitting down for a lemonade on the square, where an orchestra was playing and people were swarming. Even though the waiter tried to cheat me out of 200 lira, it was a pleasant experience. I have been tired all day, so returned to the hotel to write. So until tomorrow, good night.

 Love, Tom

Rome, Italy—Friday, August 2, 1963

Hi–
 Rome is now on my list with Paris and Berlin as a truly fascinating place, and one of my very favorites. It's a shame that we can't stay here longer since there is so much to see, and not nearly enough time.
 I got up about 7:30 this morning, and the first thing on the agenda was American Express, to see if there was more mail, and to leave forwarding addresses. After a quick breakfast at a coffee bar across from the railroad station, I boarded a bus for American Express. The line there was much larger this morning than the other day, so I left my forwarding address as London. I then returned to the hotel, stopping at the railroad station photo shop to pick up my film, which, unfortunately, was scratched, although otherwise, very good. I had to mount the slides myself which seemed like an unnecessary evil, and by the time I had finished doing this, it was about 11:00. I had not as yet seen the Colosseum, so Karl and I went to the station to catch a bus, stopping first in our old trusty coffee bar for a hamburger and Coke. We descended from the bus on the wide avenue encircling the Colosseum. As you know, this ancient amphitheater is now in a state of ruin, which actually adds to the charm of the place. The Emperor Vespasian[3] began the erection of this large structure in 72 A.D, and it is said that it was built by 12,000 captive Jews, prisoners of the Jewish War. The inauguration was a 100 day ceremony of games during which the arena was flooded with rivers of blood. It covers an area of 6 acres, the original height 200 feet. On the inside, on the left are two pilasters which are all that remains of the imperial box, which was reserved for the Emperor, the court and the Vestal Virgins. All around, at a height of 12 feet, is the Podium which was reserved for the highest dignitaries of state. Behind and above the Podium sloped up the so-called "Cavea," a ramp of step-like seats where the mass of spectators sat. The lowest part being nearest the arena and of easier access was occupied by the highest class of people; the central part was for the middle class and the highest part for the plebians. The central open part of the amphitheater was called "arena" from the sand which covered the ground and served for absorbing the blood and preventing the gladiators from sliding. The floor of the arena must have been of wood and was supported by the closely set walls of the substructure, under which was an elaborate arrangement of underground passages, tunnels, lifts, dens and trap doors by means of which the attendants, gladiators and wild beasts were admitted into the arena. The Colosseum was used for naval games, gladiatorial combats, for

hunts of wild animals, and for martyrdom of Christians and criminals who were condemned to be devoured by the beasts. Although partly ruined, the Colosseum is almost as majestic as in the days of the Caesars and always of that solemn and imposing grandeur which inspired the Mon Beda centuries ago to exclaim: "While the Colosseum stands Rome shall stand; when the Colosseum falls Rome shall fall; when Rome falls shall fall the world." Walking around the old ruins of this place, much of it covered with wild grass, you couldn't help catch the spirit of all the centuries of horror and bloodshed between its walls. It must have been quite an impressive place—and still is for that matter!

What's left of the Colosseum's arena floor

Leaving the Colosseum, we walked toward the Roman Forum, still my favorite place in Rome, to do some further investigating. This time we entered by a different entrance, on the street of the Colosseum, which took us into the Forum through the Arch of Titus on Via Sacra. This beautiful arch was built in 70 A.D. in celebration of the surrender of the Jews and the destruction of Jerusalem. We then continued down Via Sacra past the Basilica of Constantine, the last and largest of the Roman basilicas which for its colossal proportions, surpasses all other ancient pagan edifices of this kind. We then continued on past The Temple of Sacrae Urbis, built in 78 A.D. and The Temple of Romulus, erected in 297 A.D. by Emperor Maxentius. We then found ourselves in front of The Temple of Antonina and Faustina, one of the best preserved monuments of the Roman Forum, still showing its perfect architectural style. While looking at this huge, amazing ruin with its beautiful columns, still intact, we sat on the steps of Regia Pontificia—an ancient structure used as a residence until the period of Julius Caesar. In fact, it was in this building where Julius Caesar spent the last night of his life on the 15th of March 44 B.C. You can imagine the strange feeling you can get while sitting on such a historical and ancient spot. We then continued down Via Sacra, reinvestigating many of the old ruins we had seen day before yesterday—things like The Curia (Senate House) and various temples at that end of the Forum. We then decided to investigate parts of the Forum we hadn't seen, and headed first for The Lacus Juturnae, a fountain connected with one of the most important events of the republican period. The legend goes that during the battle of Lake Regillus in 498 B.C. the twin brothers Castor and Pollux, demi-gods, appeared in this spot to water their horses after the battle which they had fought for the Romans, and announced the victory of the Republican army. After looking at this we proceeded into The Temple of Augustus, ruins believed to be the remains of the temple built by Livia and Tiberius in honor of Augustus, founder of the Empire. Nearby is the Santa Maria Antiqua, the most important Christian monument of the Forum. This church was built in a hall of the library of Augustus and although it is not in a very good state of preservation, still all the different parts of the basilica are distinguishable. The really amazing thing about this place was the murals on the walls, left from the 8th century. Leaving here, we passed the Arch of Augustus, now only a ruin of a huge arch erected in 20 B.C. I must say that inspecting these old ruins in The Forum has been one of the most enjoyable experiences of the entire trip. And as I said before, the lack of tourists makes it all the more refreshing. I noticed that most of the tour buses stop on top of Capitoline Hill, not allowing the passengers to go down into the ruins. This is probably the reason for the lack of tourists.

We left the Forum by the same way we entered, deciding to walk down to the site of the old Circus Maximus. This wasn't a long walk, and before we knew it, we were there. It is now simply a huge oval-shaped track set down in a valley, but it had been at one time the largest stadium of ancient Rome, built in the 6th century B.C. We stood there looking at the place for a few minutes, generally unimpressed, since there are no ruins at all left of the place. We then decided to walk toward The Pantheon, a very ancient church. Since it was quite a distance there, we took a bus, arriving there in just a few minutes.

The Pantheon is the most perfect among all classical buildings in Rome and the monument which gives the best idea of Roman architectural genius. It was built in 27 B.C. It was dedicated to the most important Pagan Gods and to the mythological ancestors of the Julian family, Mars and Venus. It was used as a pagan temple, surprisingly enough until the year 392 A.D., when it was closed along with all pagan temples until 608 A.D. when it was converted into a Christian church. The interior, although deprived of its original decoration, is impressive, its beauty consisting of simplicity of line. The dome, the 1st and largest ever built in the world, is a striking example of Roman architecture. What amazes me about the place is its almost perfect state of preservation, and its beautiful marble walls and columns, supposedly of very rare marble. It's quite a place.

Leaving The Pantheon, we started walking toward The Trevi Fountain, the famous fountain where tourists always throw the coins. It is the largest fountain in Rome, built in 1735 from a sketch by Bernini. When we walked out onto the square of the fountain, there were crowds of people parked all around it, trying to cool off, I suppose, since it was a very hot day. The aqueduct feeding the fountain today is the same one which carried water to this spot in Rome 2000 years ago—quite an interesting fact! After throwing 200 lira into the fountain, a small ceremony performed by turning your back to the fountain and throwing the coins over your shoulder, we looked for the American Express area, as Karl wanted to check there for mail, and I wanted to get post cards. After buying the cards, I walked down to the Spanish Steps, where I sat for about an hour, writing cards and watching the people, as well as reflecting on the day.

Following tradition, making a wish at the Trevi Fountain

About 6:30, I took a bus back to the termini, where I walked back to the hotel. Rick was the only one in the room, so we decided not to wait for the rest, and grab a bite to eat. We ate downstairs in the restaurant near the hotel, and had a delicious meal of lazania [lasagna], fruit and Coke. The Italian lazania is really made the way it should be—really wonderful stuff! We then headed for the square with the Fountain of Naiads, where the piano was located, and being luckier tonight, I spent the entire evening playing. My hands are really out of shape, and I'm going to have to practice like mad to get back in condition. It was also surprising to me how much had slipped my mind—and it took a while to remember some things that I had so well memorized. I can't think of a more ideal setting for practice—the beautiful square and fountain out the window plus the atmosphere of the city of Rome itself. I played until around 10:30 and by the time I finished I had an audience of a couple of American fellows from Birmingham, Alabama, one a high school teacher of about 24, who was taking a group of students from his school around Europe for the summer. The other fellow was one of those students. Rick had been listening while writing in his diary until about 10:15, when he decided to leave. So about 10:45 I headed back to the hotel, completely pooped after such a full day.

So until tomorrow, good night!

Love, Tom

P.S. To answer some of your questions: yes, we met Al Courier in Berlin through John Rice. I thought that I had explained that very clearly in my letter. My clothes have held up well, the drip-dry shirts needing no ironing whatsoever, and very easy to wash out by hand. In fact I haven't been to a laundry yet, and certainly hope I don't have to. Granted, I do smell every once in a while, but in Europe, everyone does—so what's the difference. More later.

Rome, Italy—Saturday, August 3, 1963

Hi-

How can life be so consistently interesting? This last day in Rome was equally as interesting as the others, but in a much different way. The main things we did today were take a tour of the ancient Appian Way and see Tivoli Fountains. We slept late this morning, till around 10:00, which was probably for the best since we have really been running like crazy since being in Rome, and after arising, the first thing I did was take a hot bath, which really was wonderful. What a luxury a simple thing like a bath has become. Meanwhile, Bill went to see the Pantheon and Rick and Freddy went to the railroad station to mail some letters. Karl went to the Volkswagen dealer to see about picking up Vicki, since we had left her there yesterday to have her oil changed. Since we had wanted to get a fairly early start, and sleeping late prevented it, no one was terribly happy that I should take time for a bath. But I was determined to take one anyway, as I was sick and tired of taking birdbaths in ice cold water, and if they wanted to go on without me, let them go! But Bill's trip to the Pantheon was equally as time-consuming, and likewise for Freddy and Rick's trip to the termini. So Karl was the only one left to get Vicki and he left the room with a few choice censored words and in a puff of smoke. We yelled down the hall that we would meet him there, to which he didn't reply, so we shrugged our shoulders and decided to forget it. Somehow I let most of these minor skirmishes happen without letting it upset me.

And so after my wonderful bath, which I lavished as much as possible, Rick, Freddy and I took off for the Volkswagen dealer, located several blocks from the hotel. We arrived there around noon, and since I hadn't eaten breakfast, I stopped in a small coffee bar for some rolls and a Coke. Vicki passed her inspection and oil change with flying colors, and she was all ready to roll. Before leaving for The Appian Way, everyone wanted to stop for lunch groceries, and I not feeling like lunch, went back into the coffee bar, where I bought an ice cream cone and a Coke, which I turned into a Coke float. The Italians there had obviously never seen such a concoction, but the fellow behind the bar pointed to the bottle of cognac on the shelf, indicating that they drank cognac floats, something we should perhaps introduce into ice cream parlors in the United States. I can just see the youth of America running to the local drug stores and dairy queens after school and ordering cognac floats—quite an innovation!

And then we all piled in Vicki and headed for the Appian Way, a trip which took about a half-hour, being unfamiliar with Roman streets and highways. Upon arrival at the famous road, which in Italian is Via Appia Antiqua, we were surprised to find it just as interesting as we ever imagined. A brief history: it is the oldest Roman road, built in 312 B.C. by Appius Claudius the Censor, the great Roman general and orator, the same who built the first aqueduct. It was the most important military road built by the Romans and the first line of communication between Rome and the South of Italy, Rome and Greece, and the most remote colonies of the Empire. Many historical events are connected with this road, among them, the enthusiastic reception with which Cicero the great Roman orator was received by the people and the ruling class on his return to Rome from banishment in 57 B.C. The road, besides being the most celebrated military road, was also the aristocratic cemetery of the early Romans. Many of these ancient tombs or ruins of them still exist, and the drive along the road is filled with sights of these ruins—complete with the beautiful cedar umbrella pines which are found in great abundance all along the way. We stopped innumerable times just to investigate many of the old ruins and crawl around on some of the old Roman houses. We continued along the road for about 45 minutes, finally running out of decent pavement, but deciding to go on down the way, since this section of the road seemed almost completely untraveled. It was along here that we made a most shocking and surprising discovery. For a while we had been noticing girls sitting by the road, some of them by the old ruins. We quickly discovered by observation that these girls and women were prostitutes, who made their place of business along The Appian Way, certainly the type of discovery not made in high school Latin books. This struck us extremely funny, to think that such a situation exists along the the *Appia Antiqua*. After thinking it over, however, it did seem ridiculously logical in a way that the world's oldest profession could actually be doing business on one of the world's oldest roads. Feeling in an extremely daring mood, we decided to stop and price one, which turned out to be quite an embarrassing scene, for the prostitute, who really wasn't terribly bad looking, wasn't at all modest either, and no sooner did we stop, than she giggled and exposed herself, which surprised us so much that all we could do was laugh and drive away. All I can say about the whole situation is that it certainly did shed a new light on our images of The Appian Way. I hope that my sincerity about the situation doesn't embarrass you too much, but I thought it was well worth relating—even if it isn't exactly material for the high school newspaper. I wonder how much this letter will be circulated? (Ha!)

The Appia Antiqua—the oldest profession finds a home on one of the world's oldest roads

On our drive back along the ancient road, we stopped at the Basilica and Catacombs of St. Sebastian. The catacombs, among all the monuments of antiquity, are, with Pompeii, the only ones which, having been buried and forgotten for so many centuries, have come down to us almost intact. These catacombs show us the life of the early Christians. On nearly every tomb is carved some of their primitive prayers, their hopes, the human doctrines which animated them and the faith for which they risked and often willingly sacrificed their lives. The catacombs were actually burial grounds for hundreds of thousands of these early Christians, and many of them excavated only recently. The catacomb of St. Sebastian, where we visited, is thought to have been frequented by Peter and Paul, and they are also thought to have been buried here. The tour led us far down into the ground into these dark caves and tunnels, and it was really a fascinating trip. One can see how Christianity could have been at that time such a strong influence, as these catacombs, where the early Christians met, worshipped and were buried, were places where great bonds and ties could have been so easily developed—and obviously did.

After a tour of these catacombs, we went upstairs into the church, which seemed like so many others we've seen, interesting and full of more of these ancient relics we had seen so much of. Bill and I, having gone on a different tour than the others, came out of the church unable to see the other three anywhere. So we did our own exploring of the area, walking through the courtyard of some school, and ending up in the garden of some nunnery, a very beautiful small place overlooking some of the ruins along the Appian Way and also a clothesline loaded with habits hanging out to dry. On the way back to the car, we passed through a deserted school yard, and spying a teeter totter, both of us laughed and got the same idea. We ran over to the thing, jumping on, and practically broke it trying to do something that few 21-year-olds do—teeter-totter. But it seemed a fitting contrast to our earlier experience on the Appian Way, and we've laughed about it ever since. We then returned to the car and waited for about fifteen minutes before the others arrived. Rick had a strange coincidence occur when he was down in the catacombs: he ran into a fellow he graduated from high school with there, someone who then had been a good friend. So he and his friend, who was doing Europe on a motorcycle, planned to go out on the town tonight.

We then left the Appian Way, searching for the main highway that would take us to the town of Tivoli, where is located the Villa d'Este, a place famous for its beautiful garden and fountains. We let Rick off on the highway to catch a bus back into Rome, and with the help of some Italian fellow, we found our way to the highway to Tivoli.

This village, according to tradition, was founded 460 years before Rome, in 1213 B.C. During the Roman Empire it became the favorite residence of statesman, orators, generals and the leading classes of Rome. So during this time many beautiful Villas were built here, including those of Julius Caesar, Brutus and Cassius. The town is located on the side and near the summit of a mountain, from which can be seen Rome in the distance, and all of the surrounding countryside. It is a very attractive spot.

We arrived in Tivoli around 6:00, and since we were hungry headed immediately to a restaurant. Here we sat and waited till around 7:30 for spaghetti, but we didn't mind too much since we had a good pre-meal conversation as well as a beautiful view of a river valley and the ruins of some ancient pagan temple. After the meal, we headed for The Villa D'Este, and upon arrival there, found it didn't open till around 8:45. While waiting, I spent about $20.00 on some hand-made bags and tablecloths, which struck me as so beautiful and cheap that I couldn't pass them up.

The Villa d'Este is supposedly the most lovely Renaissance Villa in Europe, begun in the year 1571, and most impressive for the magnificence and profusion of its fountains, for the colossal dimensions of its old trees, for the charm of its lakes. This we found to be more than true, as the fountains and ancient gardens were truly one of the most beautiful sights of the whole trip. They were so elaborate and extensive, some of them over a hundred feet high, many of them running for several hundred feet along the side of the mountain. They are truly indescribable.

We left Tivoli about 11:00, heading back for Rome. While there, I developed a bad headache, which bothered me all the way back, and wasn't helped by the fact that Bill and I sat up till around 3:30, just talking about goals, ambitions, life in general.

I must get to feeling better. So until tomorrow, good night. We're leaving Rome tomorrow, a fact which I hate, since there is so much we haven't seen. Until then, goodnight.

Love, Tom

Telegram of concern from home

THE RIVIERAS
10

Monaco Sightings and No Room at the Inn

The French Riviera and the Italian Riviera comprise one of the most ruggedly beautiful seaside vistas in the world. Known as the "coastline," it is dotted with the spacious hillside villas of movie stars, millionaires and just your everyday rich and famous. The Rivieras breed wealth, glamour and a carefree lifestyle. Picture Grace Kelly, scarf flowing in the wind, with Cary Grant at her side (*To Catch a Thief*, 1955). They are driving along the winding road high above the sea in that gorgeous sapphire blue Sunbeam Alpine convertible. Classic Riviera style. Five guys in a Beetle…well, they tried.

§ § §

Somewhere on Italian Riviera—Sunday, August 4, 1963

Hi–

Today wasn't at all good as my headache from last night had gotten worse, and driving didn't help matters a lot. But at least I felt pretty well the whole time in Rome. Before I start today, I must tell of a funny incident which happened last night at Tivoli. A whole busload of young students, either British or American, since they spoke English, trooped up to Villa d'Este while Karl and I were sitting there waiting for it to open. The group was led by a priest and two nuns, and upon finding out that the place wouldn't open for a half hour or so, the priest announced that all the little boys who felt the urge should follow him. This would have gone unnoticed, except I happened to catch a glimpse of the two nuns when he made his announcement, and they were both looking at each other and giggling. It's a minor incident, I know, but at that moment, it struck me very funny.

While in Rome I broke one of the glass windows in my regular glasses, so I have been walking around, at night, at least, squinting through cracked glasses. Thank goodness I have the prescription sunglasses, which I wear almost all day.

We got up this morning around 7:30, which wasn't nearly enough sleep after my talk to 3:30 with Bill last night, and my headache was so intense I could hardly move, but managed to walk to the termini to pick up the other roll of film I had left there and my clean suit, sport coat and pants, which I had taken to them last Thursday morning. We finally got the car packed and pulled away around 10:00 after a breakfast of rolls and hot tea in a nearby coffee bar. We left Rome in a flurry, fighting the traffic thru the city, passing the Vatican, and finally reaching a highway that took us from the city. For a joke, we were all singing, "Arrivederci, Roma" while driving along, which actually seemed ridiculously anticlimactic to our wonderful 5 days here. I vow that I must someday return to Rome to see so many of the things I missed this trip. Strangely enough, I have felt that way about so many of the places we've visited, almost as if the trip this summer were merely a survey excursion, only an introduction for future investigation.

    What is amazing about the European countries is the vast difference in appearance, language of course and customs of the various countries. It seems that as you cross a border into another country over here, comparable to a state back home, you pass into a brand new rhelm [realm], so completely different from the one you are leaving. And then it seems you must do some revamping of your developed habits of the previous country, and most obvious of all, start learning some essential phrases of the new language.

    The Italians seem to be wonderful people, but you have to overlook the group that preys on tourists, and their strange custom of bargaining. Almost every store will sell a good to you cheaper than the original quoted price, almost as if it was meant to be that way—which is probably fact. Italy also seems to be the strangest of all European countries we've visited, at least by American standards. The American tourist almost needs a previous education on Italian customs and outlooks before venturing into that country. It's truly an interesting place. One nice thing about being here is its similarity, weather-wise, to the United States. It has been hot here, a condition we never believed we'd like and appreciate after experiencing sweltering hot summers at home, but on the contrary, enjoying very much after being in the colder climates of Scandinavia and Germany. Vienna, on the other hand when we were there, was miserably hot. But they were having a drought and heat wave there which for Vienna was most unusual. It's strange also to look at a world map and see that Rome is on a horizontal parallel to New York City, while in Europe, is considered a very southern city.

Admiring the old Roman Aqueduct on the road to Pisa

So we left Rome and headed for the Mediterranean. Once in the car, my headache subsided somewhat, and we were driving along, all singing to the top of our lungs. We then drove along the Mediterranean coast for a couple more hours, a drive which was beautiful, but not spectacular, since the road was set far enough back from the coast to prevent being able to see it all the time. Around 1:00, we stopped at a beach, which was covered with umbrellas and chairs, and overlooking the blue-green sea, one of the most beautiful bodies of water I've seen. I wasn't feeling at all well, as my headache was acting up again, so while the others adorned swim suits and took off for the water, I spent the afternoon sleeping in the car. Around 4:00 they returned to the car, and I felt much worse, almost like I had a fever, and their stories of how wonderful the water was certainly didn't pep me up. So they dried off and changed clothes, and before leaving the town, I stopped in a drug store, where I bought some aspirin. We drove on along the coast till around 8:00, when we stopped for dinner at a small restaurant. They all wanted to sleep on the beach tonight, which I couldn't see for myself, since I felt so badly, so while at the restaurant, the young waiter called a hotel in town which had a single room where I could sleep. Our meal was beefsteak, broth soup, which I ordered to make me feel better, and hot tea. The young waiter was extremely friendly and in his efforts to please me, brought in a phonograph and records, which he proceeded to play at extremely high volume, which was bad enough to normal ears, let alone to the ears of someone with a splitting headache. He even played his English lesson records for us, which after a while, got very boring. But the meal tasted good, and I had the satisfaction of knowing I had a place to sleep.

The young waiter led us to the hotel in his car, a thoughtful gesture, and I went straight to bed at 9:15, even knowing I had to pay 2000 lira for the room ($3.30)

And so ends another day. Tune in tomorrow to find out more about sick boy. It's quite irritating. Until tomorrow, good night.

Love, Tom

P.S. I'm writing this on Aug. 13, the day I called, so remember that I'm healthy as can be now. Love, Tom

Near La Spezia, Italy—Monday, August 5, 1963

Hi-

Today has been more than interesting, my headache gone, and feeling much better, even though we couldn't find a place today, and ended up sleeping in the car all night. The others came to the pension where I was staying around 8:00, after their cold night on the beach. I envied them their stay on the beach as the sunrise and the full moon in a semi-cloudy sky sounded like a beautiful way to spend the night, even if raincoats and sweatshirts were inadequate in the cold night. But my eleven hours of sleep had helped a great deal, even though I still had a small headache. I couldn't quite figure out why I had felt so badly, but thought it could have been constipation, since I hadn't had to go in about 3 days. But whatever, the rest helped a great deal, and I felt eager to get on the road. The town where we stayed was somewhere on the coast between Rome and Genova, probably near to Piombino, but now I can't even remember the name of the place.

The drive now was becoming more and more scenic, as we were right on the coast, and the Mediterranean is such a beautiful color, a deep blue along the horizon, and a deep shade of blue green near the coast. Another factor adding to the beauty of the trip was the foothills of the mountains near the coast, which could be seen in the distance coupled with the sea, as we curved along the road, winding in and around the coast. The coast seemed also to be filled with sandy beaches the whole way, and they were all dotted with the cabana umbrellas and easy chairs. The beaches, surprisingly enough, were almost deserted of swimmers or people, a fact we accorded to lack of enough tourists to fill all the beaches. Anyway, it was strange that these beaches were deserted, but we were happy in a way that they were, since the lack of scads of tourists kept the roads clear of burdensome traffic.

MY STORY

My construction was begun in 1174 by Bonanno Pisano and finished after 99 years by Giovanni di Simone. Tommaso di Andrea Pisano crowned me with a bell-cell.
My height is 55.863 m.
My max. height is 56.705 m
My interior base diameter is 7,368 m.
My exterior base diameter is 15,484 m.
I have 8 floors and 294 steps.
I rest on foundations about 3 metres deep.
For what I said my total weight is 14,500 tons.
My leaning is 4.500 m.
In my bell-cell there are 7 bells tuned on the seven musical notes.
My oldest bell - the Pasquareccia - rang for death of Count Ugolino della Gherardesca.
From my summit Galileo Galilei performed his famous trial about gravitation.
For alla I said I am one of the Seven Wonders of the World.

Postcard: The Leaning Tower—one of the seven wonders of the world

    Around 11:00, we took a side road away from the coast see the leaning tower of Pisa, which logically enough, is located in Pisa. We found Pisa to be a very clean and pleasant town, and upon arrival there around noon, we asked directions to the leaning tower. We were tempted to ride through Pisa without seeing the leaning tower, just to be able to say we had ridden thru Pisa without seeing the damn thing. But that being only a sarcastic thought, our curiosity led us to the tower, which is located next to a beautiful cathedral. It was originally meant to be the bell tower of the church, and is actually used as that. Believe me, after seeing the tower, we were amazed that the thing didn't topple over, so great is its angle of inclination.

We parked the car and walked up to the tower, walking around its base and investigating its lean. We then paid 200 lira to climb to the top, which turned out to be quite an odd sensation. Being inside the tower and walking around its various outdoor levels on the way up was quite a feeling, one mostly of great insecurity, as not only did you feel greatly unbalanced, but the outdoor levels had no guard rails, a condition that would give people suffering from vertigo quite a start! We were on top of the tower about 15 minutes before descending, and that was plenty long enough, for being on the thing made me feel most insecure, and I wouldn't have been surprised at the time if it had toppled over. I mentioned this to Karl, and we both laughed and decided that if one had to die in Europe, not a more spectacular death could be had anywhere else in Europe than falling from the leaning tower of Pisa. Nevertheless, we were glad to get off the crazy thing, and all breathed a sigh of relief upon reaching the ground. The tower is set in a very beautiful area, a fact we were all surprised to see, since I somehow always imagined the tower on some huge dirty piazza. Pictures and imaginations are very often deceiving. But the whole area, the green lawns, the gorgeous marble cathedral and the tower, was very pleasant, and we left Pisa, glad after all, that we had stopped to see it.

We drove on then, after eating ice cream cones for lunch, back toward the coast, and we soon, after again reaching the sandy coast, decided to stop for an afternoon on the beach. So about 1:00, we stopped at a beautiful deserted beach somewhere south of La Spazia, and spent the rest of the afternoon here, laying under umbrellas, swimming and relaxing. I felt so much better today, and determined to go swimming, I put on my trunks with the rest and headed right for the water. The waves were very high, the water warm and the undertow strong. We were warned, in fact, not to go in above our waists, since there had been trouble with whirlpools. The water, unfortunately, although beautiful to look at, was extremely salty and dirty, probably caused by the roughness of the undercurrents.

So I took several short dips during the afternoon between periods of lying in the sun. Rick and I, around 4:00, went down by the water, where we spent the next hour and half building sand castles. I built the most elaborate castle you can imagine, modeling it after so many of the ones we had seen in Europe, complete with moat, walls, small towers, windows, doors and the works. By the time I had most of it built, we had quite an audience of people gathered around watching, but alas, the tide was coming in, and some of the waves were leaping up over the sand, trying to devour my "masterpiece." Even though the moats I had built and the drainage system I had made for a while did a grand job of saving the castle, soon the waves came in farther, and the group of spectators roared with gentle laughter when one monstrous wave came sailing in, completely melting one end of the castle. Such a catastrophe! I thought it not funny at all after all my work, but it soon became apparent that no matter how deep my moats were, they would be useless. So I seceded to the tide and laughed myself as the sea crept up slowly, demolishing the castle. I think the Italians thought my great seriousness while building the castle was funny, but I was actually very intent while building the thing, working like a beaver on the moats, towers and walls. It was like a journey back into childhood, and I enjoyed the whole thing immensely.

About 5:30, we left the beach, first changing clothes and washing off our bathing suits. After tying the towels and trunks to Vicki's roof rack, we went roaring again up the coast, towels and suits flapping in the Mediterranean breeze. We stopped at a BP gas station (a leading oil company in Europe) in La Spezia, where a very accommodating gentleman gave us all kinds of maps and told us of a good restaurant there. La Spezia seemed to be a very nice town, and our meal of ravioli, shrimp, fruit and Coke was all right, but certainly nothing special. We had thought that the shrimp there on the coast would be delicious, but were surprised to find it bad, at least in comparison to shrimp back home. Perhaps it was because they failed to serve it with the hot sauce we're so used to. We then left La Spezia, heading up the coast toward Genova, where Bill and Freddy were planning on catching a train to Switzerland.

Postcard: The French Riviera

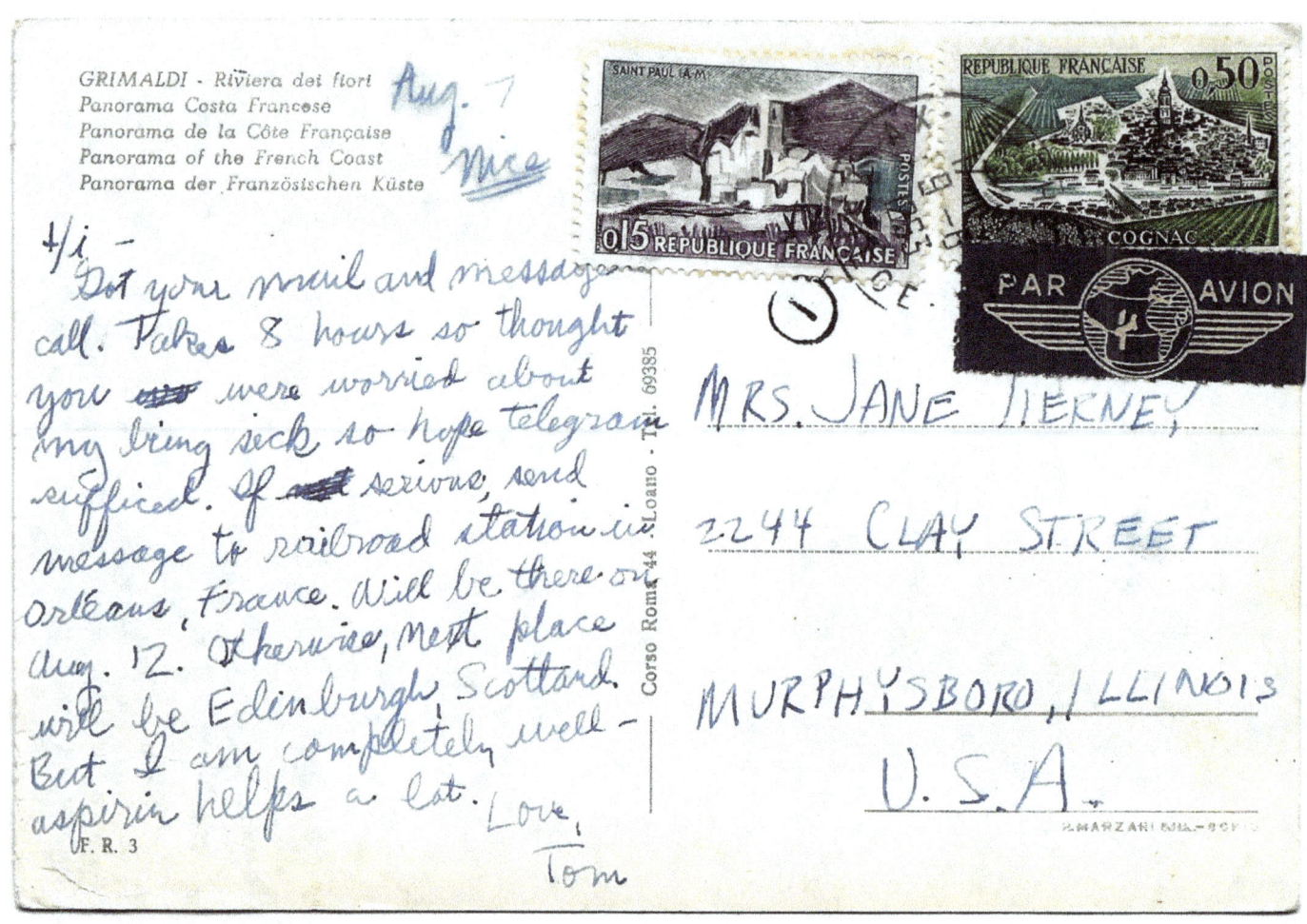

Side 2: "...completely well—aspirin helps"

    We were now getting into the mountainous part of the coast, and at night, this was a most beautiful and spectacular drive. Hugging the coast, we drove on narrow roads along the mountainous ledges, and the view of the small villages, with their twinkling lights far below along the sea and the sea itself, sparkling from the reflections of the full moon, was unusually breathtaking. We were constantly surprised to round one of the mountainous curves and see before and far below us a fantastic panorama of moonlight on the sea, small towns below with their night lights dotting the coast, and the dark silhouettes of the jagged mountainous cliffs in the foreground. The beauty of these sights had a certain mystery about it plus a peacefulness seldom experienced, there being little traffic on the road at night. We wound our way along the mountain edges, curving up and down and around till around 11:00, when we decided to try to find a place for the night. All the hotels were closed tighter than a drum, but we thought a camp site might be able to rent us sleeping bags or blankets, so with this thought in mind, we searched out one campsite, only to find disappointment. So we wound up parking the car on a lonely little side street and spent a very uncomfortable night sleeping in the car. Bill and Rick had gotten out of the car and ended up sleeping on a park bench, which I must say adds a great amount of character to the trip, even though not much comfort. I still wasn't feeling too well, but sleeping in the car was better than nothing, even though I wouldn't relish doing such through all of Europe.

So, until tomorrow, I say goodnight, which somehow today seems like an inappropriate phrase.

Love, Tom

FRANCE
11

Chateau Country and a Dressmaker's Tale

France is blessed with many magnificent country chateaux. Equally alluring are the charming villages—complete with dusty sidewalks, antique streetlamps and a statue of Joan of Arc in the middle of the requisite town square. Imagine men on bicycles dressed in work clothes and berets whisking by. Women appear carrying large baskets filled with cheese and baguettes—small children following in their wake. A choir of nuns' voices can be heard in the background.

Now, just for the fun of it, add the smell of freshly baked bread and a colorful array of farm fresh fruit and vegetables. Ooh la la! Heaven on earth to these mid-western travelers.

§ § §

Nice, France—Tuesday, August 6, 1963

Hi–

Well, here we are in Nice, France. We slept, or tried to sleep in the car last night, but it wasn't easy, so we woke up around 5:00 AM, deciding to drive into Genova to put Bill and Freddy on the train, which was only about 26 kilometers away. We sleepily put Vicki in gear after Bill and Rick returned from the park bench where they spent the night, and drove off into the sunrise, which was extremely beautiful, and made the uncomfortable night almost worth it. We found the scenery of the night before equally as beautiful in the early morning light, and almost as dramatic, with the bright blue water far below us and the misty morning fog clinging in clusters to the mountains along the way. It took us only a short time to reach Genova, which seemed like a ghost town so early in the morning, a big one at that. We saw signs leading us to the termini, which we religiously followed, and about 6:30, we poured into the station, unshaven, wearing only Bermuda shorts, T-shirts and sandals, looking I'm sure like complete bums. I had to wear those sunglasses, which I've been wearing almost everywhere since my regular glasses broke, and from the looks we got there, I know they thought we were tramps. But who cares! The freedom of living like this is wonderful, to be able to drive and act as we please, knowing that no one really gives a damn anyway.

We then got some traveler's checks cashed and walked next door to get some rolls and coffee while Bill and Freddy were buying their tickets to Lucerne, Switzerland and getting their clothes organized so that they wouldn't be taking too much luggage with them. This took nearly an hour, and by 7:00, after bidding them goodbye and good trip, Karl, Rick and I drove off in the morning, rather relieved that the crowd had dwindled. Freddy has improved a great deal over the summer, and the whole wild experience I believe has been good for him.

The ride today took us into the really beautiful parts of the Riviera, although its character changed from sandy beached coasts to rocky ones, characterized by mountainous cliffs sweeping down to the sea. Along with the beauty, however, also came the tourists, and the farther we drove along the coast, the heavier became the traffic and the people. It eventually turned in to a continual barrage of tourist shops, hostels and resort towns. But the scenery was too wonderful to really mind the time we were losing, even though driving up and down the hilly roads became irritating in the heavy traffic. We stopped about 11:00 for lunch in a very clean looking restaurant, run by a German woman who had spent most of her life in Italy. There we gourged [gorged] our stomachs with what seemed like a strange combination of Viennese and Italian food, having spaghetti, wiener schnitzel, potatoes, salad and Coke for only a nominal sum. This seemed to be a German tourist area of the Riviera, as many of the hotels boasted signs saying "We speak Deutsch." (German), which this lady did, much to Karl's satisfaction, who was really missing being able to use his German.

We then continued up the Italian coast, stopping around 1:00 at a small inlet beach, which wasn't at all sandy anymore, and very calm. Karl slept in the car the whole time we were there, but Rick and I rented 2 chairs and an umbrella, where we parked for the next 3 hours. The water was perfect for swimming, colder than yesterday, but so much cleaner and calmer, enabling one to really swim and not have to fight the waves and the undertow. I slept for about an hour, I suppose because of our sleepless night last night, and it was a quiet, relaxing time. I was feeling almost completely well by now, and glad to be rid of the horrible headache of two days ago. The time somehow has flown so fast since we've been in Italy, a bad sign, since the trip is over half gone, and in less than a month we'll be back in the old grind. I would so much like to stay over here and study for a year in Paris, and was tempted to ask you what you thought. But I suppose there will be another chance, and even if not an apparent one appears, I will do my best to invent one. Europe is quite a wonderful place—and especially for one interested in the arts. There's so much inspiration here!

We left the beach around 4:00, and in less than an hour, found ourselves at the French border. After only a brief passport check, we drove into France, and bade our final farewell to Italy. So here we are back in France, where I at least don't feel completely lost in language, but certainly more aware of what I don't know.

Now that we were on the French Riviera, we found the traffic and congestion much worse than it had been. We soon found ourselves passing through Monte Carlo and Monaco, and the percentage of Cadillacs and Rolls Royces [Royce's] began to greatly increase. Monaco was extremely touristy, and we soon passed the beautiful palace of Princess Grace and Rainier, which was perched on a plateau-like bluff overlooking the Mediterranean, a very romantic looking place. We also saw signs in Monte Carlo to the Casino, and none of us feeling in the mood to stop and fight the crowds, decided to continue on toward Nice. I could swear that I saw Princess and her husband in this huge gold Cadillac convertible as it zoomed past, but it was more than likely only a figment of my imagination plus only the desire to be able to say I had seen her while there. For a while we followed a yellow Rolls Royce, hoping to see her eventually step out like Cinderella from the golden pumpkin, but were disappointed to see only a dignified gentleman leave the car by some very exclusive looking restaurant. It must be quite the life to be able to spend vacations there gambling away basket loads of money! Maybe someday…?

And so we fought the traffic all the way to Nice, arriving there around 6:30. Nice is also a tourist town, but a very beautiful one at that, its broad busy palm tree-lined streets bustling with all kinds of interesting looking people. We went first to *la gare* (the railroad station) in hopes of finding a hotel, but the reservation window was closed, so Karl and I set off on foot in search of one, finding a nice quiet inexpensive hotel only a block from the station, where Rick enquired about trains to Barcelona, Spain, his main goal. I am having to use my French. Although very rusty, I can do the essential things, which I suppose is most important.

So, very tired after such a long day, we unloaded the car and settled down in a hotel room, which was a wonderful feeling, after last night in the car.

It's only about 8:30 now, and I'm not even hungry enough to try to eat a meal, so am going to bed to catch up on sleep. And so, until tomorrow, *bon soir* (good night).

Love, Tom

P.S. I'm writing this on Aug. 14 in Calais, France. We get to England tomorrow, and it will be wonderful to be able to speak English again. I'm trying like mad to get caught up in my writing, and have spent all day doing so. But I don't want to slight one day, as they're all so important, so bear with me. I should be caught up soon. Was wonderful to talk to you on the phone yesterday, and hope it didn't run up any terrible bill, which is probably impossible to avoid. But, nonetheless, I'm now completely well, and have been since leaving Italy, and will see a doctor if anything goes wrong again. But please <u>don't worry</u>.

Love, Tom

Carcassonne, France—Wednesday, August 7, 1963

Hi–

What a day! We have covered a great deal of territory today, as tonight we are in Carcassonne, France, which is located very far indeed from Nice, if you will check a map. We arose this morning about 7:00, and the whole night of sleep did wonders for our tired bodies, and I felt wonderful. So after paying the hotel bill, which amounted to only about $1.50, I headed for American Express, eager to see if I had any mail. Well, fortunately, I received three letters, one from you, one from Ann and one from Mark Juergensmeyer[1], but unfortunately, the message to call led me to great mental anguish, since I at first had no idea why you would want me to call, and the people at American Express seemed to be positive that calling would take as long as 6 hours, which was an impossible amount of time, since we had to be in Narbonne tonight to put Rick on a train to Spain, and it was impractical to sit in Nice all day to call. So after much discussion, mental debate and reading your letters, I finally logically figured out that you must be worried about my health. So we went to the post office, the only place where transatlantic calls and telegrams can be sent, and proceeded to write a cable. At first I wrote out a cable that if you wanted to call, that I would be in Narbonne at a certain hotel tonight, but it was so long that it would have cost more than a call, so I decided to chance it that it was only worry about my being sick and your not having heard from me for a while, and so I sent the same telegram you received. I'm still very upset about it, but hope that meaning was clear. Time will tell!

I had a terrible time trying to communicate to the people in the post office as they spoke no English, and had no patience at all, a fact which just added to my worry. As it was it cost me more than $5.00 just to send those four words, so I was having to spend money which I should have been saving. However, I was glad to spend it, but still kind of upset over the whole thing. I did figure that if it had really been something serious, that you would have sent it on a wire. So I hope my calculations are correct?!

We then stopped at a stand that sold fresh fruit juices, and I proceeded to drink two glasses of fresh grape juice and one of orange juice, which tasted wonderful, as it had been so long since any of us had tasted fresh juice for breakfast. We also had a hot dog for breakfast, a delicious one served in a thick French bread roll, and tasting very different from the ones sold back home. We then walked along the boardwalk of Nice, and what a beautiful resort it is, the palm trees in profusion lining the whole "Promenade des Anglais" and all the big luxurious old white hotels and fancy shops facing the sea. But our short stay in Nice then ended, and we piled into Vicki, heading West along the coast, our destiny Narbonne.

The traffic this morning wasn't any different from yesterday, and we literally crawled through this area, eventually passing through Cannes, another tourist resort similar to Nice, and there leaving the Riviera, deciding we'd make much better time on the inland roads, a fact which proved correct. We stopped for lunch at a small roadside stand where we had salami sandwiches and Coke, continuing on to Aix-en-Provence.

The French roads are wonderful in comparison to those in Italy or Germany (except the Autobahns), and the drive was very pleasant, as the Southern French towns were picturesque places, and the countryside was very green, in contrast to some of the barrenness of Italy. The French roads are also made much more drivable by the tall grove of trees which lines every road, giving them a peacefulness and quietness not found on roads in other countries.

We stopped in Aix-en-Provence to pick up some tourist information on France and to buy some petrol coupons for Vicki. It's a real nice town, not too large, but full of tree-lined streets and ancient fountains as well as medieval buildings, which added to the charm of the town. The tourist bureau gave me loads of information, but most of it on the region there, and hardly any on the area up north around the chateau country, where Karl and I wanted to spend most of our time. So we left Aix-en-Provence, heading toward Arles and Montpellier, passing through many small quaint French villages on our way, with names like Salon, Vauvert, Marilaque and St. Gilles. Right outside of Arles, we picked up a fellow who was hitchhiking, mainly because he had an American flag on his back. His name was Bill Lasus, and he went all the way to Narbonne with us. He was from Fort Wayne, Indiana, went to school at M.I.T. and was hitchhiking all over Europe, now on his way to Madrid, Spain to catch a plane back to the U.S. He was a real nice fellow, and sort of added to the trip as he had a lot of interesting stories to tell. We stopped in a small town outside of Montpellier around 5:30, where we bought some grapes and a bottle of wine, which we had demolished by the time we reached Narbonne. We were now back along the coast, along the area between Sète and Béziers, and all along this wild deserted beach were countless tents and campers, which we later found out belonged to refugees from Algeria, who were recently kicked out of there. We reached Narbonne around 10:30, and went directly to the train station, where we found Rick could get a train to Barcelona at 4:00 AM certainly an ungodly hour. We then hunted all over Narbonne for a hotel, but every damned hotel in the town was *complet*, so we went back to a restaurant near the train station, where we fed our starved stomachs with soup, jambon (ham) sandwiches and tea. We were all dead after the long drive, but there was not a hotel in the whole damned town that had a vacant room. While eating we met some chap from England who was also going to Barcelona, and finally at midnight, Karl and I decided to head toward Carcassonne, since we couldn't find a place here, and we might be able to in Carcassonne. So we left Rick with only a pack on his back, unshaven and tired, in Narbonne, wondering how his journey to Spain would turn out, and wondering also what we would be doing. Upon arrival in Carcassonne, there wasn't a light in the town, so Karl and I pulled off onto a small side street, flipped a coin to see who would sleep in the back seat, and turned Vicki again into a hotel, something she should never be, as I ended up in the front seat, and had to straddle the damned clutch over the bucket seats for the night.

After such a day, I must say goodnight.

Love, Tom

Aix-les-Thermes, France—Thursday, August 8, 1963

Hi-

So here Karl and I were, at 5:30 in the morning, waking up very uncomfortably after the poor sleep in the car in Carcassonne, a small, seemingly obscure town located less than 150 miles from the Pyrenees, both of us tired. I more than him since I had to fight the damned gear shift all night. Feeling ultra grubby, we knew perhaps some food would lift our spirits some, se we started up Vicki, heading for what might be the center of town. The car was parked by a very high wall, and upon turning the first corner we saw what is perhaps the most fantastic sight we've ever seen, for looming high on a hill were the walls and towers of a huge medieval city, and so early in the morning, with the sun barely over the horizon, and the early morning haze just visible enough to give the sight a rare mysterious enchantment, we could have been living 500 years ago, so ancient it looked. And there was not an earthly sound except for the singing of the birds and a few greeting calls by some farmer's rooster, giving the experience even a more authentic air, one so authentic that Karl and I both were stunned. The huge ancient wall surrounding what looked like the old city of Carcassonne and the castle there, with its frequent towers and drawbridge, almost gave us the feeling two knights must have had, centuries ago, when approaching the same town. After gazing at this sight silently for a while, we came back to earth to see a bakery nearby, and upon entering, saw that it was probably the place that bakes the city's supply of bread for the day, and we then purchased some freshly baked rolls, and stood there munching and shivering, as it was chilly in this early hour of the morning. Leaving the place, we headed for the old city drawbridge, so fascinated were we by the previous sight. We drove Vicki thru the narrow, quiet ancient streets, winding up toward the old city, finally reaching it and parking the car. There was not a soul in sight, and we walked in silence toward the drawbridge, pausing there to see before us the old moat which was now empty, and the old wall and towers that at one time had so faithfully guarded the city. Beyond this sight was a view of the hills and valley below, lying there very peacefully and fitting into the picture perfectly. We then crossed the old wooden draw bridge, noticing that its pulley system was still in perfect condition and laughingly wondering if it indeed might be used on us, so fitting seemed the silent crossing. We walked up the winding street, soon spying a breakfast shop that was open, and feeling very much like a cup of coffee, we went in. Upon entering, we were greeted in German by a good-looking family sitting at one of the tables with a hearty *"Gooten morgin"* [guten morgen]—obviously a sign that they thought us German. Karl, with his extreme German look, and I, with longer hair now, probably do look anything but French, so the father of the family's calculated guess was good, but not correct. But regardless, he seemed pleased by Karl's ability to exchange a few words in German, and I wonder still if he ever realized we weren't. Anyway, we each had a cup of café au lait, the French coffee consisting of half very strong coffee and half milk plus a few croissants before having to do some further investigating of Carcassonne. I'm now quite easily able to converse the simple things in French, and I'm enjoying it immensely. I'm also able to have simple conversations with people with the patience and the will, and these are the things which help me most.

Postcard: Carcassonne—Europe's best-preserved medieval wall and castle

    Karl and I then left the shop, and spent the next hour or so just walking around the town, the walls, and many of the small squares and gardens. It was still early, but around 8:00, the town began to come to life, shopkeepers arriving and going about their routine business of opening up, old ladies dressed in black carrying armloads of very long loaves of the French bread, and early morning delivery boys going from house to house and shop to shop with whatever they had to deliver.
    We strolled around taking in all these sights until the castle gates opened at 9:00, when we took a tour of the old palace. The castle was very elaborate for its date (15th century), and the tour (in French) led us all through the castle and out into the city wall, where we climbed towers, saw how the ancient defense system worked, and observed so many interesting sights and views of the old city from various places along that wall. We learned that Carcassonne was the only town in Europe that had retained its original medieval wall and castle almost perfectly intact, mainly because the city had such a wonderful defense system, that no one was ever able to seize the town. From the high walls of the city to the South we could see what

looked like the beginnings of a mountain range and our expectations proved correct when we asked an English couple if they were the Pyrenees. So intrigued were we by the sight of these hills that we suddenly decided not to head north right away, but instead to go South into the mountains. This turned out to be a wise and promising decision.

So at 10:45 this morning we left that ancient village of Carcassonne, and headed for the Pyrenees, the very same thing the Romans did centuries ago on their conquesting journey to Spain. Driving along the Aude River and passing through small towns like Limoux and Quillan, we soon found ourselves in country so different and yet so much more beautiful than any we've yet seen. The mountains were upon us before we knew it, and they were much more spectacular than any part of the Alps had been—at least the parts we had seen. We drove along following rushing, clear mountain streams, which wildly lashed their way down toward the valleys, ripping over the stones and the smooth rocks, and roaring over them with a fresh, rough and invigorating sound. We often found ourselves climbing higher and higher, winding up the sides of some of the cliffs on the narrow road, passing only a few cars and an occasional truck, which put us on edge every time, since the road in parts was almost too narrow for both a truck and car—a situation not always greeted with enthusiasm. But the ride was so beautiful that we soon got used to the narrow road, and besides, we had insurance! Still climbing, we stopped in a small store where we bought some bread, cheese and cider before we reached what must have been the highest altitude, where we parked the car to eat lunch. At this point we could see a magnificent panorama of not only the scenery we had just passed through, but also the scenery that lay ahead. Here also were patches of snow on the peaks of some of the mountains and a few lonely clouds hovering at the same altitude before us, which was an amazingly beautiful combination. It was also cold this high, and I dug my trench coat out of the suitcase, which from then on was very useful. We were also at this point above the tree line, giving the view a wildness and barrenness we had not seen in Bavaria.

After lunch we reluctantly continued on, this time going down the sides of the mountains, heading toward scenery that seemed even more impressive. And down we kept going, until we came upon an interesting looking town called Aix-les-Thermes, which was located far into a valley completely surrounded by enormous mountains, and looked like a wonderful place to spend the night, as we were both tired after the few hours of sleep we'd had in the car last night, and anxious to find a bed as soon as possible. Aix-les-Thermes seems to be a bustling tourist village, as it was loaded with hotels, and there was even a casino there. Near the center of town we saw the town's namesake, a square pool of steaming water, where a group of people were seated, feet dangling down in the pool. So here we are in what must be France's version of Hot Springs, and we soon, upon arrival, found that the town's frequenters were people looking for such a health resort. We immediately checked in to a hotel, which is extremely nice as well as cheap, only $1.20 for the night. And after waiting until 2:00 for them to get the room cleaned up, I went immediately to bed, sleeping until around 7:00, when Karl, who had spent the whole afternoon writing a letter, woke me up.

I then got up and took a sponge bath in the wonderful hot water, the first we'd seen in ages, and it felt great to at last get some of the salt from the Mediterranean off my body—something that should have been done ages ago.

Karl and I took off around 8:00, exploring the town while looking for dinner. It's a quaint (I hate using that word) place, with the usual winding streets, and the very old shops and stands lining the way. It also has its share of sidewalk cafés, something we've discovered as a French institution since Paris, and the people are very friendly, glad to give directions and advice, even if it is in French.

We at last stopped in a restaurant, where we not only were blessed by a cute French waitress, but a delicious meal of *soup du jour* (my favorite part of the French meal), porc [pork], green beans, peaches and wine for only around $1.50. After dinner we returned to the hotel, passing by the casino, a lively place which appeared less a gambling joint than a night club.

The streets were swarming with French tourists of all kinds and ages, and for such a small town located seemingly in the middle of nowhere, it was tonight really "jumping."

So here I am, on the nightly (or almost nightly) vigil, and it's nearly 2:00. So must say "Until tomorrow, goodnight."

Love, Tom

P.S. A traffic ticket was discovered on the car tonight. It seems that in France we just can't avoid them. Remember Paris? By the way, we are ignoring it!

Saverdun, France—Friday, August 9, 1963

Hi–

What a crazy day this has been! Karl and I, in our adventuresome travels, have gone biserk [berserk], for not only have we traveled through three countries including Spain, Andorra and France, but we aren't at all far tonight from Aix-les-Thermes, even though we spent almost all day driving. Does that set the mood? Read on and find out how we "accomplished" such a crazy thing.

We slept till around 10:00, when we got up, dressed and packed, going downstairs for a typical French breakfast of "*café au lait*" and croissants. I then gathered together a huge pile of postcards, some even from Rome, which I ashamedly wanted to at last mail. So Karl and I crossed the square, I stopping at a bank to cash a traveler's check, proceeding on past the steam bath through the winding street to a post office, where I must have spent $4.00 on stamps, so much did I have to send. On the way back to the car I bought some envelopes, since I'd run out, and around 11:30, we were finally off. While boarding Vicki, we saw two policemen, the same that had probably given us the traffic ticket yesterday, and before I had the chance to avoid his stare, he gave me a short nod and a slight smile, probably realizing that we had disregarded the traffic ticket you now have. It was very funny!

And so we left Aix-les-Thermes, and rather than heading north we figured since we were so close to Andorra, a very small country in the Pyrenees between France and Spain, that it would be fun to see exactly what it was like. Leaving Aix-les-Thermes, we again started climbing, and in less than 10 minutes found ourselves high in the mountains, and able to see Aix-les-Thermes nestled far below in the valley. The drive was similar to yesterday's, just as wild and just as barren, especially in the high altitudes beyond the timber line. The road seemed to get rougher and more narrow the further south we drove, and wound its way around and thru the mountains, hugging their ledges. There was also a complete lack of guard rail along most of the way, except a scarce run of stone wall in isolated spots. Again the rushing clear mountain streams added to the beauty of the trip, along with the small patches of snow and small clouds clinging to some of the higher peaks.

We were peacefully driving along, when suddenly, as rounding a curve, we came upon a whole herd of cattle right in the center of the road, a herd that wasn't about to get out of our way, and were going to need persuasion to ward off some of their curiosity for us. We managed to get past a few, and after some time of sitting there, honking furiously, and putting up with their large black noses against the windows, a strange sensation indeed, we cleared a path through the creatures, and rode on through, with the clanging sound of their bells in our ears as we proceeded down the road. It was one of those experiences which can be both amusing and irritating.

At 1:30, as we rounded a curve in the road, we were forced to stop quickly behind a huge stream of waiting cars, which we assumed to be the French border. Our expectations proved correct after about a 45 minute wait, and we slowly creeped [crept] along during that time until we crossed the border, which lay right in the middle of nowhere near probably what was one of the highest altitudes in the Pyrenees. We were extremely irritated that the French should run such an inefficient border, but found out later that there is much smuggling between France and Spain by way of Andorra, where there is no tax on goods.

Once in Andorra, we continued on our way over the only road which runs through the whole country, passing through several small villages before reaching the city, or village I should say, of Andorra. We stopped there for gas, which was half as cheap as anywhere in France, driving on through the town. It seemed to be quite a Spanish-French tourist stopover as there were many of them there, probably because of the low prices. Our original plan had been to have lunch here and then head back north, but again, being so close to Spain, we thought we might as well cross over the border, have lunch there, and then return. And especially since Andorra didn't appeal to us that much.

So we drove on through Andorra toward the Spanish border, crossing it about 2:30. It was already amazing to us how different the weather was in Spain, as we were forced to roll down the windows and take our coats off, something we would never have done an hour ago in the chilly weather of France. But too, we had almost crossed the Pyrenees by now, and we presumed that that mountain range serves as a catchall for the cold weather drifting down from the North. The Spanish border guard was adorned in a magnificent uniform of light beige with red and gold trim, quite amazingly proper for a representative of the only Fascist government left in Europe. But there was no problem for us at all in crossing the border. Most borders, when finding out that we are Americans, let us through with very little formality, probably not really caring what the hell we take into the country, only worried about what their own countrymen try to smuggle in. It was the very same here.

So here we were in Spain, and Karl and I both laughed when remembering our original plans which completely omitted it. The roads were terrible, much narrower and not nearly as well kept as roads in France and even Andorra, which we found had better roads even than France. We drove on to the first Spanish town, Seo de Urgel [La Seu d'Urgell], stopping in the outskirts to get a couple dollars-worth of Pietas, the Spanish money. So now that we had money, we had to spend it, so we stopped at a restaurant for a bit of lunch. It was much nicer inside than it looked on the outside, and when we discovered that the waiter spoke English, we knew this wasn't for us, and when he was in the kitchen getting us some water, we sneaked out the side door. I bet he's still wondering where we disappeared to!

So we walked toward the center square of town, where we found the ideal place for lunch—a strange looking tavern where seemed to be gathered a representative sampling of Spanish local gentry, including ten or more members of the Spanish army, all dressed in uniforms similar to the one I previously described, but a huge diversity of rank included in the group.

The gentleman at the bar was very friendly, and even though they didn't serve sandwiches, he was willing to scrape up some bread and sausage, which wasn't delicious, but nonetheless adequate for our starved palates. And Karl, who had served so well with his German in Germany began spouting off with his high school Spanish, and it was an interesting meal. The bartender asked me if we drank Coke in America to which I casually replied affirmatively, while roaring hysterically inside, and between all this, he kept fixing some kind of coffee with gin or some kind of liquor. So our only meal in Spain was deemed a success as we left the tavern. Since we hadn't spent nearly the $2.00 we had changed, we proceeded to do so first buying huge ice cream cones, and then post cards. We found a relic of a post office which looked straight out of the 19th century and was topped off with a huge picture of Franco peering down over the place and a scratchy old quill pen which Karl had a heck of a struggle with.

So, after we had spent our money, we headed back for France. Strangely enough, Spain seemed Spanish, and very different from nearby France, not only in weather, but in appearance as well, for the architecture was characteristically Spanish if you can imagine that, and the whole air was entirely different. I still maintain that Europe's language barrier has done the most to keep the countries apart. So off to Andorra we went, anxious, now that we had satisfied our curiosities about Spain and Andorra, to get up to the chateau country in France, which was actually quite a long way from Spain. When crossing the border, the guard who had checked us before gave us a bewildered look, but evidently concluded we were honest, and didn't say a word. On the trip back we were surprised to find, once in the mountains, that we were driving through "solid" clouds, clouds which had drifted into the Pyrenees since we had driven through earlier in the day. And what an odd sensation it was, driving on these narrow ledges through those clouds, a feeling that you were somewhere either on top of the world or at the end of it, take your pick. But all along the way, all you could see was the mountain wall to one side, the ledge which you remembered as dropping off to eternity on the other. It was a peculiar feeling, but very exciting and beautiful at the same time. We again had to wait at the French border, but this time on a downhill slope, which made things much simpler, since all I did was put Victoria in neutral and whenever we had to move, simply release the brake. We were on the same road that we'd been on before, and around 4:30 we passed through Aix-les-Thermes, feeling almost like it was home, and continued North to Foix, where we stopped for dinner. Of course, once out of the high altitude areas of the Pyrenees, we were no longer in the clouds; and reaching Foix about 7:30, we were both starved. We went into a small insignificant looking restaurant, and I told the single waitress (and cook) we wanted dinner. She said "fine" and not another word, disappearing into the kitchen, soon to return with a huge silver bowl of noodle soup, a sign that we obviously had no choice in what we wanted to eat. The soup was delicious and was followed by a plate of freshly fried fish, which we thought to be the main course since it was Friday. We were soon surprised after finishing the wonderful fish, to see a huge plate of sausage and spaghetti as the third course, fruit as fourth. All this plus a whole bottle of wine and bread was only about $1.20. See what I mean about European prices?

Leaving here, we headed north until we stopped around 9:30 in Saverdun, finding a wonderful hotel with bed and breakfast for only $1.10 apiece. What really makes it nice is the gorgeous French girl who works here. She is beautiful and friendly too—and my French seems to be working beautifully. I just went downstairs for a soda and she said, *"Vous avez soif,"* which I could not think of the meaning of while there to save me. My imagination has been running wild ever since until I remembered what it means. "You are thirsty."

And so I say, until tomorrow, good night.

Much love, Tom

Loches, France—Saturday, August 10, 1963

Hi-

I think it impossible to have one dull day all summer! And today is no exception even though we spent all day driving—about 9 hours in all.

We got up around 7:30 in Saverdun, and after packing and shaving, we went downstairs for breakfast, where we were greeted royally by our beautiful French friend and served a typical breakfast, but with the best coffee we had had in France. It's funny that even in the small "poor man's hotels," they seem to serve food in silver dishes. Very nice custom!

We left Saverdun, heading north toward Toulouse. To trace briefly the great distance we made, leaving Toulouse, we went through Montauban, Cahors, Brive, Limoges, Bellac, Lussac, Chauvigny, Chatellerault, D'auge, Ligueil and to Loches, where we are spending the night, and near the heart of the chateau country. The countryside was rather flat and uninteresting until we reached Cahors, where we found ourselves in a string of beautiful rolling hills. Actually, all of France is attractive country, but this section in particular was very scenic, everything being so green, and the haystacks dotting the fields. We stopped at a small roadside restaurant right outside of Cahors where we bought a cheese sandwich and a Pepsi, which we ate in a small deserted clearing off the main road. The scenery continued until we reached Limoges, where the land again began to flatten out. Even the flat lands were pretty to drive on because of the inevitable groves of trees which seem to line every French road. Around 5:00, we stopped in a tiny town outside of Châtellerault, where we bought a huge narrow long loaf of French bread, which we munched on while driving on. We pulled into Loches about 7:30, our drive into the city greeted by a huge medieval castle and walled in city high on the hill—a pleasant sight to see. We found a hotel right away—Hotel Du Palais (Hotel of the Palace) which charged a modest 12.50 francs for room, and expected us to eat dinner. After unloading into the hotel room and cleaning up, we went downstairs for dinner, a mediocre meal of soup du jour, ham, potatoes (English), cheese, wine and plums for dessert. After dinner we decided to investigate the castle and old part of the city, and we walked through the near-empty streets, through the old city gate, turning left and walking toward the castle, which was closed and looking good and spooky. There was not a soul in sight, and the few ancient streetlamps added very little light to the scene. From the top of the hill we saw the most brilliant sunset I've seen since Sweden, one that was a brilliant shade of orange, casting red and purple streaks in the clouds far above. We then walked to the other end of the old city near the city wall which was high above what used to be a moat, and found ourselves by the walls of an old prison or dungeon. Directly beside this was the most serene and well-kept park I've seen, a very peaceful and beautiful place. It seemed strange that there was not a soul around, but this fact added to the beauty of the place. These old medieval places possess a rare enchanting air at a time like sunset when there are not a lot of people around. We were there for about an hour when we decided to walk back.

On the way back we stopped in a small old French tavern, complete with wooden beamed ceiling, black leather seats, and huge dark wooden tables. It was a small place, and very old-worldlike in character. It seemed to be a favorite hangout for all the young adults of Loches, and was really interesting. Karl and I splurged, ordering our first scotch and soda since being in Europe, doing so more as a preview for England and Scotland, but the place was overloaded with atmosphere and we sat there for more than an hour soaking up that plus observation of all the pretty French girls who kept running in and out. We left there about 11:00, more than ready for bed after the long day's drive.

So here I am, and the time is again right to say: Until tomorrow, good night.

Love, Tom

Blois, France—Sunday, August 11, 1963

Hi-

Today has been wonderful—and I'm so glad I decided to come to France during this part of the trip, as the chateau country is beautiful, and the chateaux equally so. We arose this morning about 9:00, and after packing, having petit dejeuner and paying the bill, we left Loches, bidding the castle on the hill goodbye, and anxious to get into the heart of chateau country, most of which surround the Loire River. We headed first for Chenonceaux, a town located about 30 kilometers northeast and where is situated a very famous palace or chateau (castle) which is built over the Cher River. We arrived at the chateau, parked our car, and after paying 2 francs for our entrance ticket, walked through a huge wide grove of trees or path through trees which took us straight toward the castle. We passed through two statues of lions into an entrance lawn, where to the right was located a series of beautiful stables. Upon reaching the chateau itself, which is flanked by 2 huge formal gardens, we first investigated a tower on the right hand of the entrance, which must have been either a guest house or gardener's residence during the heyday of the castle. We were then taken inside the castle by a young man who proceeded to give the information in French, most of which I couldn't understand, so fast did he talk. But he had an outline in English which he gave us after finding out we didn't understand French well, and we were then taken through most of the downstairs rooms, which were really beautiful, including a chapel, elaborately paneled greeting and game room, sitting room, a huge hallway which spanned over the river, and numerous other rooms, all lavishly decorated and filled with all kinds of family heirlooms, paintings (one even by Rubens) and furniture. The strange thing about the place is that it is still privately owned, and obviously the family must show the place off to tourists to keep up tax payments. It's sad in a way! While inside we met a wonderful English couple who told us of a Sound and Light Spectacle at Angers that we shouldn't miss, as it had a "cast of thousands" and was really terrifically produced, with the knights in costumes, traditional dances, etc. So Karl and I decided to at least think about it and check the map upon returning to the car. Leaving the chateau, we walked out through the impressive garden along the riverbank, where we could get a view of the castle over the river. And what a beautiful place it is, so old (15th century) and yet so pleasing architecturally, with its symmetrical towers and ornate trim very tastefully in place. The entrance hall's ceiling, I forgot to mention, is an isometrical [isometric] gothic arch structure, one of only two in existence, and unusual as well as pleasing in looks. The whole chateau, with its formal gardens, surrounding wood and peaceful river beneath was well worth the visit. On the way out, I stopped to buy some post cards, and there met an interesting couple from New York City, who were trying to explain something to the fellow who was selling tickets. For once I felt my French was really useful, as I had to help them translate what they wanted into French. It was loads of fun! Upon reaching the car and checking the map, we decided that Angers was too far out of the way for the "Son et Lumière" tonight, as we are to meet Bill and Freddy tomorrow in Orléans.

Leaving Chenonceaux, we headed for Amboise, passing first thru the small village of Bléré. The country here is characterized by beautiful green trees, ripe looking fields, some dotted with yellow haystacks, and small quaint villages, which all "reek" with tradition and history. The highways which follow the small rivers, as well as the Loire, are lined with stone fences, which also seem to be relics of an unknown (at least to us) past, about which they only know. Your imagination wanders and you start thinking about the countless people over the centuries who have traveled these same roads, being observed by the same stone wall, and you wish it could share some of its secrets. Amboise was a larger city than Chenonceaux, and its castle seemed just as interesting, but we decided not to stop, but drove on through, knowing that there would be plenty more to see today, and stopping would be wasting valuable time. So we continued up the Loire River through

Chaumont, another beautiful town, to Cheverny, by way of Ponlavoy [Pontlevoy] and Contres. The drive along the Loire River was very scenic, but strictly in the peaceful sense. As we drove into Cheverny, we approached by way of a road through a forest of trees which headed straight for the Chateau of Cheverny, a very handsome looking structure, a bit more square than others we'd seen, but nevertheless, just as beautiful, with its golden entrance gate and perfectly kept huge lawn. We at first wanted to stop, but decided to go on to Chambord, where an even more beautiful chateau is situated.

At Chambord we saw what is perhaps the most ornate and yet most impressive castle we'd ever seen. It is the very picture of what you always imagine one of these chateaux to look like—it must be the one that's always used in pictures. We stopped here, walking toward the castle on a huge green lawn, and before taking the tour of the place, we investigated a small old church close by. The tour of the castle through all the various rooms, up and down ornate staircases and through an old carriage room where are located some gorgeous old carriages, was almost impossible for me to understand in French, and all I got out of it was possible dates and the fact that Louis XIV had slept in one of the beds—a fact which made Karl and I both roar thinking of all the G. Washington[2] beds in the U.S. The interior was actually disappointing compared to the exterior and we almost wished we hadn't gone inside. We were here for about an hour before taking off for Blois.

Postcard: The ornate Chambord chateau

We stopped in a small town right outside of Chambord where we bought some lunch. I had a wonderful conversation with a little old lady here in one of the shops—the type of person who really enjoys talking to foreigners. I also picked up a few forgotten words from her—exactly the best way to learn French. Granted, the conversation was far from deep, but it was interesting anyway. Here I bought potato chips and bananas, not a very substantial lunch, but all I felt like eating, and Karl and I drove to a small clearing near the house, where we stopped to eat.

After eating, we headed back along the Loire until we reached Blois, a picturesque and interesting looking town, situated on and seemingly emerging from the Loire. We headed first toward the old city wall and castle, located, as usual in these towns, on a high bluff-like plateau in the center of the city. There we parked the car and walked in to inquire about the "Son et Lumière" spectacle that was scheduled to be presented tonight at 9:00. We decided not to take a tour of the castle, and instead made our way on a stairway down the hill from the old relic toward what looked like the center of town, in search of a hotel. We turned left up a side street and came upon a very nice-looking place, serving dinner tonight, and having room for us both, and certainly reasonable enough to take. It was still fairly early, around 5:00, so I went back to the castle to get the car, and Karl went off in search of a Newsweek or Time, since we hadn't heard or read any news from home in ages. I then returned to the hotel, and after finding out that dinner would be served at 7:30, spent the next hour or so writing. Karl soon returned, and at 7:30 we went downstairs to probably the best meal we've had in France, soup, roast beef, English potatoes (boiled), peas (*pois à la francais*), lemon soda and neopolitan [Neapolitan] ice cream for dessert. The dining room was cozy—thick green carpets, white paneling halfway up and bright red walls. It was a delicious meal.

After eating, we walked back toward the castle, where we found out that the "Spectacle de Son et Lumière" was all in French, a fact which discouraged Karl to the point of returning to the hotel, but not me. So I paid my money and went in to see a production in sound and light similar to the one in Rome, but not nearly as impressive since it was in French plus the fact that any castle cannot hold quite the interest a Roman Forum does. In fact I was so tired that about half-way through I went to sleep. But the part I did see was beautiful, particularly the extremely romantically written music. It was interesting! I did catch Joan of Arc saying "Mon Dieu" (My God) in the chapel several times, if that means anything, but most of it was too fast for me to catch anything but the simpler words.

So afterwards, around 10:00, I returned to the hotel, and being tired, the letter probably reads that way. And so, until tomorrow, good night.

Love, Tom

Somewhere in Northern France—Monday, August 12, 1963

Hi–
What a hell of a day! We not only spent all day waiting for Freddy and Bill here in Orléans, but there was "no room in the inn," so to speak, and we're spending another one of those horrible nights in the car!

Karl and I arose to a beautiful sunshine day in Blois about 9:00, and after getting cleaned up and dressed we went downstairs to pay the bill and eat breakfast, only to find out that it was too late for petit dejeuner, so we paid and took off, heading for the main street in hopes of buying an American newspaper or magazine. We found a *New York Herald* and found out about the Kennedy baby[3]—certainly a shame, and the "Great Train Robbery in England."[4] Perhaps we'll find some of the money when we get to England! We then walked down the street where we entered the only coffee shop that seemed to be open, where we had breakfast. I exchanged a few words with the gentleman (*monsieur* if you please) at the bar, and he was a very friendly sort. The French you know, have quite the reputation for being rude, but I heartily disagree. The more proper description would be "independent" and reserved, but certainly not rude. They are, however, very proud about their language, and simply refuse, in most cases, to speak English. And we certainly can't blame them for being proud of that. The English speaking peoples are not a bit different about their own language. Before coming over here, I had one of those naïve misconceptions that everyone in the world spoke English—and that is so very far from right. The United States, unfortunately, seems to breed a proud sort of person who cannot help but know one culture—and one culture only! Americans are so sheltered, and it is obvious over here that the older Americans especially, the ones with set ways and ideas, seem to be almost afraid to face new language or custom. They simply don't know how to cope with it, and unfortunately their reactions are defensive, taking on the form of rudeness and haughtiness. To young Americans, those who are still able to accept and face new surroundings, this action by their fellow Americans is repulsive, creating a feeling of shame. I've had this feeling numerous times myself.

At any rate, we finished eating breakfast and left Blois around 10:00. We took the "back road" along the Loire, which was a beautiful drive, and led us all the way into Orléans, a city of great charm which impressed us immediately upon entering. Orléans is a city of about the size of Decatur,[5] and seems very clean and well-kept. It is the famous home of St. Joan of Arc, and there are all sorts of statues, etc. over the whole city in honor of her. Since we were to meet Bill and Freddy here at the main railroad "*gare*," we went there first, but not a sign of them could be seen. I inquired of a young man in the information booth if messages could be left, but unfortunately this was impossible, and at the same time we found out the horrible news that trains do not come directly to Orléans from Switzerland, and the only other possible way to get here from there was to go first to Paris, which was further north, and thus, a longer distance. That's a good example of "preplanning!"

So Karl and I then walked to the central post office in hopes that some kind of message would be left there or that we could leave one, but once there, we got into all kinds of trouble with the language barrier, etc., trying to explain to the clerk what we wanted to do. Finally some distinguished gentleman who knew some English came to our rescue, suggesting that we leave a message for them under "General Delivery," which was just what we wanted. But then we changed our minds, after all that trouble since we figured they might never check here in the first place.

So—Karl and I said "to hell with it," and decided not to worry, and noticing a huge cathedral which emerged beautifully from the Orléans skyline, we headed in that direction. We went inside and found an interior similar to other French cathedrals we'd seen, however with statues and commerative [commemorative] monuments mostly to Joan of Arc, the heroine of the town. It was a beautiful place though, but I'm getting almost sick of going through cathedrals. Don't misunderstand, they're far from all alike, but their atmosphere is, and that I get tired of; even though it is quiet and religious, at the same time it's damp and dingy. Leaving here, we headed back to the central square where is centered a huge statue of Joan on a horse, and surrounded with flowers. There we collapsed in a sidewalk café, where we sat for about an hour, munching on "jambon" sandwiches and beer. I swear, the French bread with that ham and hot mustard is one of the best things France has to offer. I could "live" on them!

Postcard: Jeanne d'Arc—"The Maid of Orléans"

We then walked back toward the *gare*, me stopping on the way to see if I could get my glasses lens replaced. The darn things are still broken, and have been since Rome. Guess I'll have to wait till London! At the station there was still no Bill and Freddy, so Karl and I decided to wait it out, and we parked in what must be the dingiest, dirtiest snack bar in the world there in the station—and we sat there almost all day waiting for trains from Paris. I got my writing materials out, and thought it a good chance to get "caught up," and Karl bought newspapers, magazines and all sorts of things to keep himself passified [pacified].

And so we kept waiting and waiting. Around 8:00, we were both famished and trying to console our stomachs, so went next door into the station restaurant, which, surprisingly enough, was beautifully decorated in wood paneling, had clean white tablecloths on all the tables and smelled wonderful! We here had a most embarrassing thing happen, and due to me and my poor knowledge of French. The cheapest meal on the menu gave us two choices for main course, an egg omelet and something else, which I couldn't translate. So I asked the waitress what it was, to which she gave no reply, and instead quickly hurried off to the kitchen saying that she would show one to us. So she returned moments later with what looked like some kind of meat loaf wrapped in skin and fried, looking "lovely" with its decoration of green parsley. So Karl and I both hungrily nodded "wee," [*oui*] and everything seemed fine. She then brought out two bottles of "rosé wine" and a huge silver bowl of a delicious vegetable tomato soup, which we greedily devoured in only a few minutes. Then it happened. We were served the "meatloaf" on silver trays along with a huge bowl of mixed vegetables. She also brought a jar of mustard indicating that we would put it on the meat. Upon cutting open the skin, out rolled not only a whole bevy of what looked like little wiry intestines, but a horrible wiff [whiff] of steamed smoke, which had a stench I can't describe. We both sat there stunned for a minute, each wondering what the hell this stuff was, and wishing we didn't have to wonder! My theory was that they were intestines, but Karl upheld the belief that they were what he called "rocky mountain oysters" or hog's testicles, something that repulsed us even more. So—I spent the meal eating loads of vegetables and pushing the... whatever they were... around in my plate, while the French couple at the next table kept looking over and smiling. When we told the waitress that we were through, she got a very hurt expression on her face, and I laughed and said in what must have been miserable French that I was sorry, that we didn't know what they were, and that we never eat them at home. So she unloaded the table, and obviously feeling guilty, brought out a huge tray of assorted cheeses for us to choose from. But dammit, I didn't want cheese for dessert, I wanted ice cream ("glace"). But it wasn't the time or occasion for doing anything but accept her hospitality and eat the cheese, which wasn't bad, but had a strong flavor and taste that didn't agree at all with what we'd previously smelled. At any rate, it's a meal I'll never forget, and I'll laugh about it later I'm sure.

So Karl and I returned to the snack bar, where I again began writing. Some of the characters who came in the place were really amazing—and of all sorts. Somewhat later, we both walked out into the place where the trains were arriving, to see if perhaps our comrades would be around. Karl sat down on a bench where he was reading "*Playboy*" and I was walking around, looking at all the travel posters lining the walls. When I returned to the bench where Karl was sitting, I noticed a strange looking character sitting next to him, bumming a cigarette and asking to look at his magazine. I then happened to change my glance long enough to notice, on the bench which was back to back with the one where Karl and his friend were sitting, another fellow, who was motioning to me at the same time giving horrible glances at the direction of Karl's "friend." I smiled to myself and walked around the bench where he was sitting and he motioned for me to sit down. He then proceeded to tell me in sign language that Karl's bum was crazy and that he begged money, liquor and all kinds of things from people. But he kept carrying on this way for quite a while till I began to think that he was equally as nuts as the bum sitting next to Karl, so I suggested to Karl that we go inside to get something to drink. I bade my friend goodbye and then waited while Karl retrieved his *Playboy* from his friend. On the way back I told Karl what my bum had been doing, and we both roared when Karl told me that the whole time his bum had been making exactly the same kind of motions at my bum as my bum had been making at his! We're still laughing about it.

We sat in the ugly, dingy snack bar writing and watching the people till around 11:00, when hallelujah!—Bill and Freddy came bouncing in from Paris, where they had spent an hour changing trains. We talked over coffee for a while, before deciding suddenly that if we wanted to find a place to stay, we had better get going. So we packed Vicki and spent the next half hour futilely trying to find a place to sleep in Orléans. So we left Orléans and drove through town after town, stopping in each one looking for a hotel, but it was too late. We even drove through Chartres, getting a fleeting glimpse of the cathedral with its two different spires against the dark skyline, bringing back memories of the early days of the summer.

We decided to drive on all night, and Karl took the wheel about 2:00, at which time I went to sleep. And so, until tomorrow, I say good night.

Love, Tom

Calais, France—Tuesday, August 13, 1963

Hi–

I woke up very early this morning to find the car parked right on the coast of France on the English Channel, which comes as somewhat of a surprise, to say the least, and feeling perfectly miserable, my legs cramped and half my body still asleep. I also felt so filthy—as it has been quite a while since I had had a bath, and train stations at Orléans aren't exactly the most conducive to cleanliness. The others were soon awake, all feeling equally as miserable, and feeling even more that way upon finding out it was about 5:30 in the morning.

We then started up Vicki and headed up the coast, destination Calais, where we were planning on meeting Rick on the 14th as well as departing from France to England. I was too sleepy to notice much about the drive, but near Calais, we stopped right there on the coast where were located thousands of the defensives used by Germany during the last world war. The country here along the coast was unbelievably beautiful, as not only could one see the sea, but also the white cliffs of Dover lurking across the channel. The flat green fields, the rolling hills and the tiny villages which dotted the coast in this section added to the beauty. The wind was biting, and seemed to serve to wake us up, at least temporarily. We wandered around upon the old bunkers and investigated a monument erected to the French and English for all those who were killed during the war. The Germans seemed to have had quite a defensive as it was amazing how heavy the coast seemed to have been fortified—it's no wonder the English felt hemmed in. It must have been horrible. But along with the horror of all the war relics was also the beauty of the scene itself. The cold deserted sandy beaches were covered with the debris left from the last tide, and the sight of those white cliffs across the channel from the top of those windy bluffs was gorgeous.

Tired and cold, we didn't stay there long. Instead, anxious to get to Calais and find a hotel where we could sleep, we got in Vicki and continued up the coast. The English Channel looks just as rough as we always imagined and equally as cold.

We pulled into Calais around noon, and by accident came upon one of the most wonderful places to stay that we've been able to find all summer. It's Hotel Albion, run by an elderly French woman by the name of Madame Campagnolle, who lived in London as a dressmaker for 40 years, and speaks almost perfect English. She told me that we couldn't go to sleep until around 1:00 since she had to get the room ready, so we decided to get a bite to eat before that time.

ALBION

11, RUE VAUBAN
CALAIS

Comfortable Hotel

in the centre of the town

H + C water - Central heating

Garage Berliet - Nord Auto opposite

English Spoken

PHONE 34.31.51 CALAIS

Pr. A. CAMPAGNOLLE

IMP. R. MARTIN · CALAIS

Calling card for Mme. Campagnolle, hotel proprietor (and dressmaker)

    I forgot to mention that we stopped for breakfast in a small town about 6:00. We were amused to see there that many of the gentlemen who came in at that hour started the day off with a shot of some kind of liquor, chasing it with a sip of coffee. That's a custom that I wouldn't care at all to pick up no matter how much I like France.

    We walked around the corner of the hotel and sat down in a sidewalk café for jambon sandwiches and beer. I again have to say that those sandwiches can't be equaled anywhere. I wish we ate more of the French bread.

    At 1:00 we returned to the hotel and found the very nice and spotlessly clean rooms all ready. I had been feeling guilty ever since Nice about not calling, so decided that since Madame Campagnolle spoke English that she could give me some help or at least some information on how to make the call. It then came as a great and pleasant surprise to find her taking care of the whole thing for me, and I was lucky at that time also since the New York line was open, something unusual from what I could gather. So she told me to go upstairs and wait, and in less than 45 minutes, the call went through. However it seemed to me the most mass confused operation I've ever seen with half the operators speaking French, half of them English. In fact, I could hardly believe it when I finally heard your voice, but it was certainly a good thing to hear. I was sorry that the conversation was strained, but I had to yell as you know, and at the same time I could hear you perfectly. I must say that it did ease my mind on the whole thing even though it made me guilty again over how much it was going to cost. We must have talked for 15 or 20 minutes—and at several dollars per minutes, the bill must be colossal. I dread to find out what it was. Anyhow, it was wonderful to hear your voice, even though the whole conversation seemed impossible. It's just

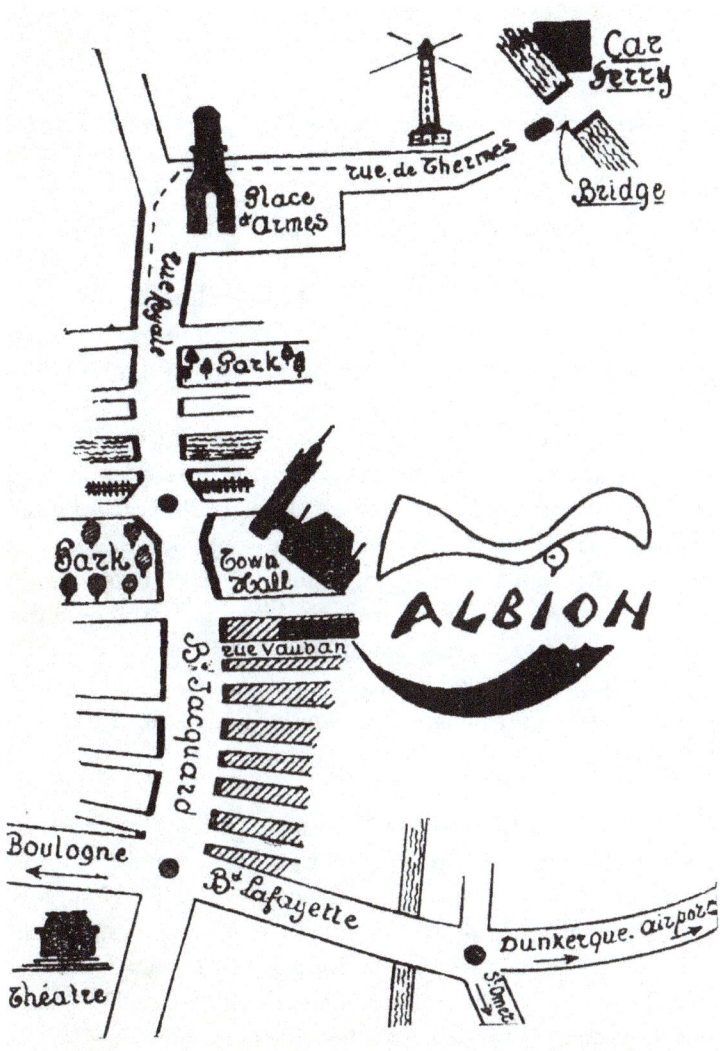

Side 2: Map of Calais—*au revoir* France

that when you are so far away from home, the thought of talking to someone that far away seems impossible.

I then went up to try to sleep, which took me about a half hour, so keyed up I was after the call. We all slept till about 7:00, when Madam C. came up to the room, yelling in her very French accent that if we wanted to get a good meal, that we had better get up and get ready. So that we did, and I took that unopportune [inopportune] opportunity to shine my shoes. Sure enough, it was too late to go to the place she suggested had wonderful food, so instead she called a nearby hotel-restaurant, and found out for us that they had food left and would be glad to give us dinner.

So we walked around the corner to The Atlantic Hotel and there had a fantastic meal of steak, soup du jour, French fries, rose wine and a lettuce and tomato salad. Afterwards I returned to the hotel, the others going off on a walk. I spent the next hour or so talking to Madame C., who is a wonderful person and full of all sorts of tales about the war and her various experiences in life. She is one of these persons who says exactly what she thinks, making one feel on guard at all times, but at the same time, unable to conceal her heart of gold. She has already done so much for us, it is almost like being at home. And she is giving me great tips on my French.

The others soon returned, and we went to bed around 12:30, after reading and writing for a while, and so, until tomorrow, good night.

Love, Tom

Calais, France—Wednesday, August 14, 1963

Hi–

Well, here we are, still in Calais, since we weren't sure whether Rick would be coming in today, so changed our reservation on the ferry until tomorrow morning at 7:30. But in a way I'm glad we stayed since I had my best meal of the summer tonight in the restaurant that Madame Campagnolle suggested.

I woke up this morning about 8:00 feeling wonderful after sleeping yesterday afternoon and also all night. It's really wonderful to have a bed to sleep in—and you don't realize it until you don't have one.

Unshaven and looking sloppy we went downstairs to breakfast, and sat there around the table hoping that Rick would show up and then deciding that we should stay another night and take the ferry that leaves early tomorrow morning since we would have been getting into England late at night if we went tonight and might be taking the chance of not finding a place to spend the night—God forbid!

Also in the small neat breakfast room was an English couple with their son, who must have been about 15. Madame Campagnolle kept popping in and out giving us *petit déjeuner* and at the same time telling us some of the stories she had collected. Quite a woman! We soon got into a conversation with the English couple and ended up talking with them for quite a while. They were wonderful people, and even gave us a hard-bound atlas of the British Isles, which would be wonderful to have while traveling in England, as well as a guide to good hotels and restaurants in England, including such things as price, quality, number of rooms, etc. This made us all the more anxious to get over to Britain, as they told us many things about what we should expect. For one, the prices in England are supposed to be much lower than in France and Germany—a fact which was wonderful to hear. It also seemed that the British were going to be friendly, and best of all, we would at last be able to talk to people, a situation which appealed to us tremendously. You can't imagine how confining it is not to be able to converse thoughts deeper than how much a room or meal is. The thought of at last being able to trade ideas with the Britainers is really great!

They soon hurried off, as they had a boat to catch, and Karl and I then hopped in Vicki, heading for the "*gare maritime,*" the ferryboat station. Upon arriving there we found that the office didn't open until 11:30, so we wouldn't be able to change our reservation until then. While waiting, I got into a conversation with an Englishwoman who had lived in France for most of her life. She had married a Frenchman, and all her children were raised French, but as they grew up, she taught all of them English, and they are perfectly bilingual. She told me that she has her own system for teaching language to small children—and that is by omitting translation and using motions. She was now using this same system on her grandchildren, and she seemed to think that it worked beautifully. She said that the secret to languages is being able to switch your train of thought so that you are thinking in that language—a fact which must be so true since the same things in one language cannot be always said in the same way in another language. I was very envious of anyone who could be bilingual, as learning perfect French is one of my new ambitions—and I wouldn't mind learning German either. The opportunities for one who does well in more than one language are priceless—and one can learn if one puts his mind to it. (I hope I don't get complacent upon returning to English-speaking countries.)

Karl and I also met while standing there an American couple who were with the army and just changing from a French base to an English one. I was quite amused at this couple, as the father was the bashful sort and very narrow—while the wife seemed to wear the pants, as she kept telling him what and what not to do. Their little girl was raised with French children and could speak French much better than I—although I couldn't persuade her to say anything there.

Finally the office opened, and we not only were able to change our reservation to tomorrow morning, but we changed our message to Rick, which we had left yesterday. We just hoped that he would find it. I was very curious to find out all about Rick's trip as he had no idea what he was going to do, and had talked about going back to Paris—something I would give my right arm to do. (That is still my very favorite place—a truly perfect city.)

Karl and I then returned to the hotel, and we told Madam C. that we would be spending another night and that we would like an extra bed for Rick—that is, if he shows up. So I spent the next hour or so writing, and about 1:30 the four of us went to the main street to the same sidewalk café for the same lunch of jambon sandwiches and beer. Afterwards, I took a trip to the post office with Bill and Freddy while Karl went to the Railroad Station in case that Rick might have come there and not to the ferry station. Freddy was in an especially bad mood today and seemed to do nothing but complain. I've really gone out of my way to be nice to him—and I think that he really likes me. There have only been one or two major skirmishes, mine included. Well, enough rambling on a subject I should not be talking about anyways.

After mailing the letters, I strolled back toward the hotel with Bill, leaving Freddy in a shoe store to get a shoe fixed. I then started writing again and wrote till about 7:00 this evening. During that time, the doorbell kept ringing, and I answered it almost every time, not only to save Madame C. from coming to the door each time, but also to see if it could be Rick, who we were expecting to come at any time. Karl, Bill and Freddy went down to the Railroad station about 6:15 to check on trains from Paris and at 7:00 I answered the door to see Rick and the others standing there. Well, he had had quite an exciting trip, having spent the last three days in Paris, and also met some very interesting people. I was green with envy as Paris is my ideal, but managed to control myself while listening to all of his adventures. He also hitchhiked from Spain to Paris with a fellow he met from London.

Madame Campagnolle then came butting in, and after shaking hands with Rick, told us that we had better get our fannys in gear if we wanted to get to the "best" restaurant tonight before the crowds. She has a way of saying things that reeks of authority, so we scurried upstairs, cleaned up and left for dinner about 7:30.

Well, she was so right, for the meal was by far the best we've had all summer. It started off with a delicious pea soup du jour, was followed by a whole cantaloupe, charcoaled steak, French fries and ice cream. We also had a bottle of wonderful rose wine, and the price of the meal was only $2.20. Feeling fat and contented, we left the restaurant, I heading back to the hotel to write some more, the others off for a stroll along the water. It was a chilly night and the long way back seemed too long tonight in the cold, but the sun was just setting across the Calais skyline and I could hear the call of the gulls and birds out over the water, which made it all seem worthwhile.

Once back at the hotel, my plans for writing were ruined as I spent the rest of the evening chatting with Madame C. and she told me how it was in London during the war. She said that she went to a shelter only once after the bombing started, and after that, stayed in her own room, in her own bed. She said that the bombings at that time were so frequent that after a while, they didn't bother her at all. The only thing that upset her were hysterical people—and she said that there were many high-strung people who would easily get in that condition when the bombings started. But she would just lay [lie] in her bed and "have to be bothered by the noise" of all the bombs falling around her. But the worse thing about the war to her was the rationing. But that didn't stop her from having a good time! She had a friend who could get gas stamps for her, and she used these to get poultry from friends of hers in the country who couldn't get gas. In fact, at that time she dressed (she was a dressmaker) the Queen of Albania who was living in London at the time with the King who was trying to protect himself from the war, and this woman was able to get her all sorts of stamps for things which she couldn't get otherwise. Even funnier, she knew a French chef in one restaurant who would do a wonderful favor for her when she had friends to take out for dinner.

During the war in England, one was allowed to spend only 5 shillings for a meal, which as she so pompously put it, didn't "keep a bird alive." So when she would go to this restaurant, her chef friend would put her in some little quiet corner with her friends and would give them a royal feast. She also became very good friends with an American soldier who would also bring her things that she needed. He was in some job that took him back and forth to the United States, and he would always bring shoes back to her—evidently a product that the English couldn't get easily during the war. At any rate, she managed to survive beautifully at that time, although it must have been hectic. I suppose you know what I mean about the rationing, but it sounds strange to me, as I remember nothing whatsoever about that, except some talk about food stamps. A trip to Europe seems to make you aware of so many things!

The others soon returned, and after loading the car and bidding goodbye to Madame C., we went up to bed. You see, we were to be at the ferry station at 6:30 tomorrow morning which means that we won't be able to eat breakfast here and she assured us that she would not be up to tell us goodbye in the morning. She also hoped that we would enjoy England, and assured us that we would love Scotland, as it is so beautiful, and made us promise to send her a post card from New York. We didn't bother to disappoint her by saying that we wouldn't be in New York, but I'm sure a post card from Chicago would do.

So it is again time to say goodnight, and tomorrow, you will be reading about England. I'm extremely excited at the prospect of finally getting to England, and feel even more enthusiastic about Scotland. And so, until tomorrow, for the last time, I say, *au revoir, bonsoir*, etc.

Love, Tom

ENGLAND 12

*Sherwood Forest, Very English Hospitality
and a Wise Fortune Teller*

England is our kissin' cousin in so many ways. Besides giving us the Beatles, *Downton Abbey*, bulldogs and the corner pub, we share a common language and belief in a strong democratic government. One can only admire Great Britain's courage and ability to withstand German aggression in World War II. They were forever thankful to the Americans for coming to their rescue. However, that did not prevent some good-humored banter: "The Yanks came. They were overpaid, oversexed and over here!" Following the allied victory, England quickly worked to regain her rightful place among the leading countries of the world.

Great Britain commands our respect as does the enduring warmth of its people. "Fancy a spot of tea?" is both a welcoming invitation and an opportunity for some lively conversation. Guess who happily indulged?

§ § §

Cambridge, England—Thursday, August 15, 1963

Hi-

And so we're in England! God save the Queen, pass the mustard, if you please! England is living up to all my expectations and even more so. To at last be able to communicate is wonderful, and to communicate with a people who are so friendly and hospitable as the English is even better! And they all have British accents!

In all seriousness, it has been a great day, and we have already covered a great deal of territory as well as seen a lot of sights, if that is possible in one day.

We woke up at 10 minutes after six this morning and panicked as we had to be at the ferry station in 20 minutes. But when we have to mobilize in a short time, we do it, for we were dressed, packed and roaring into the ferry station at exactly 6:30. After waiting in line for quite a while, we finally pulled trusty Victoria into the boat, and made our way upstairs into the dining room, where a real English breakfast was being served. You know, everywhere on the continent the breakfast consists only of rolls and coffee, but no sir, not in England! They start off with juice, then cereal, then bacon, sausage and eggs, followed by toast and jam or marmalade, to top it off with a cup of tea with milk, if you please. In other words, in England a breakfast is a more than substantial meal. I presume that that is where the Americans get their big breakfasts. But, not really worrying why the English eat the big breakfasts we were more worried about eating one ourselves this morning, so we sat down and did just that—eat! After breakfast, I changed all of my francs to pounds, shillings, pence, etc, and then learned that handling English money was not going to be at all easy. Their money system is not based on tens and hundreds, but instead is divided as follows: One pound is equal to twenty shillings. One shilling is equal to twelve pence, a half-crown is equal to two and a half shillings, etc. To say the least, it is at first confusing, but by the end of the day I got it straightened out, which makes me believe that I'm lucky, as I've talked to Americans who never could figure it out. To draw an analogy, their money system is similar to many measuring systems which we have borrowed from the English, for example, the weight system or the distance system. That reminds me, the English also use miles and inches, yards, etc., which again puts us back into more similar surroundings.

After eating, we learned that goods were duty free on the boat, and if there was anything that we needed, that this was the place to get it as there would not be any kind of tax at all. We all sat down with a glass of apple cider, an English drink with a similar consistency as beer, and equally as alcoholic. The ship "Free Enterprise," called by the ferry company a "luxury liner" was clean, modern and full of people. It also was rocking back and forth, as the Channel was particularly rough today. I took a walk out on the deck and was greeted by a cold whiff of wind and a slap of mist, and could see nothing but water, water, everywhere. The mist was so heavy today that I couldn't spot the white cliffs of Dover that we had seen the other day from the French coast, but I was confident that they were there, and after a short walk around the wet deck, returned inside to get warm. The others were sitting around sipping cider and as I walked inside, I noticed that Rick was talking to some lady whom I had never seen. I soon found out that her name was Mrs. Hilton, that she was from Nottingham, England, and that she and her family were traveling back to the Isles from France where they had been taking a "holiday."

And to our surprise, she made the most wonderful gesture, inviting us all to stay with them when we passed through Nottingham, as they had six bedrooms and would love to entertain some boys from America. We were all flabbergasted, to say the least, and could hardly believe it. But she kept insisting, and even gave us her name, address and telephone number. While sitting there, she recommended that if we wanted to buy any "spirits," that this would be the perfect place to do so, since they are much cheaper on the boat. She soon bade us a friendly goodbye and returned to the other side of the lounge. With her, I noticed two sandy haired children, a boy and a girl, who both had the most winning smiles I've ever seen on children, and seemed to be the epitome of what English children should look like. Rick and I went up to the bar where we both purchased a half-fifth of Haig Scotch, which only amounted to about $1.50 apiece. On the way back I stopped to thank Mrs. Hilton for her kind offer, and she assured me that she meant it and introduced me to her husband, a distinguished looking gentleman with a well-groomed mustache and looking more like King Arthur than someone of this day and time. He seemed to have just stepped down from some dusty picture frame of a family's hall of fame, as he had those deep-set eyes, a very serious expression, but a slight smile beneath that mustache which assured one that he wasn't really as serious as he looked. The children, the picture of wholesomeness and politeness, both beamed at me and said, "How do you do," and I was extremely impressed by the whole situation. She did all the talking, which somehow seemed fitting, and their British accents were perfect, lending an even more interesting tone to the scene. I talked with them only a few minutes, returning to the seat.

The boat landed in Dover at about 9:15, and after a brief customs check by a very British looking gentleman, we found ourselves in England, and as we drove off, we were frequently reminded by signs to be sure to keep on the left. It is just lucky that we had the experience of driving on the left in Sweden because it is amazingly hard to get used to at first. The worst thing about it is trying to see to pass, because it is impossible, and you have to rely on the person's judgment sitting on the right side to tell you when the way is clear.

We were immediately amused by the variances in signs and expressions. On the back of one car was a sign "Please toot before overtaking," which means in American, "Please honk before passing." We had secured a copy of the "British

Rules of the Road," which were hilarious to read, as their prim expressions were very comical and strange sounding to us.

But how weird it seemed to again see signs in English and not have to worry if we were translating everything correctly. We drove on, destination Canterbury, passing through almost a solid mass of villages and towns before arriving there at 10:30. The Canterbury Cathedral was looming high above the city, and we soon parked the car in a small "Car Park" nearby. The older buildings and houses of England looked just as I expected, their timbered walls, Tudor leaded windows, severe gabled rooves [roofs] and protruding dormers crowning the quaint windows underneath.

Canterbury Cathedral—
the oldest and most famous of English churches

We walked into what looked like a business section of Canterbury and were immediately impressed by the appearance of the town itself. Part of it was very, very old, with the half-timbered houses converted to small shops, combined with a brand-new section of stores down the street, looking very much like our shopping centers. Near this old section was the gate to the cathedral, an ancient looking structure which seemed appropriate enough for the cathedral beyond its limits. I have to admit that this is the most interesting cathedral I've seen since being in Europe. It's loaded with beautiful stained-glass windows as well as tomb after tomb of famous Archbishops dating from the 11th century. Karl and I wandered about inside for quite a while, overjoyed at being able to read the inscriptions on all the ancient relics and getting quite a kick out of some of the wording. Some of these tombs of the ancient knights and bishops were quite ornately decorated, and the dates alone were worth a trip inside the place. We soon walked out into a center courtyard where we spotted a distinguished looking priest adorned in a purple robe, and we both wondered just who he could be, as there was a striking resemblance to the Archbishop himself, and it looked as though he was being interviewed by a young gentleman with a portable tape recorder. We strolled along the corridor surrounding the courtyard and noticed that the Gothic arched ceiling was decorated with crests, all of them different, presumably crests belonging to the families who contributed to the building of the church through the centuries.

We soon walked back inside, and before long found ourselves almost on top of the gentleman in the purple robe whom we had thought to be the archbishop. We both stood there listening for a while, and after he left, we asked some people standing nearby if it was "he." They replied that it was not, but that it was the Bishop of Edinburgh, a Bishop Warner, who was retired and living in Canterbury, frequently coming over to the church and giving interested people personal tours of the place.

All in all, I was mostly impressed by the sheer beauty of the church itself, as some of the small chapels with their elaborate windows, the decoration in marble, and the wood paneling was [were] beautiful. Since most of the churches we've been through this summer have been Catholic, their layout has been similar, but the Church of England's plan was entirely different. Parts of the church are separated by different levels, and it lacks a transept that the Catholic churches all possess.

I left the others and went to a nearby bookstore, where I bought Stone's "*Agony and the Ecstasy*," the book about Michelangelo, as well as some post cards. I then exited through the gates, turning left and heading through the interesting and bustling street toward the post office, where I mailed a letter and the post cards I had just purchased. On the way back I noticed a quaint looking restaurant by the name of the "Old English House." I continued on down the street, and even found a camera shop that had some film that would fit my camera.[1] I've had a terrible time finding the darn stuff in many places we've been.

I walked back to the cathedral and sat down on a bench just to relax for a while when I spotted the others coming out. We all decided to go down to The Old English House for lunch, and this we did. There we had our first English meal, and not a more typical one at that! I had fish and chips, tea with cream and ice cream for dessert. Chips, by the way, are English for "French fries." The fish was delicious, and although I've never been much of a fish eater, this stuff I devoured like I'd never eaten before. But I suppose that fresh salt-water fish can't be beat, and especially when it's fried so well.

A proper English greeting—a bulldog welcomes the Yanks!

    We then left Canterbury, and headed northwest through Rochester to Gravesend, where we took a small ferryboat across the Thames River. We did this to avoid going through London on our way north. We then headed for Cambridge, avoiding the larger highways to try to pick up some scenery. The drive was a very beautiful one, as we passed through quite a bit of hilly country, and there could be seen great examples of the uneven plots of ground, the hay mounds and many fields where herds of sheep were grazing, the first we'd seen on the trip. Around six, we decided to try to find of a place to spend the night, and we drove through numerous towns, stopping at some of the quaintest inns, the kind you imagine—with their deep carpets, wood paneling, fire in the fireplace, deep easy chairs, etc., only to be disappointed as they seemed to all be full. Also their prices were more than we wanted to pay—about 25 shillings, which is over $3.00. I stopped in one of these places that was run by a distinguished looking gentleman who was willing to give us all kinds of advice and had an extremely friendly way about him. I soon learned that he was Scotch, and then told him about the family and asked him if he knew any Rollo's[2] in Scotland. He laughed and said that if I wanted to find any Rollo's, that I should check all the jails in Scotland, a reply which surprised me, but completely amused me too. We all left the place in uproarious laughter, and it made us all the more glad that we were in the British Isles.

We continued on without any luck, and were advised at a petrol station that if we wanted to find a fairly inexpensive place, that we'd be most wise to drive on to Cambridge, which we did, and here we are! We stopped in the first hotel we saw, and they had room for us at 17/6 per night apiece, which is $2.15 a night including breakfast. That was still a bit stiff, but we were too tired to really care at that point, and decided to take it.

After unpacking and relaxing for a while, we walked down the street to a snack place that seemed very much like home. There I had a hamburger steak, chips, chocolate shake and a sundae for dessert. It was great to be able to eat a snack instead of having to order a four or five course meal as in France, a fact which you can't seem to avoid no matter where you travel in France, except Paris.

Leaving here, Bill and I decided to take a walk to the college, the others heading back to the hotel. We spent the next hour or so wandering about on the various campuses of Cambridge, extremely impressed by the beautiful courtyards of each college, all of which had a plot of grass not like any I've ever seen, as it is not grass like we know it, but more like bent,[3] the grass found usually on golf-course greens. We then finished off the evening in a small college pub that must have been serving ale for hundreds of years, before walking back to the hotel. Cambridge is a pleasant town. It's late, so off to bed. Until tomorrow, good night.

Love, Tom

Cambridge, England—Friday, August 16, 1963

Hi–

Well, we're still in Cambridge, and it has been a quiet, pleasant and rainy day. We went downstairs to breakfast this morning about 9:00, and were greeted by a huge meal, consisting of cereal, bread, jam, eggs, bacon, sausage, hot tomatoes and coffee. We were seated around this huge table with some of the other guests of the hotel, and I, still asleep, upon sitting down, asked Freddy to pass the coffee pot, which was sitting next to him. This he did, and I poured myself a big cup, only to soon find that the pot belonged to the girl sitting next to Freddy. Needless to say, it was embarrassing, but I laughed and apologized, not letting it bother me as much as it seemed to bother the rest of the crew, who were more embarrassed than I. At the end of the table was sitting this huge old woman, who kept rattling off all sorts of crazy things, to which those who seemed to know her, paid no attention. Upon finding out that we were from America, she (her name is Mrs. Dawson) started telling us that she was in America when she was four, and went on and on about the skyscrapers in New York, the Indians, etc. She asked us if all the little girls still wore the huge bows in their hair, to which we smilingly answered that that had gone out of style years ago, and at the same time we were wondering if there had really been skyscrapers in New York in 1905 when she was there. I looked up during one point of her ramblings to notice the landlady motioning to me that Mrs. Dawson was crazy, and after breakfast, we were informed that she had never been to America at all. You certainly run into all kinds!

I spent the rest of the morning washing clothes and myself, and it was a relief to again feel clean. Baths are no extra charge in English hotels, a fact which leads me to believe that they are civilized in the way I like them to be. I can't think of one hotel on the continent that didn't charge us for a bath! Karl and I were to meet the others at King's College at 2:00, so about quarter of we left, feeling cleaner than I've felt in ages, with all clean clothes and a clean body.

Upon arrival at the college, the others were waiting, and we found to our disappointment that there would not be an Evensong tonight. The Evensong is a nightly thing in most of the churches in England, and consists of a boys choir singing religious songs—supposedly a very beautiful thing to hear and see. So with that news, Karl and I left the rest to find a place to eat, and ended up in a restaurant I had noticed last night directly across from the pub where Bill and I had downed our first English ale. It was very old and picturesque, and Karl and I enjoyed a delicious meal of Hungarian goolosh [goulash], rice, chips and beer for a good price. Food in England is wonderfully cheap compared to the continent, and in this meal the beer (imported from America) was almost as expensive as the food itself.

After eating, we went back to King's College, one of the more famous schools at Cambridge. Here we went into the famous chapel, where we saw Freddy talking to an elderly gentleman. We both sat down and spent the next fifteen minutes listening to some of this fellow's stories about Cambridge, a very interesting experience. The chapel is beautiful, and is enhanced by Ruben's painting "Adoration of the Magi." Leaving here, we went to Trinity College, equally as beautiful and there entered the chapel, which wasn't so impressive as the one at Kings, but more interesting for the many famous people who had been a student at one time there, for example, Tennyson and Isaac Newton. As I mentioned last night, the lawns surrounding the colleges and found in their courtyards are of bent grass, and look even more perfect in the daylight. The Cam River flows behind each college, and peaceful canoers can be seen drifting down its still waters. I've never seen such a beautiful campus, but after all, they've certainly had time to make it that way—centuries.

Leaving Trinity, we crossed the street going into a bookshop, where I went wild looking at all the wonderful books at such low prices. In fact, I bought a huge volume of all of Michelangelo's paintings and sculptures for $6.50, an unbelievably low price for such a beautiful book, as I'm sure it would be at least $20.00 in the United States. I also picked up some post cards and some stationery and envelopes here.

The others then returned to the hotel, and even though it was raining, I wanted to take a walk back of King's College along the Cam. This I did, and what a beautiful place it is. I found a dry spot under a huge tree on a small bridge that crossed the river, and there I stood for quite a while, stunned by the beauty of the scene. There were ducks fluttering their feathers near the water, and the rain was light enough to allow me to stay dry under the tree. About 6:00 I put up my umbrella and headed back to the hotel. For some reason, I don't seem to mind the rain in England—it fits in!

Back at the hotel, we decided to bring out the "spirits" and have a nip or two before dinner, and the landlady and her husband were very nice about giving us glasses and ice. Freddy abstained, but the rest of us managed to polish off one of the half-fifths that Rick and I had bought on the boat.

At 8:00 we returned to the place where Karl and I had eaten lunch, which tonight was even more atmospheric with candles on all the tables, and there enjoyed a delicious meal of fried chicken, fried pineapple, chips, peas and coffee. Afterwards, Rick and Freddy returned to the hotel, Karl, Bill and I deciding to take a walk down by the Cam near the Bridge of Sighs, obviously named for the Bridge of Sighs in Venice, which we had remembered seeing.

Postcard: Another Bridge of Sighs—this one in Cambridge

    This walk tonight is one of the things about the trip that I will always remember. The sun had not quite taken away all of its light, and there was not a soul around. We walked through the courtyard of Kings college, taking a path toward the Cam. Crossing a bridge after passing through a grove of huge old trees, we walked toward John's College where the Bridge of Sighs is located. Against the sky were the silhouettes of the ancient towers and buildings of the university, and the bridge was dimly illuminated from the inside. We stood on another bridge opposite the Bridge of Sighs for about a half hour, no one saying a word. It seemed as if the whole world must be asleep, for there was not a sound except for the very quiet rippling of the water. At ten o'clock, the bells of the various colleges took their turn in tolling that hour, and the sound of those bells seemed to bring the type of frame of mind of finality, like the tolling of funeral bells, and they seemed to be saying that this was the end of the day, so lonely was their ring. I can't really describe how beautiful this moment was, but it is one of those things that happens rarely, and when it does happen, you want to cling to it unrealistically, not wanting to let it pass. Looking around, I could also see the black outlines of the trees across the lawn looking like skeletons, and just moments later the spell was broken by a voice off across the river.

"Yo Ho, who's there?" the voice said. "I'm locking up now and you will have to leave." Startled after our contemplation, we hurried down the dark path, crossed the bridge, and headed back toward the college. The voice was now shining a light toward us, and we soon found out that the voice was really the groundskeeper, who was locking up the place for the night. We were not supposed to have been in the grounds at all after 8:00, and upon learning this, we were amused in remembering how we had entered. We had strolled up toward the college, and even though noticing a guard standing at the gate, didn't break our stride at all, but nodding a brisk "good evening" and brushing quickly past the guard, who stepped aside, probably thinking that we were some of the fellows, walked through the gate. This particular guard was a friendly chap with an intelligent air, and a perfect British accent, and on the way out, he told us that we were walking along the corridor where Newton had supposedly paced countless times while thinking up some of his famous theories.

We then headed back to the hotel, and upon arriving found that Rick had been locked out of our room, since I had the key and it was the only one. I found him asleep in the other room and felt guilty about forgetting to tell him. Oh, I forgot to mention that we stopped for a beer in a place called "The Turk's Head" on the way back, an old looking pub where there were all ages and types sitting around on barrel stools sipping ale and beer. While there I was amused by an elderly woman sitting at a nearby table, who kept talking with a cigarette dangling out of her mouth, between trips of running up to the bar for another drink. I wouldn't have been so aware of her had it not been for the couple she was with—for they seemed to be not at all amused by her actions, even though the rest of the place was.

And so, after writing for a while, it's late and I again must say goodnight. Tomorrow we are going to head for Nottingham and then find out if our friends on the boat really meant what they said. So until then, good night.

Love, Tom

Nottingham, England—Saturday, August 17, 1963

Hi–

I am constantly amazed at how wonderful people can be! This day has been truly unbelievable, for here we are, all five of us, being entertained in the home of the most wonderful family you can imagine, the Hiltons. As you recall, they are the family we met on the ferryboat from Calais to Dover, and we took them up on their offer, and the result is terrific!

We arose this morning in Cambridge about 8:15 and went down to the same breakfast we had yesterday, except today I had grapefruit instead of cereal, a fact which I'm sure is of profound interest to you. Anyway, the funniest thing about the meal this morning was Mrs. Dawson, who repeated her tale about living in America when she was four, and we had to be equally as agreeable and equally as restraining in our amusement at this peculiar woman. She seems to be living in a world of fantasy, and is only satisfied when surrounded by people who are willing to agree with everything she says. Another inhabitant of the hotel is an old gentleman who happened to be in the breakfast room at the same time we were. The whole time Mrs. Dawson kept on her babbling, he sat there grumbling under his breath, and every once in a while, she would say something to him, which would go completely unrecognized, and at one point during one of her questions to him, I heard some fowl [foul] language emit from under his breath, and sitting directly across the table, trying to cut the toughest grapefruit I've ever dealt with, it was hard to control the laughter. But the old gentleman soon left, and we spent the remainder of the meal trying to explain to Mrs. Dawson that no, the little girls in American didn't still wear big bows in their hair and dressed with little buttons which reached to their ankles. It was quite a time!

We wanted to leave there as soon as possible, as we hoped to reach Nottingham at a decent hour, and wanted to stop in Ely, where is located a very famous cathedral. So after excusing ourselves from the table, we made our way upstairs, after which we started packing and cleaning up. The couple who run this place are pre-middle age and quite characters. They seem to be bright people, but obviously uneducated. The wife calls everyone, including us, "love," and the husband has an accent that we can barely understand. It borders on a cockney, but is somewhat more refined, if that is any kind of accurate description. Their four year old son, Bobby, is quite a pistol, and since being here, we have spent a great deal of our time entertaining the little brat, who keeps coming up to our rooms, pounding on the doors, and wanting us to play with him. He really is a cute little bug though, and last night, while downing the bottle of Scotch, we had a great deal of fun teasing him.

By the time we had paid our bill, packed Vicki and pulled away, we were great friends with everyone there, and the couple and Bobby escorted us out and waved goodbye or "cheerio," as we zoomed away. Before leaving, we ran into Mrs. Dawson and the old gentleman who were sitting together in the front hall. We couldn't avoid a short conversation with them, even though being in a hurry, and they were quite a pair! They both had the nicest way of bumming cigarettes, which we were really glad to give, and during this exchange, Mrs. Dawson was muttering something about how poor the old man was, while he sat there stone-faced with probable embarrassment, and we equally as tongue-tied. But that moment passed and he covered up with telling us of all his world travels, while Mrs. Dawson kept interrupting with some completely irrevalent [irrelevant] comments. And that was all.

We stopped on the way out of town at King's College to pick up Freddy, who had gone there earlier to get some pictures. We left Cambridge, heading straight for Ely, stopping outside of town to take a few pictures of the beautiful cathedral that loomed up over the city and the surrounding countryside, which was nearly flat, but a beautiful shade of green. Once in Ely, we parked the car and went inside the cathedral, another very impressive place, particularly for its stained glass windows, which were enormous and structured in gorgeous colorings. After walking about there for a while, I left and asked an elderly woman directions to the post office, which she not only gave, but practically led me all the way. After mailing a letter and some post cards, I returned to the car, and Karl showed up, without the others. Before long we were a group again, and decided to get some lunch in a bar adjacent to the car. There I had a ham sandwich and a glass of cider, and tried to eat it while playing a horrible piano which sat in one of the tiny rooms of the pub. On the way out of town as we passed the cathedral, on the lawn we noticed one of the funniest signs I've ever seen: "Please Don't Let Your Dog Foul the Green!"

We spent the remainder of the afternoon driving through the relatively uninteresting English countryside toward Nottingham, passing through Chatteris, Peterborough, Stamford and Grantham, arriving there about 4:00. The first thing we did upon arriving was find a phone booth, and Rick called up Mrs. Hilton, who to our surprise, got all excited about us being there, and gave us explicit directions on how to get to their place, agreeing to meet us at Church Road. So off we roared all wondering what the rest of the day would bring. Sure enough, she was waiting there for us, and seemed thrilled that we had decided to stop. She is an attractive woman of about 35, and was well dressed; she has a way of rattling off the language at an enormous rate of speed, and speaks in an accent that sounds different somehow from what we had come to know as the standard "English" English. She told us to follow her and we found ourselves in a beautiful residential area, full of huge old English houses, surrounded by high stone walls, and boasting the most beautiful flowers and green lawns I'd seen in ages. We quickly turned up Arlington Drive, and in a minute were in front of her house.

In a few minutes, up strolled Mr. Hilton, looking just as much like a distinguished relic of the past as he did the other day, and saying bashfully just about as little, as Mrs. Hilton hardly stopped talking long enough to let him get a word in. But he had an intelligent look that didn't go unnoticed, and before long we were carting all of our luggage into the house.

We were immediately impressed by the lawn and flowers, which looked like they should belong to some greenhouse or national monument rather than someone's home. Again, we were surprised to see that instead of grass in the lawn was the bent again, looking more like a carpet of green than a lawn. On the way up to the house, Mr. Hilton muttered through his huge mustache that gardening was his hobby.

Once inside, she showed us the bedrooms upstairs, and pointed out which ones would be ours. The house was one of these large Victorian two-story homes, and had been Mr. Hilton's father's residence, the large size accounted for since there had been eight children in the family. Many of the windows have the leaded panes of stained glass, and at the head of the stairs was a huge oil painting of Mr. Hilton's father, a distinguished looking man who seemed to have probably presided with dignity and authority over the Hilton household. They explained that they were glad to have us stay since there were only four of them living there and such a big house should get more use. Trying to hold back our excitement at the whole situation, we restrainedly agreed, and she proceeded down the hall, pointing out three bedrooms that we could fight over.

She then explained that she must go to the market for some groceries, and led us downstairs, where she insisted that we sit down for "high tea," as it was about 4:30, the usual time to enjoy this custom. So Mrs. Hilton and Rick went off for the groceries, while the rest of us sat around their living room with Mr. Hilton, having tea and biscuits (cookies) and discussing everything from Kennedy to mad dogs and Englishmen. Upon entering the living room, I immediately spied the piano, a huge upright sitting along one wall. After banging out a few chords, I found to my delight, that it was almost in perfect tune, and was the best piano I'd had my fingers on all summer since Heidelberg, which seemed like ages ago.

Mrs. Hilton and Rick soon returned, and all of us sat around getting acquainted and talking until the children came in. Upon finding out that the children got quite a big kick out of our western movies, we were going to all talk with western dialects upon meeting them, and someone suggested we get a lasso and some "ten gallon" hats to greet them at the door. But this plan failed, and the children were too smart to be fooled by such nonsense. Two such polite and wholesome kids I've never met, and they each took turns shaking hands with all of us. Both with near white hair and broad beaming smiles, Christine is thirteen, and Michael is ten. With all of their politeness, they were somewhat bashful too, and after all the formalities, they didn't add much to the conversation.

After tea, the group broke up, the other fellows going upstairs to clean up for dinner, Mrs. Hilton to the kitchen, Mr. Hilton to the lawn, and the children out to ride their bikes. I stayed in the living room, and spent the next hour at the piano, naturally in pure ecstasy, since it had been Rome since I had really been able to play—and even longer, since I could play <u>and</u> sing some of my songs. Mrs. Hilton kept running in and out of the room, telling me how much she was enjoying it, and at one point she confided that she was thrilled to have some American boys in the house, that she had seen her chance to do so on the boat, and decided not to pass it up. Really stunned that someone would consider it an honor to put up five fellows, I thanked her, and she went back to the kitchen. The whole afternoon, I could hardly believe that life could be so beautiful, and felt like pinching myself to see if it might have been only a dream—which of course, it wasn't!

Before long, the rest began drifting in the room, and until 8:00, when Mrs. Hilton announced that dinner was ready, everyone sat around relaxing and reading. We had insisted earlier that she shouldn't fix a meal for us on such short notice, but she refused to listen, saying that it was a pleasure. For dinner we all assembled in the dining room around a huge old walnut table. The meal was terrific and had that home touch that we hadn't enjoyed since Sweden. We started off with chicken noodle soup, which was followed by sausage, bacon, beans, eggs for those who wanted them, chips and a delicious dessert of peaches topped with a fresh thick cream. This family is so much fun to be around, as we spent most of the time between bites, laughing over all sorts of things. They invited us to go with them tonight to see some friends of theirs, whom they had previously made a date with, and then insisted that we stay another night, as tomorrow being Sunday, Mr. Hilton could drive us around Nottingham and show us some of the sights. After a short conference we agreed, as we were having such a wonderful time, and as long as they were so sincere, it was hard to refuse.

At 9:30, after everyone had cleaned up and changed into suits, we left for a pub in Sherwood Forest, half of us going with the Hiltons in their Jaguar, half in Vicki. In England, these old country inns or pubs, as they call them, are where most of the townspeople go for a night out.

We drove through the pouring rain, through Nottingham and out into the country, arriving at the pub in about 15 minutes. It was a totally atmospheric place, decorated in the Old English style, with the timbered beams and the old stone fireplace lending the finishing touches to the place. There we met some of their friends, a couple by the name of Tom and Madeline and another woman by the name of Gwyn. Tom is a respectable and distinguished looking gentleman of about 50, his wife Madeline, a good-looking and giddy woman in her probably early 40s, and Gwyn, an even more giddy woman of about the same age. They immediately bought us drinks, and we stood around in the place for about an hour small-talking and getting to know them. I was most impressed by Tom, who seemed to be above it all, yet knew what to say at the right time, and behind his serious facade, had a bright humor and interesting wit. Of the whole group, Fred and Dorothy Hilton, (they insist that we call them by their first names) stood out to me as the most down-to-earth and sincere, but the rest had been drinking most of the evening, which probably accounted for my opinion. The whole place seemed so very English, not only because of the atmosphere, but because of the people themselves, the men with their mustaches, tweed suits and pipes, and the women, frank and naughty in a prim and proper sort of way. And the English accents were there too!

At 11:00, the inn closed, so the Hiltons insisted that the rest of the group come home with us, and so we all left in a grand processional, driving through Sherwood Forest back to Nottingham. On the way back, I drove with the Hiltons in the Jaguar, and they promised that if I looked close enough, I could see Robin Hood, riding through one of the glens in the wood, a statement which sounded funny indeed. It was the first time I'd ridden in a car with the steering on the right, and it was an odd sensation.

Before long, we were back home, and we gathered in the living room, while the women were off in the kitchen preparing tea and biscuits. After the tea, we spent the rest of the evening drinking scotch, and it was truly a wonderful time, as we had many interesting conversations, especially with Tom, who is the district manager for Heinz (57 varieties), and who had many interesting comments about their views of our integration problems and also about England's particular problems, not only politically, but socially as well. They also insisted that I play the piano, and this led to doing all sorts of things, including our journalism Stunt Show[4], which they all got a big kick out of.

I was most amused by Tom's wife, Madeline, who had been earlier to see the Bolshoi Ballet, and was one of these types who is not happy unless she is the center of attention. She was a pretty woman, and knew it, and seemed to use this to guide her actions, of which some seemed ridiculous to me, as I could see right through them. The other woman, Gwyn, was bordering on crazy, and the men seemed to enjoy kidding her. They all left finally at 3:30 in the morning, after many a round of scotch and many cigarettes. But it was a great evening, and I can't remember when I've enjoyed myself so much. These English are very hospitable, and would not allow us to provide one thing, even a cigarette. I suppose that it is the custom, but who's to argue?

Regardless, it has been a long and totally interesting day—and I'm dead—so I'll say goodnight. Until tomorrow–
Love, Tom

Nottingham, England—Sunday, August 18, 1963

Hi–

After last night's festivities till 3:30 in the morning, I slept like a log until 11:00, when I awoke feeling wonderful. I was the last one up, and went downstairs to find the rest waiting breakfast on me, but they had arisen only a few minutes earlier, so I didn't feel too guilty.

The breakfast was terrific—orange juice (the first since Nice), toast, syrup, marmalade, jelly and coffee. While eating, in hustled a woman whom we had not seen, and very soon we found her name to be Mrs. Bennett, and what a card she is! About 60, she acts 25, and is the perfect maid for the perfect English household. She's full of those bright anecdotes that English maids are supposed to be full of, and flits about the house like she owns it. She is full of those wonderful English expressions I thought only existed on British films imported to the United States for late late shows, and always has a keen sparkle in her eye, mostly to assure her audience that she's only kidding about the things she says. We soon found out that she frequently comes in to help Mrs. Hilton with meals. At one point during the meal we were all sitting around quietly when, all of a sudden, we heard a shriek, and the door flung open. Christine and Michael came running in, half laughing, half screeching, and were nearly around the table when sure enough, screeching louder than the whole lot, Mrs. Bennett came galloping in, chasing the two around the table. After several rounds, they all went running in the hall, where Michael tripped, sending all of them sailing to the floor, where they all lay laughing and winded. Mrs. Bennett got up, stuck her funny gray head in the door, gave a quick apology, and closed the door, leaving us stunned and in complete darkness about what had just happened. As a matter of fact, we never did find out!

Soon after eating and cleaning up, Mr. Hilton announced that he wanted to take us for a drive and show us part of Nottingham to which we enthusiastically replied, and about noon, we were off in the Jaguar on a personal tour with Mr. Hilton and Michael. We first drove by the main factory where Player cigarettes are made, the leading brand in Britain, then passing the factory and warehouse of Raleigh Inc., famous manufacturer of bicycles. We next drove to the campus of Nottingham University, where we took a drive through while Mr. Hilton pointed the various buildings out to us. We parked the car beside one of the student dormitories, and noticing a plump middle aged gentleman locking up one of the buildings, asked him if he could show us into one of the rooms, so that we could compare facilities with those back home. This he was more than happy to do, and we were most impressed by the Nottingham students' set up. Each student had a room to himself, including desk, shelves, bed and sofa, dresser, and in most cases, a private lavatory. A bath was shared by the very most, four students. The man who showed us around was accompanied by his small bright red-haired and buck-teethed daughter, Margaret, who kept opening doors for us, giggling, and making eyes at Michael, who seemed equally adept at making eyes right back. She was a cute little thing, and I was most entertained by her frivolous manner, bright freckles and horn-rimmed glasses. She obviously wasn't pretty, but she showed signs of turning into a typical English housewife, or any typical housewife, for that matter. Women seem to be the same all over the world—the same flirt, the same manner, the same cunning method they have for preparing the trap—at any age!

Leaving the university, we headed toward the center of town and the bluff where is located Nottingham's castle. But it wasn't the castle we were going to see, but instead, the "oldest inn in England," called The Old Trip to Jerusalem, and established in 1184. This ancient building is located right beneath the castle, and its interior is carved out of the rock of the bluff itself. There we met Tom (from last night) and his 15 year old daughter Jane, who was quite impressively serious and mature for her age—also good looking. They immediately bought a round of dark beer, and we all stood around the bar drinking, as Englishmen have been doing (there at least) for 779 years—truly an amazing number of years. We got into a conversation with Jane, who is surprisingly intelligent, knowledgeable and frank, especially in her opinion of the United States and America. It was refreshing to meet a girl of her age who could not only discuss world affairs, customs and politics, but discuss them well. She impressed me very much, even though she couldn't cover a slight insecurity and still was young in many of her ideas about things. At least she was opinionated! Tom was in his usual good humor and he and Mr. Hilton stood around laughing and talking while the rest of us were much more interested in his daughter. This whole time, poor Michael had to sit outside, as children under 12 aren't allowed in pubs or bars, so we took him a lemonade, to find him entirely happy, as he was making friends with some little girl who also was sitting outside. About 2:00, we bade them goodbye, and returned home to the wonderful smell of lamb and Yorkshire pudding and the sound of female voices in the kitchen.

Ye Olde Trip to Jerusalem—England's oldest inn, established in 1184

I found my home at the piano and banged away until 2:30, when Mrs. Bennett came marching into the living room announcing dinner. What followed was a feast fit only for the Queen, and I stuffed more food down than I'd stuffed since Christmas, and how delicious it was! The main course was roast lamb with gravy and mint sauce (made from crushed mint leaves, vinegar, salt and sugar), my first Yorkshire pudding, boiled and browned potatoes and peas. The dessert was unbelievable. We had two kinds of pie, hot lemon meringue and red raspberry, which was served with a fresh thick cream, and tasted delicious. Of course we all had to try a piece of both, but my favorite was the raspberry, mostly because of the cream! And to top it off, after dessert, Mrs. Bennett came in with a huge tray of assorted cheeses and a basket of biscuits (cookies) and crackers. The meal was a barrel of fun, as the children and Mrs. Bennett were full of wit, and Mr. Hilton would soberly and wryly comment on things being discussed, in such a manner as to kid whoever made a statement. He and Mrs. Bennett would constantly get into a humorous argument and we spent most of the meal in peals of laughter. It was great fun! In fact, it's still all too good to be true. It's hard to believe that such friendly, generous and hospitable people like the Hiltons exist—yes, here they are, and all of it resting on fate…

After dinner, everyone retired to the living room for coffee, and I spent most of that time at the piano. All of us spent the rest of the afternoon relaxing, mostly doing such things as reading or writing. We also listened to records on Christine's new stereo and it was a quiet, pleasant Sunday afternoon. I also was able to get some writing in, but it seems I can never find time enough to really catch up. At 7:00, Mrs. Bennett suddenly filled the room with a loud announcement that dinner (supper) was ready, and I could hardly believe that it was again time to eat. Well, I might as well have forgotten about the five pounds I lost and the baggy pants, for the food we were eating here forced me to do so. For supper which they called a "light snack," we had cold corned beef, chips, 101 varieties of pickles, jellies and for dessert, orange jello with mandarins, caramel custard, delicious strawberry pie, pound cake and fresh thick cream. And with our coffee we again had an assortment of cheese and biscuits—wow!

After dinner we all helped clear the table, which was quite a production, with Mrs. Bennett giving orders, and all of us following like blind dogs. We spent the rest of the evening watching television, which was interesting—as some of their programs are quite different than ours, and their BBC (British Broadcasting Company) is a government sponsored channel, thus no advertisements. The news was comical to us, as much of the local happenings which made the news was typically British. One news item concerned a church of England service which was held in some tavern—and the film showed the priest in a background of liquor bottles and bar stools—very funny! After the last show, they flashed on the screen a picture of the Queen, during which an orchestra played a patriotic version of "God Save the Queen."

Soon everyone went to bed except Bill and I—and we stayed downstairs to do some writing.

Mrs. Hilton insisted that we have a nightcap, and disappeared into the kitchen, returning moments later with a bottle of scotch and two glasses.

Since Mr. Hilton would be gone by the time we will arise tomorrow morning, we all bade him goodbye, and Bill insisted on taking a picture of him and Mrs. Hilton before they retired. So he rushed upstairs for his camera, and soon we took the picture of Mr. & Mrs. Hilton sitting on the sofa. We certainly hope the picture turns out.

Fred and Dorothy Hilton (the photo turned out!)

After writing for about an hour, I konked [conked] out—as it has been quite a long and full day. We are going to miss this home atmosphere, but I suppose all good things have to come to an end. It's been wonderful meeting these people, and we wonder what we can do to repay them.

Well, again it's time to say: Until tomorrow, good night.

Love, Tom

Whitby, England—Monday, August 19, 1963

Hi–

Here we are in Whitby, and it again has been an interesting day. We got up this morning about 10:00, and after dressing and throwing some things together, we went downstairs to another feast for breakfast. This morning we had cereal with bananas and fresh cream, grapefruit, toast, jelly and marmalade. The rest of the family had already eaten earlier in the day, and the five of us sat around the huge dining room table, contemplating the wonderful stay with the Hiltons, and talking about future plans. Mrs. Hilton kept coming in and out with more food—she must think that we have been starved! After breakfast, we helped clear the table, and immediately set out to pack the car. I was sidetracked by Michael, Christine and a girl friend of theirs, Julia, who asked me to play some numbers on the piano for them. So I entertained while the others got all the luggage together. They are such nice kids—and seem very intelligent. I played the kind of stuff that I thought they would enjoy—"Mustapha's Song" from that children's musical I was working on and some other things from the same show. I was amused by their typically British comment when I would finish a number: "Jolly good!" Christine would say—and I would thank them laughing to myself. Of course, over here, it is us who have the accent. They seem to get a big kick out of the American pronunciation.

Soon we all gathered in the living room and spent the next half hour discussing some of the British customs with Mrs. Hilton. We talked for quite a while on the British school system and then the conversation changed to the Queen and the British Royalty. We soon insisted that the whole group gather in front of the house for pictures, and proceeded to have a real press conference, with everyone clamoring to take pictures of everyone else—and even Mrs. Hilton taking a shot of all five of us with the children. Let's hope the pictures turn out well!

The five guys bid farewell to the Hiltons

After this episode, we took all of the luggage down to the car and went through the regular ritual of packing—which by now we have down to a system—with each guy doing something different. If there have been any nuisances on the trip, packing has been the biggest of them all—so I guess we shouldn't complain. And after the usual goodbyes and the usual exchange of comments when you leave hosts, we sailed away—cramming [craning] our necks for several moments waving at the children as we left. The Hiltons couldn't have been better people to meet—and we all sung [sang] their praises as we headed for Edinburgh.

Last minute travel advice from our charming Nottingham hostess

By this time it was noon, so we resigned ourselves to the fact that we would not be able to make Edinburgh in one day. It was a beautiful day—the sun shining, the English countryside looking extremely green and well-watered. It was cool, however, so coats and sweaters were in order. It sure is nothing like U.S. weather in August. We stopped for lunch in a town, the name of which I've forgotten, and after mailing some letters, Rick and I found a small café where we had a good and cheap meal of sausage, peas, chips, ice cream, cake and Coke. The whole meal amounted to about 50 cents, and we thought we had a pretty good deal. After mailing the letters we had lost the others, and upon returning to the car, found them there waiting. It seems that they had not found a place to eat and had waited almost a half hour for us. Needless to say, nerves were on edge, and directed at us—I suppose for not trying to find them before we went to eat. However, I am sick of always worrying about the whole group and am able to let these things slide with no worry whatsoever. If I couldn't, my life would be miserable. For there are always those who are hurt over some little point or another, and it would be a tremendous waste of time to always worry about their feelings. But Rick and I had full stomachs, and that was all that was necessary to us—so the others hadn't eaten—tough! I don't mean to sound cruel, but they surely could have found a place. I sometimes think that people have to be led around by the hand.

We then headed for Scarborough, and the drive this afternoon was really beautiful. We were near the East coast of England and the farther north we drove, the wilder and more beautiful was the country. At points we could see the water over the hills, but most of the time we were on roads that wound in and around fields, hills, and grazing sheep. There was an abundance of heather the closer we drove toward Scotland, and those fields of nothing but purple as far as you can see are really a beautiful sight. We passed through Scarborough, heading farther north toward Whitby, where we are spending the night. Between Scarborough and Whitby, we stopped once at some of the country houses that boasted signs of B and B (bed and breakfast) but there was never an opening. The day finally became overcast, and at one point where we stopped, there was an old dirt road heading toward an old house which was nestled down in a valley between some of the heathered hills, and looking very picturesque in that hazy sky. There were sheep grazing on each side of this road, and we had to get out and walk, so bad was the condition of the road. But as I said before, we had no good luck for lodging, and so continued on to Whitby, where we stopped in a small red brick house which had the B and B sign, and is run by a little old lady, who luckily gave us an affirmative to our request for a room.

We unpacked the car, and she showed us upstairs to the two bedrooms where we would be sleeping. This gal had a wonderful Scottish brogue upon greeting us, and we knew from the very beginning that it would be an interesting stay. It was still only about 6:00 so we weren't at all hungry. Someone had the idea that we could finish up the other bottle of Scotch which we had purchased on the ferry from Calais to Dover, and this we agreed upon. We went downstairs for some glasses and ice, and our little old lady, upon hearing that we had some Scotch became so enthusiastic that we offered her a nip, to which she replied her acceptance enthusiastically, and soon we were all sitting around in the room sipping on the scotch and talking with her. She was spinning tales in a brogue which made it hard for us to understand everything she was saying, but we really didn't mind, since it was so amusing. She told of her daughter who is engaged to a fellow, excuse me, "lad" from Scotland, and how she was in a tither about the wedding that was coming up in only two weeks. This gal was somewhat off mentally, or slow, but she told us also that she had been having blackouts, so we decided that she must be sick. Some of her ramblings seemed to make no sense whatsoever, but she did enjoy the Scotch, and also about hearing of the United States. We laughed hilariously later about some of the statements that she made. She was extremely mixed up on her geography, for she thought that the United States was no farther from England than Ireland—and that she thought was quite a distance away. She also seemed to be mixed up about American cities, confusing them with British cities, and we almost laughed in her face several times. But she was entertaining for the moment, and I suppose she has been worth meeting.

Her daughter recommended that we have dinner in a Chinese restaurant in the heart of the town—as they were supposed to have the best meals—and be reasonable too. So around 8:00 we headed for this place—it is nice, and the meal of beef chop suey, rice, tea, ice cream for only seven shillings was delicious.

Whitby is an interesting town. It was here that many of the ships were built for the early English explorers—and now the names of some of them slip my mind—but regardless, it is a very famous ship-building town. Tonight Whitby was in gay spirits due to a traveling carnival which is in town. After dinner, we walked across the bridge, and along the waterfront, or harbor. The small booths of the carnival were set up, and the people of Whitby were out in full force taking in all of the festivities. The sparkling lights of the carnival shone on the water, and off in the distance across the harbor was a fantastic display of fireworks. To add to the confusion, the Scottish fleet was also in town, and scores of Scottish sailors were roaming the waterfront. There were all kinds of concessions typical to any carnival, and the people seemed typical too. The whole atmosphere was very picturesque. Across the water the silhouettes of the Whitby houses made an interesting skyline against a sky highlighted by the moon as well as an occasional flare of the fireworks.

At this carnival I did something that I've never done in my life. We passed several "palm-readers," and someone in passing suggested that we get our palms read. It was said as a joke, but I decided that I would like to try it, as it was cheap, and I was curious to see just how perceptive some of these palm readers are. I was most amazed to be greeted inside by a very serious woman who asked me politely to sit down. She had a sharp look in her eye—or perhaps a more proper description would be "wise." I was also amazed that she came very close in some of her comments about me and my future. I cannot see that the palm is actually any clue, but that these people can tell a lot about someone by the way they talk, the way they dress, and their manner. This is obviously the method that she used. The first thing that she told me was that I was a very traveled person. I assumed that she recognized my accent. She next told me that this following year that I would be put to some kind of test that would affect my whole life. This is debatable, but of course, there are always exams at school. She told me that I have a very lucky "hand" and that I am determined to do what I want—and that meeting and knowing people will be a very important part of my future. Her next comment was something to the effect that I didn't believe in people like her, to which I had to reply "yes," for I have never been superstitious, and I have always had my doubts about these so called "palm-readers." Her next comment floored me! She told me that I come from a family that is good in business—and that I possess qualities that make me a good business-man. But she said that there is a conflict in that I am also artistic—and that whatever I do will be a combination of these. She went on to say that I would travel a great deal in my lifetime, and that I was funny about girls, but that I would go a long way for the one I really care for. She said that I probably wouldn't meet her for several years. She also said that there had been many girls that had cared for me more than I cared for them, and that I was not going with anyone seriously at the present time. She predicted a very successful marriage and a happy one. I was surprised at some of her comments, for I could see no way in which she could have gotten a clue for some of them. Most of it of course was probably malarkey, but she did say a few things that really hit me. I was extremely curious just how one gets started as a "palm-reader," so I spent the next five minutes or so asking her about her background and how she became a palm reader. She said it was a family thing and was passed on from generation to generation. We had quite an interesting chat—and she seemed to have a great deal of perception and wisdom. Even though I still take most of what she said with a grain of salt, I still was impressed, especially with some of the things she said. It will be interesting to see how close she comes on some of these things!

We wandered around the carnival for about an hour before returning to the hotel, and it was a lot of fun. There were groups of young people who were wandering around with huge bottles of liquor, getting louder and drunker, singing Scotch and English songs.

We returned to the house about ten, and after finishing off the bottle of scotch, we wrote and talked. As usual it is too late, and again time to say—until tomorrow—good night.

Love, Tom

SCOTLAND
13

The Moors, Bagpipes and Family History

Oh, ye'll tak' the high road, an' I'll tak' the low road,
An' I'll be in Scotland a'fore ye;
But I and my true love will never meet again,
On the bonnie, bonnie banks o' Loch Lomond.
—"Loch Lomond"—Traditional Scottish Song, circa 1841

§ § §

Edinburgh, Scotland—Tuesday, August 20, 1963

Hi–
This is my first letter from Edinburgh. I'm already fascinated by this city—it is one of the most picturesque places we've been yet—it has the kind of charm that no other place we've seen has. But what a confusing time we've had today—and the weather is bad to top things off.

We got up this morning about 7:30 and after dressing, went down to breakfast of bread, tea, bacon, eggs and the usual. The old lady was extra confusing this morning, and seemed to be off in her own little world. She repeated many of the stories she had told us last night—and Rick and I, remaining after the others had gone upstairs to pack, could hardly get away from her. She had a polite way of bumming cigarettes, so we gave her about five Players, since she raved on and on about how good that brand is, and how it is very seldom that she has a chance to smoke one. She is quite a character. She again repeated her stories about her daughter—the same ones she told us last night. Her daughter came in the room shortly—and although not a bad looking girl, she seemed bashful and embarrassingly aware of her mother's mental deficiencies. It seems that her future husband, from Scotland, is building a house right down the street from here. Perhaps that is the custom—that the son-in-law joins the neighborhood of the wife. At least in this instance, that is the way it works. The old lady told us that she had a lot of trouble with her daughter. She quit school at 16, and has been working in the dress-maker's shop ever since. That isn't so bad, except that she has worked there longer than any of the other girls, who have all managed to get husbands. The lady said that she thought that her daughter would never nab herself a husband—but finally, she did manage to do so.

Rick and I finally got away from her, and before long we were off, heading north for Edinburgh. The drive today was unbelievably beautiful. I keep saying that so many of these drives are the "most beautiful of the summer" but so many of them have been so—in different ways, but yes, very impressive. Today, we drove along many of the bluffs that line the coast, and one particularly scenic spot was right outside of Whitby. Here we stopped to take pictures. Below us was a sandy beach, virtually deserted, and from the spot where we were standing, we could see the coast opposite us as it wound its way north. The fields of heather in back of us added something extra to the scene, but the softness of the rolling hills and the bluffs sweeping down to the water were really impressive. The road we were on is undoubtedly one of the most extreme, angle-wise, that we have driven on yet. We found ourselves going up and down, almost vertically, over these hills and bluffs, and even the Alps and the Pyrenees didn't compare to this. Adding to the beauty of the drive were the small towns, with their quaint squares, and the countryside itself, with its stone walls lining field after field. We by now had passed out of the densely populated areas of England, and the deserted roads and small farms had a charm never seen in the United States. It was quite an impressive drive.

    We soon stopped for lunch in a fair size town near Scarborough. It is here where I must make an amendment to yesterday's letter. It was today that Rick and I had the lunch, after mailing the letters, to return to the car to find that the others hadn't eaten. Yesterday, we stopped in a small crumby restaurant for a lunch of sausage, peas, chips, ice cream, cake and Coke—and there was a particularly bad waitress who seemed to be A number one in stupidity. Today Rick and I had the cheap lunch of mushroom soup, roast lamb, peas, mashed potatoes, apple pie with custard. So I have made an error in recording that will have to be someday straightened out in these letters. So you can make the mental adjustment, and just switch days of lunches. Our lunch today was only 3 shillings, 6 pence.

    The day had become rainy, cold and misty between the rainfalls—which dampened everyone's spirits somewhat, but not enough to spoil the scenery, which managed to look good with or without rain. We soon found ourselves in the country of the moors—and what wild country it is. These fields stretched out before us for miles and miles—and most of it seemed to be uninhabited. There was still an abundance of heather—and the mist over a dull sky made the country seem even farther away from civilization.

The moors, the sheep and the heather on the hill

We wanted very badly to arrive in Edinburgh before 5:30 since that is usually the time that American Express closes, but unfortunately, we were too late. But what a chase we had! We drove into the city limits of Edinburgh about 5:15, and hit Princes Street, the street where American Express is located, about 5:25. But alas, the traffic was heavy, so Freddy and I got out of the car, taking everyone's passport, and half-walked, half-ran toward American Express in the rain. No sooner than we would run 2 blocks, than Vicky would catch up with us. Then she would get caught in a traffic jam, and Freddy and I would go hurrying off, getting ahead another block or so, when all at once we would hear Vicky's beep, and sure enough she caught up with us again. Freddy and I finally huffed and puffed up to the door of American Express, but we were too late—they had closed just 5 minutes earlier. By this time the car had gone on ahead, and we weren't sure how they were going to come back around the block, since part of the street was one way—it's really too confusing to explain in detail. But before long, Vicky came roaring around one corner, and Freddy and I hopped in.

We were now faced with the typical problem of where to stay, so we headed for the most logical place—the railroad station. We drove down Princes Street to Waverley Station, located on Princes Street opposite the side of the street where many of the finest shops of Edinburgh are located. Bill and I were elected to find the information window where we could make reservations, but there we found out that we would have to go all the way to the other end of Princes Street to an information bureau. So it was decided then that I would go on the excursion for rooms, that Bill would meet the others, and then bring them down to the information center.

So I went carting off down Princes Street in the rain again—and it is here that I must pause to make a few observations about what I had thus seen in Edinburgh. Princes Street is one of the most impressive streets I have ever seen. One side of the street is devoted exclusively to the nicer shops, in other words the "North Michigan"[1] shops. The other side is adjacent to a huge park area with trees and fountains that sweeps down into a gully. Rising out of this area is the Edinburgh Castle, an ancient thing which looms up over all of this area. Beyond the castle is a row of very old looking houses and buildings which form the beginning of the Royal Mile—the street which runs from the Edinburgh Castle down to The Palace of Holyroodhouse, the place where the Queen and all Royalty stay when in Edinburgh. Today, in the midst of the rain and haze that covered the city, the castle and the silhouettes of the skyline of these buildings looming high up over the park below the castle and consequently, over Princes Street, looked very much like you have always wanted someplace to look. The huge castle, in particular, impressed me. It had a dignity and a heritage that few others we've seen have. I was awe-inspired.

Meanwhile, back on Princes Street, hurrying toward the information center, I made my way past the Scots and other tourists who were here for the Edinburgh Festival—a famous international festival held here every year to further the causes of music, theater and art. I soon arrived at the center, and a gentleman inside told me that I would have to go right around a corner to the Festival Office, where reservations for rooms were made. So consequently, I had to wait for the others to show up before I could do anything more. I stood out in the rain for about 20 minutes, when finally I saw Vicky pull around the corner—and unfortunately, there was no place to park, so she went sailing by, and I was still standing there. Shortly, however, Bill and Karl showed up, and the three of us made our way to the Festival Office where we waited for about a half-hour before we finally got a room. Nevertheless, this was the most cordial, the most well-organized reservation counter that we have seen all summer. And she found us a place to stay for 12 shillings, 6 pence per night, a price that was way under anything we have been paying. So we were quite happy about the whole affair.

We then decided that since we were downtown, that we would stay here to eat, then go to a show, since it was already 7:00 and to go all the way out to the hotel would be a waste of time. So the lady called our hotel and told the landlady that this is what we would do, and she agreed. We told her that we would try to show up about 11:00.

We then passed a restaurant that looked like good food, and Karl and I went in while Bill went to the car to get the others who were waiting. The name of the place is the Capri, and we had a very cute Scotch lassie for a waitress. We flirted with her through an entire meal of Welsh Rarebit, scotch (very fitting, don't you agree), chips, a banana split and milk—and flirted with her when we paid the check. She was very wry and kept making remarks about money which I thought were typically Scotch—and we hadn't even encouraged her. However, she may have been just kidding.

After dinner, we decided to see the movie "Heavens Above" with Peter Sellers. I had to wear my sunglasses through the whole thing because my others are still broken, but it didn't seem to bother me as much as everyone else around. Granted, I must have looked like some kook, sitting in a dark movie house with sunglasses on, but who cares? No one knows me in Edinburgh, anyway. A very "funny thing happened" right after the movie. The lights went on and we all scrambled toward the aisle, when all of a sudden I noticed that everyone was standing still, not saying a word. To our embarrassment, they were playing "God Save the Queen" on an organ and everyone was standing in humble and rapt attention. But it was too late for us to mend our error. Freddy and I noticed it in time to cause little attention, but Karl, who was sitting down in front of us, was paying no attention whatsoever, and was still scrambling up the aisle, pushing and talking to Bill by the end of the first phrase, when he finally noticed that everyone was at attention but him. It was a very funny and embarrassing situation—and one we'll never forget, I'm sure! But Karl is the one who will remember the best!

After the movie we walked outside to find it pouring down rain—and I didn't have a jacket. So I asked them if they'd mind coming back to pick me up. Bill snapped something back nastily, and went marching off, playing martyr—and the others followed. Since I wasn't in the mood to cause trouble, I went too, the rain soaking a sport jacket I didn't want soaked. We finally reached the car, and nerves were on edge, especially after the previous episode. But it blew over soon enough, and our next task was to find the hotel. We had some general directions on where the place was, and after driving on several wild goose chases, we finally found the right turn and arrived. It is Hotel Nirvana, certainly a strange name for a hotel, and is run by a Mrs. Clement, a friendly Scotch woman with a wonderful brogue. She must be about 42, is short, and has reddish blonde hair. She talks a mile-a-minute, and is quite a character! We're in a room for five, and the remainder of the evening was spent in making plans, writing, and talking. We still had some scotch left from last night, so we asked Mrs. Clement for some ice cubes. She wryly smiled and told us that she would charge us a shilling apiece (14 cents) and then reminded us that we were in Scotland. The Scotch seem to be aware of what the world thinks about them and their money belts—but we could tell she was kidding—and we all got a big laugh out of the whole thing. It's a very nice place, especially for the price, and I have the feeling that I'm going to enjoy Edinburgh very much.

And so until tomorrow, I again say: good night.
Love, Tom

Edinburgh, Scotland—Wednesday, August 21, 1963

Hi–
Edinburgh has been called the fairest city in Europe, and even though I imagine that there are those that have more charm in some ways, or more art treasures, or more interesting culture, Edinburgh does have a fascination that merits its being called "the fairest city in Europe."

We all piled out of bed at 8:30 this morning to the call of our typical Scotch landlady, Mrs. Clement. Her breakfast of bread, jam, bacon, coffee, etc., was similar to other British breakfasts we had eaten, but there was an added item on the menu—a dish called "black pudding" or is it "black blood pudding"(?) It's stuff in a sausage skin that seems like half dough, half meat all ground up—and I really can't do a very good job of describing it. In the breakfast room in the basement of her hotel was a Canadian family, the husband a colonel in the Canadian Navy. His wife was a real character—all three hundred pounds of her! She never stopped talking, and with many it would have been irritating but she had some sort of witty way about her that was refreshing. They had about five children, all under twelve, and they were running all over the breakfast room, screaming and acting like they didn't know how to act any other way. Mama was trying in vain to discipline them, but it wasn't easy. And it didn't take long for her to give up in her disciplinary procedure and simply act as if they weren't there (which wasn't the most enjoyable action for the rest of us in the room). But anyway, we lived through the breakfast and left immediately for downtown Edinburgh, as we were anxious to get to American Express. It had been so long since we had gotten mail. For me, the last place was Nice and for the others, as far back as Rome.

We parked the car in a crescent type drive beyond the main shopping district on Princes Street. We all made a beeline for Am. Express and I was happy to get three letters, two from you and one from Joel Suffield,[2] which I was most happy and surprised to get. After getting the letters, I took off down Princes Street to look around and see for myself what Edinburgh is like. Princes Street is colorful. That seems to be the best word I can find for describing it. There are many nice stores along the street, many of them capitalizing on the tourist trade from the International Festival. They were colorfully decorated, most in some sort of reminder of Scotch heritage—of course the tartans leading the list. I entered a tartan shop, and inquired if the Rollo's[3] had one. To my surprise, they did, so I bought six of them, as they weren't that expensive and I know that it would be a long time before many of us have the chance to pick up anything like that again. I could have ordered a complete set of kilt, cap, and shoulder sash, but upon hearing the price, decided not to. They told me that there was a limited demand for the Rollo tartan, but they kept it in stock because there were a few Rollo families in Edinburgh who asked for it—and also some Rollo's from America who asked for it on occasion. As it was explained to me, the Rollo's were not a clan, but a family, so the tartan was made for them specially some time after the regular family clan tartans were originated. A very attractive Scotch "lass" waited on me, and I enjoyed a brief conversation with her about America, why I was here, etc. From the way she talked, many Americans come to Edinburgh, but that during the festival, there weren't as many as at other times of the year.

Due to the tartan purchase, my interest was kindled in Rollo family history, so I took off for the Register House at 3 Princes Street, where many records are kept, simply for those seeking information in their Scotch ancestry. In the Register House, I inquired about the Rollo's, and since I had no specific dates, I couldn't do anything but look through the Parish records for the church at Cowdenbeath[4] from 1820 to 1870. So a girl led me upstairs to an old dusty library with the birth and death records and I started plowing through the book, having to look at every birth recorded. After about 45 minutes I finally found a Rollo and being so ignorant as not even knowing Great-grandfather Rollo's first name, I thought it must be Jim. This is what I found in the book—word for word:

"James Rollo and Margaret Penman, his wife, had a child born to them on the 2nd day of March, 1854, baptized on the 2nd of April and named JAMES ROLLO in the parish of Beath, Fife."

Ecstatic after finding this, I decided to do some more research. I found a book giving a history of Scotch names and families, and inside I found this:

"Rollo, Rollock

"Two forms of the same name, found mainly in Perthshire and Fife. A transformation of the personal name Rudolph.

A family named Rollock were long eminent in Dundee. John Rollow, cleric of diocese of Moray and notary public, 1373, another John Rollow was burgess of Edinburgh, 1381. Duncane Rollo or Rollowck, servant of Alegn of Bollone (? Boulogne) of Edinburgh, 1394, in 1396 had a safe conduct to purchase goods in England. He is doubtless the Duncan Rollok, juror on an inquest in Edinburgh, 1402 and the Duncan Rollo, burgess of Edinburgh, 1412. William Rollock of Findone gave his bond of manrent "to ryd and gang" with Lawrence, Lord Oliphant, 1476. Rook, a not uncommon pronunciation of the name accounts for David Rook in Glasgow, 1552 referred to in the same record as David Rollock and Jacobus Rollok, provost of Dundee, 1485, appears in the following year as Rwok, and in 1490 as Rook. Robert Rouk resigned the lands of Buteland in the sheriffdom of Edinburgh in the reign of Robert III. Agnes Ruke held a tenement in Glasgow and in 1486 James Rouk had a lease of the teiuds of Clova. George Rollog is recorded in 1528 and Lamont referring to the Rev. Alexander Rollock, minister of Perth, spells his name Rogge and Rogus! Robert II in the 11th year of his reign confirms a charter of Duncrub and other lands granted to John Rollo by David, earl palatine of Strathearn.

"Rolla

An Aberdeen surname, probably a variant of Rollow, q.v. Meg Rolly of Fatz, Aberdeen, was described as a common "piker" in 1411. John Rollie was a trade burgess of Aberdeen, 1617.

"Lang[5]

Lang "long" i.e. "tall." Used as a byname, this occurs in O.F. charters as early as 972—92, e.g."

So this was all I had time to find today, but perhaps if I am here longer I will be able to do some more research. It is pretty interesting. I also found something on the name

"Tiernan, Tiernann. From Ir. MacTighearnain, son of Tighernan (diminutive of Tighearna, a lord) with omission of Mac."[6]

As soon as I had found all this information and paid a dollar I headed back down Princes Street. On the way back to American Express, I stopped in Smalls, a distinguished looking clothing store, and there bought a very sharp sweater. The gentleman who waited on me was a character, Scotch brogue and all—and I had a good time talking with him. Arriving at American Express, I found that Bill had met some girl from home or at least America and was spending the afternoon with her. The rest of us showed our purchases—the others had bought sweaters too—and we took off back down Princes Street. I am still amazed by the beauty of this street. The garden and castle rising high up over this part of the city make a beautiful sight.

Postcard: For kilts and tartans, it's the world-famous Princes Street, Edinburgh

 We stopped back in Smalls and Rick bought a sweater just like mine (different color). We only paid $6.50 for them—a real deal. I also picked up a tartan tie that is equally as sharp—and only $1.50. My friend again waited on us and cut up more than ever. We then left and quickly found a restaurant, where I had some fish and chips (sole). During lunch we talked about ways we were going to get the car back home—so decided that Karl and Rick could inquire about that after lunch and Freddy and I could go after some tickets to the Tattoo. The Tattoo is a spectacle of bagpipes given every night during the Festival. So Freddy and I went to the City Chambers office located on The Royal Mile (the street that runs from the Edinburgh castle to the Palace of Holyroodhouse.) We first had to walk all the way down Princes Street to pick up the car. Upon arriving at the City Chambers I was lucky to get four of their few remaining tickets. (Bill had already bought his.)

The Black Watch Battalion on their way to the Tattoo at Edinburgh Castle

    After buying the tickets, we were supposed to meet Bill at American Express around 5:00. Since we didn't have a lot of time, we quickly headed there and arrived shortly after five. But there was no Bill. Since there wasn't a place to park on the street we would have had to go around several city blocks in order to drive back by, so I got out of the car and waited by Am. Express. Our plan was also to meet Rick and Karl there and go to St. Mary's Cathedral for Evensong. (The Church of England has this so called "Evensong" several times a week and it is supposed to be very beautiful.) So Freddy let me out of the car and when I saw Rick and Karl I told Karl to go around the corner and wait for Freddy when he came back. So Rick and I waited and waited—and still no Bill. After a while we got tired of waiting so decided that if we wanted to get to St. Mary's in time for the Evensong that we had better get going. Then I saw Freddy come around the corner, but no Karl! He had obviously missed Freddy and was still looking for him. So Rick and I hopped in the car and drove once around the block—but now Karl was lost. It's things like this that have made the trip irritating. We consistently had to worry about meeting someone somewhere—and at times this ritual becomes very old. So, thinking to hell with the whole mess, we took off for St. Mary's, knowing that Karl would probably walk over to meet us.

After all this trouble in getting to the church, upon arrival we found that there would be no Evensong tonight, but that it had been postponed till tomorrow night. Completely irritated, we walked out of the church and sure enough, we see Karl trotting along the church lawn, not looking too happy. He had gone around the wrong corner, thus missing Freddy completely. After appeasing him, we headed back to the Nirvana, anxious to rest before going to the Tattoo tonight.

At about 7:45 we took off for the Tattoo, leaving Rick behind. He was so pooped out that he couldn't see another evening out. The military spectacle is held in the esplanade of the Edinburgh castle. We had a parking problem when we arrived as most everyone wanted to park their car on the long drive which winds around the bluff toward the castle, but there were guards instructing us that we couldn't park there, so finally parking the car about a quarter mile from the castle, we made the climb. I gave Rick's ticket to one of the officials at the gate—and he seemed confident that he could sell the ticket and to check with him afterwards.

The Tattoo itself shouldn't be missed by anyone going to Edinburgh. It is the ultimate in Scotch tradition and expectancy, and all of the Pipers and Drummers, the Highland dancers, etc. combine to make this a real spectacle. We had cheaper seats on the bottom row; I sat by three British girls from Southern England—and that was half the fun—as we were kept busy throughout most of the thing exchanging ideas, customs, etc. I am constantly amazed by the small difference in the way they live over here in contrast to so many of the things that we take for granted. There were families sitting near us—and the children in particular got a big kick out of all of the ceremonies. The gate official sold Rick's ticket—and I tried in vain to give the official something for doing it—but he refused.

Afterwards we went to a small restaurant for fish and chips located on this side of Edinburgh—quite a different one from Princes Street—and obviously, the old part of the city. Returning to the hotel, Rick was up writing letters and feeling much better. He had had an interesting experience with the landlady. A woman of about forty, and suffering from an acute case of diarrhea of the mouth, she had told him of an affair she had with a boy from Pana, Illinois during the war. He was stationed in Scotland and she was endless in her appraisal of him. The whole thing made Rick kind of sick after a while—as she went into all kinds of dull details about her "wee American lad—Bob."

Bill, who had been gone all day, finally pulled in about midnight. He had eventually become bored with the girl he had been with—as she, according to him, had nothing worthwhile to say and was typical of the false snobby girls from America who talk of more money than they really have.

I decided today that I wanted to stay in Edinburgh and not leave with the others tomorrow. Karl wants to go to Ireland and Rick wants to visit relatives of his Mother in Glasgow. We greeted Bill with this news, and tensions were mounting since Bill wanted to see more of the English countryside and Freddy as usual had made no commitment about what he wanted to do. But Freddy was going to wait till everyone was committed before making his decision. I was feeling chipper; was glad to be staying in Edinburgh as there was so much more to do in connection with the Festival and I also wanted to make a trip to Cowdenbeath, which is only a forty-five minute train trip from Edinburgh.

Bill finally concluded to take the car for more touring of England and sure enough, Freddy decided to go with him. So it's the end of another day, and I must get to bed. Until tomorrow—good night.

Love, Tom

Edinburgh, Scotland—Thursday, August 22, 1963

Hi–

We arose this morning about 8:45 and for fear of missing breakfast went downstairs right away looking like a bunch of slobs! Afterwards we spent the time until 9:30 getting ready to see the others off. Bill and Freddy had definitely decided to take the car up to St. Andrews golf links and then head down to London by way of the Lake District and Stratford-on-Avon. Rick was going to see relatives in Glasgow, and Karl was going to make a pilgrimage to Ireland to see if he could find long-lost relatives of his Mother.

We all drove to downtown Edinburgh and Karl and I let the others out to do further sightseeing while we took Vicki to a VW garage for her oil change and check-up. We left there at 11:20 and headed back to the hotel, after picking the others up at American Express. Very soon after we got back at the Nirvana, Bill and Freddy shoved off. And in less than a half-hour after that, Karl left to catch his train to Glasgow. He plans on taking a steamer from there over to Ireland. Rick then decided to take a shower before he left and so I wrote and relaxed while he was cleaning up. It took me more than a half-hour to sort all of the travel posters that we had gathered. I had a couple cardboard tubes in which to send them—and by the time I had finished this, Rick was ready to go. It was 3:00. Rick told Mrs. Clement goodbye and took another fifteen minutes as she was telling us how many Americans she had had stay in her hotel—and telling Rick to be sure and look up Bob when he went back to Pana! We were soon off on a bus toward Princes Street and we grabbed a short-order lunch in some grubby restaurant. I ate cream chicken soup, the first in a long time, and not satisfied, finished the lunch off with two sandwiches—a corned beef and a ham. We tossed the food down quickly as Rick's train left at 4:00, and we hadn't much time. I agreed to mail his posters too and he took off down Princes Street to Waverly Station.

I'm now alone in Edinburgh. Not knowing quite what to do with my newfound freedom, I decided that first on the list would be to get rid of these posters. I went into several places asking if they could sell me some wrapping paper, but no one was willing to help. They advised a nearby department store, which I tried, and was successful. I wouldn't have been had it not been for an elderly woman by the name of Mrs. Blair who waited on me. She was so helpful that she even insisted on wrapping the tubes herself, and gave me instructions on where to mail them, etc. There are nice people in the world: I especially enjoyed her because of her wry sense of humor and her dirge of stories about relatives in the U.S., etc.

I then headed up Princes Street to American Express to do what I hoped I wouldn't have to do: write home for more money. I hope not to have to spend all of it, but it would be good to have in case I run into an emergency. I was furious in American Express that I had to wait in line behind an American woman of about 60 who had to sign about fifty traveler's checks. All I had to do was write a telegram, but the gentleman behind the desk would not wait on me until he was finished with her. She argued with him for fifteen minutes about how much it should be—and in the end she was wrong. And I could see the anger on the man's face. No wonder these people in American Express look like they have chips on their shoulders.

Going now to St. Mary's Cathedral to catch the Evensong we missed yesterday, I arrived there after it had started. It was nothing as I had expected, and after sitting there for about fifteen minutes I left, heading for the Festival Office to see if I could get a ticket for the play "The Rabbit Race." Upon inquiring there, I found that they had sent all of their tickets over to the Assembly Hall where the show was playing, so I set out for there, passing the Edinburgh Castle along the back route. When I got there, the office wasn't open, so I sat down in the courtyard to wait. There was another fellow waiting, sitting with his legs sprawled up against the ticket booth reading a book. I asked him when the place was going to open, but he wasn't sure, so I sat down on a bench and waited too. Shortly, a young girl came up and sat down on the same bench, reading a book in French. I assumed her to be French and asked her a question in French to which I received a perfect English reply. I about fell off my seat, but we struck up a conversation and I found that she had been studying in Paris for a month this summer and she was only trying to keep up on her French by reading French books. She was at the Sorbonne and had met quite a number of American students there and had become friendly with them. She described to me the way Americans go through museums, and the tone of her description was sarcastic. "They go into a museum, whip through it in two hours and think they have seen all there is to see. It takes most of us days to go through a museum and feel like we have really accomplished something." She came from several miles from Edinburgh and our conversation ended as a woman came up to us to see if we wanted to buy one of her extra tickets to the show. I agreed to buy it, but the Scotch girl said she would wait to see if she could get a cheaper one, and they opened the doors to the theater, so I was gone and I didn't see her again. I had hoped to, but that's the way it is.

The seat was good, the play even better, concerning Germany during and after the war. It was primarily concerned with the German experimental camps where they performed operations on men in order to find the perfect race. The hero of the play had been castrated during the war and the plot concerns his relations with his wife as well as his abnormal feeling toward rabbits, of all things! It was unusual, but acted well and left one with a sour feeling about the war in general. By the way, his relations with rabbits was not sexual as it might sound!

"Programme" from an interesting night at the theatre

The most interesting thing about the evening was not the play however, but the old gentleman who sat next to me. He hailed from Oxford, came to the Edinburgh festival every year, and was as British as could be. He at first didn't believe that I was an American. My accent by that time was certainly not British, but it must have been sharp enough to fool him. He chattered away at all sorts of things, including President Kennedy, American foreign policy and the fact that America was certainly becoming strong—perhaps even stronger than Her Majesty's country. I chuckled to myself at this, and spent most of the time just listening to the character. He knew quite a bit about a lot of things, but his knowledge seemed to be finely edited by himself, leaving many obvious points out of his statements, points which led me to believe that he had taken current history and re-written it for himself—perfectly contented to let it go at that. I soon grew very tired of his rattling's and during intermission I made the excuse of going out in the hall to have a cigarette, thereby getting away from the old fellow. And I didn't go back until after the second act had begun.

Afterwards I looked for the Scottish girl I had met before, hoping to have some kind of companionship for the rest of the evening, but she was nowhere to be seen, so I walked down the side of the hill toward Princes Street. While walking I happened to run into the two ladies who had sold me the ticket and we talked briefly until we went separate ways on Princes Street.

After getting a quick bite of food at a cafeteria on Princes, I spent the next hour or so just strolling along Princes Street, observing the sights and people. I was entertained for a while by a group of Austrian students who were obviously visiting the festival for some reason or other, and who were very adept at singing folk songs of their country. They were gathered in the brightly lit entrance of some store and before they had sung for 5 minutes they had a huge crowd enjoying the concert and applauding enthusiastically after each number.

Pleasant as the surroundings were, I somehow felt lonely and caught a bus back to the hotel, where Mr. and Mrs. Clement were visiting with Mr. Clement's sister and her husband. They invited me to join them for some white sausage, chips and scotch with lemonade, and feeling in the socializing mood, I accepted. The conversation was interesting, and the food and drink were good. They wanted to know about my situation in America and seemed very interested in what I had to say, although they were seasoned in the ways of Americans, there having been so many here during the war and so many tourists since. About 1:00 I could take it no longer and retired. So until tomorrow. Good night.

Love, Tom

Edinburgh, Scotland—Friday, August 23, 1963

Hi–

I went downstairs for breakfast about nine and there met an American couple with their two children on route back to the U.S. after serving a military stance in some African colony. They were nice but rather dull people. Sure enough, the Canadians were down there again with their son, and they offered to give me a ride to the Palace of Holyroodhouse, where I was going this morning. They were in the process of leaving Edinburgh for good and it must have been 10:00 by the time they were ready. They stopped for gas on the way and got many chuckles from the gas attendants who very rarely saw a car as huge as their Oldsmobile.

The palace was quite interesting, but seemed typical of all the other miles of tours that I had already been on. It is the place where "Her Majesty" stays when in Edinburgh and is considerably more livable than most of the other places we've seen (Versailles, Schönbrunn). We saw the spot where David Rizzio was murdered during the reign of Mary Queen of Scots, and it was no more than a spot on the floor (I have become amune! [immune]) The palace is at the end of what is commonly known as the "Royal Mile" leading from the Edinburgh castle. So after the tour I took off up the Royal Mile to gather in what historic sights it has to offer.

I stopped in the "Huntly House," built in 1517, where is located a museum and a tearoom. Not feeling in the mood for museums I instead spent my time here eating. I passed "The Tollbooth," the old town hall of Edinburgh, known mostly for the jutting clock which sets it off from the other buildings on the street.

I next stopped in Jon Knox's House, built in 1490 and owned by the Reformer from 1561 to 1592. Inside were interesting old relics and museum pieces, most of which I remember as being typical to this type of thing. Too bad I'm not some old document hound! Across the street is the Museum of Childhood, where can be found a unique collection of old toys, pictures, books, costumes and examples of forgotten hobbies and sports. The Canadian couple told me not to miss the place but I couldn't bring myself to go in.

Leaving John Knox's house, I passed the present City Chambers and the Parliament House and soon found myself in St. Giles' Cathedral, the St. Peters to Presbyterianism. A beautiful place, but seeming not much different than the scores of cathedrals I've seen. I didn't bother to do more than go in, sit down to rest, and left, without observing any of the details.

Leaving St. Giles, I found myself at the castle, which marks the end of this winding, historical street, and I was a little disgusted with the weather—it had rained off and on all morning. I ducked into a tartan shop to get out of the rain, and just for curiosity's sake, inquired about the Rollo tartan. The gentleman pompously informed me that there was no Rollo tartan, that there never had been, and that he was an expert and should know! So I pompously informed him that there was a Rollo tartan, and that I had just purchased six scarves in it yesterday in the Tartan Shop on Princes Street. To this he gave nothing but an open-mouthed reply of silence, and I being irritated anyway, left the store, rain or no rain.

I soon found myself on Princes Street again, and went back into Small's where I purchased four more ties (I am really impressed with these ties!). After buying some drugs and post cards, I decided to find out some more of Rollo history, and headed for the Scottish Ancestry Bureau where I was treated well, but informed that there would be a fee for such family information. Not feeling in the mood to pay any fees, and realizing that the history had probably been traced anyway, I went to the Hamilton Tartan Shop, Edinburgh's largest and finest, and inquired there about the Rollo name. I faired [fared] better here, as the gentleman knew a Lord Rollo from Perthshire who has done business with him in the past and who is currently serving in the House of Lords in London. The man went searching through his files and came up with some Rollo information which I am passing along to you now:

"Barron Rollo is a title in the Peerage of Scotland (Lords of the country-knighthood). The Rollo's were descended from a Norman Baron who settled in Scotland in the time of David I. The Norman progenitors of the Scottish Stem were de Rullos, from Rullus (now Ruelles) near Vernon in Normandy. The Rollo's have been a distinguished family in Scotland (see Anderson's 'The Scottish Nation.')"

He gave us the address of the Lord Rollo as follows: T. Hon. The Lord Rollo, Pitcairn, Dunning, Perthshire. (I'm not sure of all the spellings!)

Leaving here, it was about 4:00 and I took a bus back to the hotel, where I borrowed Mr. Clement's typewriter—and worked on the letters till about 8:00. Mrs. Clement had moved me into another room and had given me a new roommate—a negro sailor from Africa. He was a friendly fellow and we had an interesting conversation. He has a brother in the United States and wants very much to get a passport to visit. He moaned over the fact that it is almost impossible for negroes to get passports. Discrimination is even bigger here than it is at home in many instances.

At 8:00 I walked about two blocks to a small fish and chips place where I stuffed down a very cheap and delicious meal, returning immediately to the hotel where I continued working on the letters.

At 10:45, the door bursts open and who should come bounding in but Rick, who has returned from Glasgow. He had enjoyed the visit with his relatives, but said they were a trifle old for his prolonged pleasure and due to this, decided to come back to Edinburgh before going to London. We talked for a while, but he was so pooped out that he soon went to bed. I went downstairs, where I found Mr. and Mrs. Clement having their evening "tea," and after joining them, talked until about 12:45. It's again time to say, until tomorrow, good night!

Love, Tom.

Edinburgh, Scotland—Saturday, August 24, 1963

Hi–

In order to avoid missing breakfast, I got up at 9:00 and went downstairs looking like a bum, unshaven and hair not combed. Rick got into a conversation with the American military man who was from Springfield and they continued tossing around stories for quite a while. I went back upstairs and worked on the letters until noon, and then Rick and I took a bus downtown. Rick had to catch a train for London as he was anxious to get there, but I still had some things to do here, one of which is taking a trip to Cowdenbeath to see if there is any more Rollo history that I could gather. So I bought a ticket to that town and had until 2:05 to eat. So I wandered into the restaurant at the train station and enjoyed a pretty good meal of fish (haddock), orange juice, chips, cabbage, mashed potatoes and peach flan (a fancy name for peach cobbler). I sat at a table with two other gentlemen, one a Scot from Glasgow, the other, an Englishman from London. They were both of a curious type, rather bashful, but talkative once you could bring them out of their shell. But nothing fascinating came out of the conversation, and before I knew it I was aboard the train headed for Cowdenbeath. The train was of the commuter sort, and seemed to be full of all kinds of people who had come into Edinburgh for the day to shop, etc. I sat across the aisle from a kindly type Scotch woman who was very generous with advice about Scotland, Cowdenbeath, Edinburgh and all the surrounding country. I was usually just half listening to her babberish [blabbering] as the scenery was beautiful, particularly when we crossed the Firth of Forth[7]. From the window of the train I could see the new Road Bridge being constructed across the Firth, and it was a mammoth structure, only three-quarters finished, and looking very strange indeed, its two ends reaching toward each other from the extremes of the banks of the waters—the only connection being the steel girders which swoop down like descending and ascending roller coaster tracks.

Arriving in Cowdenbeath about 2:50, I soon found myself on the main street of town, not knowing quite how to go about finding out what I wanted. So I stopped a woman who had the air of knowing about or being sympathetic to such inquiries, and she was most friendly, first telling me that she had just returned from a trip to Detroit, Michigan, and that the lady on her right was her sister from that city, visiting her now in Scotland. Well, about that I could have cared less, but nonetheless, she did tell me that the man to talk to was Mr. Brown, who was sauntering down the street toward us now.

I'm not so sure that Mr. Brown was the man to talk to, but he must have been the "oldest" man in town, and immediately handed me a card which read: "P.W. Brown, M.F., F.S.A., Scot., Consultant," and in the upper right hand corner: "The Beeches, High Street, CowdenBeath." So this was the kind of man Mr. Brown was, and upon my inquiring about the Rollo's, he shook his head sadly and said that there were no more Rollo's about, but that we could inquire of some of the other older town residents.

What he meant by this I wasn't quite sure, but soon found out. We headed toward the Cowdenbeath square, and Mr. Brown led me up to a bench impressively laden with a group of old men, and I immediately had a whole crew of piercing, beady eyes gaze up at me in one chorus. Mr. Brown asked them if they knew anything of the Rollo's and most shook their heads negatively. One old man seemed to take an interest in this however, and he feebly stood up, announcing that the provost of the town might know the Rollo's or their whereabouts. Another gentleman also stood up, and he was probably the most sprightly of the crew, dressed immaculately in a very handsome tweed suit, with cane and shoes polished sparkling. He said that I should try the town hall, which wasn't open today (to that I cussed violently to myself), and when I informed him that I wouldn't be able to come back on Monday, as I must go to London, he said that the best thing to do would be to go see the old provost—who without question would be the oldest man in town—and that if he didn't know of the Rollo's, no one would.

So I quickly learned that the only way to see this gentleman would be to walk out to see him, and this I did, accompanied by the first old gentleman who stood up on the bench in town (I can't remember names). Mr. Brown said that he had other business to attend to, so I took off with this other old man, and he was so feeble and so old that I wondered about the wiseness of his actually walking all this distance. He talked to me the whole way, in a brogue that I could just barely understand. In fact, I had to have him repeat most of what he said, and at times it was embarrassing, as he seemed to understand me quite well.

Upon arriving at the home of the provost, we found him not to be at home, which I felt doubly sorry for. One, that I did want to learn more of the family history, and two, that this old gentleman had walked all this way with me, something I could see was quite a feat for him. Well, upon learning this, the old man said that I should go out to the old church and see who of the Rollo's were buried there, but that he did not feel up to going all the way out there. This was fine with me, but very soon another older man came up and asked us what the trouble was. The two gentlemen exchanged words in a tongue that I doubt could ever be claimed by the English speaking countries, and very soon I gathered that this other man would walk out to the cemetery and old church with me. He was considerably younger, was extremely well dressed, and I soon learned that he had recently retired. He had a very generous personality and obviously had nothing better to do than to go out to the cemetery with me.

The town of Cowdenbeath struck me as a type of place that is inhabited by a small-town type of person, mostly with small outlooks on life, but probably very happy. I found out that it was still a coal-mining town, but actually few Scotchmen worked in the mines anymore, that most of the work was now done by Italian immigrants. The day was rather dreary, the sky overcast, but yet having some blue spots intermingled with breaks in cloud groups. We walked toward the church, and found it to be a small stone building, almost made obscure by the huge graveyard which surrounded it. The gentleman said that the old graves were nearest the church. We approached the church by an old road that gave the whole scene a peculiar air, at the same time restful. We stopped at the stonecutters shed, and he informed us that the caretaker was out of town for the day, but that he would be back later on tonight. This aggravated me all the more, as I couldn't have picked a more inconvenient day to visit. The stonecutter said that he remembered seeing the name Rollo somewhere in the yard, but yet he couldn't remember exactly where. This also didn't help matters, so we decided to start looking. I also mentioned the name Lang, thinking that might help in giving me a lead.

So here we were, searching through the graveyard, going from stone to stone, a situation that was indeed unusual and weird. But it was a restful (that's a pun!) and scenic place. After searching almost all of the old graveyard with no success, the man announced that he must get to town, and after giving me instructions on how to get back to the main section of town, left. I thanked him profusely for all of his help, and continued my search. Thinking that there might be some Rollo stones over in the new section of the graveyard, or rather newer section, I crossed the road. Over there, I met two other old gentlemen who were strolling in that section. I told them my problem, and they offered to give my name and address to the caretaker and have him send me some information, and after a half-hour's more search with no rewards, I started walking back toward town.

I stopped in a small restaurant for dinner, and left Cowdenbeath on the 6:30 train. Even though I didn't find anything of any significance, it was an interesting afternoon.

When I arrived in Edinburgh I didn't feel like doing much of anything, so took a bus home.

I spent the rest of the evening writing, and so it is again time to say, until tomorrow, good night.

Love, Tom

P.S. Tomorrow I'm planning a day on Loch Lomond. And I hope to get to London as soon as possible.

Edinburgh, Scotland—Sunday, August 25, 1963

Hi-

I went downstairs for the usual breakfast this morning at 9:30 and there got into a very interesting conversation with a fellow from Africa. He was from one of these very small African countries that has recently gained its freedom from England, and he was telling me about the situation there. There are three such countries which have recently tried to unite. He told me that it was not working out at all because one of them is much stronger than the other, and has been extracting raw materials out of his country for manufacturing, and very little of the manufactured goods have been poured back into his. I was ignorant of any background, so spent most of the time trying to acquaint myself with the situation, which is difficult, since this gentleman had trouble expressing himself well in English, at least so that I could understand.

I wrote until about 11:15, and then took a bus to Waverly station, where I purchased a ticket to Glasgow, where I would change trains and go to Balloch Pier, where the steamer leaves for the trip up Loch Lomond. It was raining fiercely, and I thought that it was going to be miserable. But after we finally were on the Loch, the clouds parted, and it turned out to be a brisk but beautiful day. I then spent the rest of the afternoon (until 7:30) on this steamer "The Maid of the Mist," and found out how memorable the loch is, and why the song was written. There were all kinds of people on board, families from England, as well as people from Scotland taking an afternoon off. Feeling rather lonely and bored other than the scenery, I bought a ticket for "High Tea." The high tea was really a meal, and tasted extremely good. The dining room of the steamer was real elegance, white tablecloths and sturdy silverware making up the table. The main part of the "tea" was sole, which was delicious, as it is all over England, and the rest was salad, cold pancakes served like rolls with jelly, and of course, tea! Afterwards I strolled out on the deck and continued enjoying the scenery.

I got into a conversation with a congenial family from Glasgow, the Walkers. Mr. and Mrs. Walker, their daughter and Mrs. Walker's mother were taking a "holiday" for this Sunday afternoon, and I gathered that it was rather unusual for a family to do this often. The best thing about the trip was a group of people from England who gathered on the deck for a song fest. One gal had an accordion, and they all took turns singing many of the English and Scotch folk songs. One woman brought tears with her rendition of "the bonnie bonnie banks of Loch Lomond." Never did I think that I would hear this song in such an appropriate setting.

One man from England was a real veteran at entertaining and he did some songs that were quite humorous and entertaining.

At 5:00 the bar opened and the Walkers insisted on buying me a drink. So we retired to the bar and spent the rest of the time there talking. They were quite a friendly group and I enjoyed the whole thing quite a bit. Mrs. Walker had some friends that had moved to America and she had a skeptical outlook on the country as the reports by her friends were not the best. I assured her that America wasn't really that bad, and tried to do the best selling job I could. After we landed at the Balloch pier, I sat with the Walkers all the way to Glasgow and they even asked me to come stay with them for a while, which I thought was most honorable, but unfortunately I didn't have time.

After changing trains in Glasgow, I got on the train headed for Edinburgh. This time I found myself in one of those train compartments that you see in the movies. You know, the kind that almost needs a Marlene Dietrich slinking in with a trench coat on and whispering very sexy or mysterious things to the man in the corridor. But there was no Marlene and it all seemed normal enough, and we arrived in Edinburgh on schedule at 9:30.

I took a bus back to the hotel, stopping in a small fish and chips place on the way for some steak pie and chips, which I took back to the Nirvana with me. I wrote the rest of the evening and went to bed early. So until tomorrow, good night.

Love, Tom

P.S. I'm sure that I've done a great injustice to the beautiful scenery on Loch Lomond, but I'm almost all sceneried out!

LONDON
14

"Kings, Queens, Saints and Worthies"

So much could be said about this great historical city. Shall we talk about the Tower of London, Piccadilly Circus, Big Ben, Buckingham Palace? The list goes wonderfully on. Our five guys took it all in, on this, their last stop.

Maybe, just maybe, what they will remember the most is the pubs. The best "fish and chips" in the world. Accompanied of course by a refreshing pint or two...be it bitter, stout or an ale.

What a finale... "Here, here! Three cheers all around! Well done Yanks!"

§ § §

London, England—Monday, August 26, 1963

Hi–

Well I finally made London and it has been a long day! This morning at breakfast I had a conversation with a fellow from Rome, who was there studying at the U. of Edinburgh. He was trying to learn English and was having a rather difficult time. After breakfast I went upstairs, washed out some of my shirts and sat down to write. I continued at this till 1:00, when I went downstairs for a shower. After paying and going through all the motions of bidding goodbye to Mrs. Clement, I finally took off about 2:15. She insisted that I sign her guest book and include my address, as she prides herself on all of the visitors she has from all over the world. I must admit that my stay in Edinburgh has been most like home except in Nottingham. I suppose the main reason is the language, but there are others too, one of the most important being a free bath!

After buying my ticket at Waverly station, I took my last look at beautiful Edinburgh, mailed some letters and post cards and boarded the train.

I had expected to spend my time on the train reading "The Agony and the Ecstasy," the book by Irving Stone about Michelangelo, but ended up talking to people almost the whole trip. I met some fellow from Northern Scotland, a salesman who was heading for Newcastle. He had bright red hair and his personality matched perfectly. He had some funny opinions on British foreign policy and spent a great deal of time trying to feel me out for opinion about the Perfumo [Profumo][1] scandal. He seemed to be very ashamed of the whole thing, and was wondering if that type of thing could happen in the United States. I told him that it probably has happened many times, but that it has never reached the public.

Then he got out at Newcastle and I went back to my car and there got into a conversation with a woman from Sydney, Australia. We talked until 7:00 when we went back to the dining car for dinner. The meal was very good, but kind of expensive, and I felt guilty in a way, paying that much for a meal. We continued our conversation until arrival in London. I told her that I had no one to contact, and she suggested that I call the British Travel Association, but I thought that even that would probably be too expensive, so after getting into the station, called John Pickton, Rick's friend whom he had hitchhiked with in France. I knew that Rick was staying with him, and I secretly hoped that he would invite me also. He was very friendly on the phone, but said that he didn't have enough room for anyone else—I didn't invite myself, he mentioned it first.

He told me that Rick had gone to the theater that night and that I should call back about midnight.

I was now stuck with trying to find a place to sleep and I wasn't about to pay any exorbitant prices. Knowing nothing about London, and not seeing any information booths in the train stations that could give me any help in this matter, I walked out into the street and started walking. Someone mentioned that there were some reasonable hotels near here, so I started ringing doorbells.

The hotels in this area were clean looking and small. They were no more than three stories high and looked a great deal like townhouses converted.

After finding that the going price was about $3.00, I finally resigned myself to a place for 25 shillings, slightly less than that, but nevertheless, a place to sleep. London had obviously completely closed up for the night so I decided to retire and save my sightseeing for tomorrow. I called Rick about midnight and we agreed to meet at American Express tomorrow morning. I read for a while, wrote also, then went to bed. So it is again time to say, until tomorrow, good night.

Love, Tom

London, England—Tuesday, August 27, 1963

Hi–

Well, it has been a long day, and London is a fascinating place. It is so different from other European cities and yet at the same time very different than any American city I've seen. It is uncannily orderly and clean and no buildings are over five floors high, even in the very heart of the city.

I went downstairs for breakfast at 7:45 and sat at the same table with an English teacher from Paris. He was quite a character, the kind who goes traveling all over the continent and England when he feels like it, and seems to enjoy life immensely.

After breakfast I took a subway to Piccadilly Circus, known as the very heart of London, and found it to look a great deal like our large cities, with the bright neon signs, and the thousands of swarming people, but with such low buildings. I headed for American Express and found it to be the impressive place I'd expected, much like the one in Paris.

Piccadilly Circus, central to the West End theatres

    It was great getting mail again, and I sat down on the floor in the basement of American Express reading it when Rick came in. Before this, I saw one of the girls from Illinois and she at first didn't recognize me, I suppose because my hair was so long. (I haven't had my hair cut all summer.)

    After getting some money, Rick and I bought a copy of "Punch," to find out what some of the best shows are. We decided to buy tickets for "*Oliver*"[2] and after stopping for some tea, we went for the tickets, after which we headed for Trafalgar Square, a huge expanse where the pigeons and people gather to loaf away London time. Two fountains adorn the thing and it is surrounded by many ominous buildings, including the British Museum, White Hall and other such buildings.

    Believe it or not, here we ran into Bill and Freddy, whom we had not seen since Edinburgh. After exchanging stories for a while, we went to the place where Rick's friend John works as Rick had agreed to meet him for lunch. We found that Bill and Freddy had had an interesting time, going up to St. Andrews golf course, heading up to Loch Lomond, and then down to Stratford-on-Avon through the Lake Country. They had a close call with the car, almost getting into an accident. After hearing this, I was glad that I had decided to stay in Edinburgh.

We marched up en masse to the firm where John works and found it to be a very sedate, established looking place. John soon came downstairs and we adjourned to a pub nearby. Here we had a delicious lunch of corned beef sandwiches, sausage and beer—and also met some of John's friends. John is an interesting fellow, but is impressed with many things which we are not. He is wild over a group of singers whom we had not heard of, a group called the Beedles [Beatles],[3] and to this we nodded in approval, but secretly thought that there were certainly more important things to be concerned with. He talked at great length about the Queen and the Royal family—and this we listened to with somewhat more interest. He has a great desire to come to America, and told us that he was fascinated by the names of our cities, and I wondered if that was the only reason he wanted to visit my country.

After eating, Rick and I headed for Russell Square, the area where one can find a cheap hotel that is fairly decent. Rick had paid for two nights in one of the hotels there before deciding to stay with John. He said that the place was kind of "grunchy" [grungy] and upon arrival there I had to agree with him. I have never seen such a filthy, low class flophouse in my life. The woman who runs it has red stringy hair, and looks honestly like a prostitute who grew too old to do anything but run such a place. Anyway, I paid the pound for the room (actually I paid two pounds for two nights) and she then announced that we would be sharing a room with two other Americans. We weren't too happy about this, and even unhappier when she showed us the room. It was dirty, smelled and looked like the only care it ever had was someone making the beds every day. Soon we found out who does make the beds, and we could hardly believe this woman. About 35, she had long stringy brown hair, was fat and had only one breast. In addition, she was pregnant, and made no bones about the fact that she was unmarried. She talked in a drone about nothing in particular, and her manner led me to believe that she must be out of balance mentally. Rick and I could take no more of this, so we took off down the street, stopping in at the hotel where Bill and Freddy are staying. They weren't in, so we continued toward Russell Square, stopping in a hotel called The President (quite a contrast, by the way, to the one we're staying in) for a nip of Scotch.

We shortly returned to the hotel, changed clothes, and walked from our hotel all the way through the heart of London to St. James Park, a beautiful place dating from the time of Henry VIII. It is now known as the most attractive park in London, and it is probably that. We watched the birds in the water for some time and then walked back toward Trafalgar Square, where we found a restaurant. Our meal of minestrone soup, veal, chips, salted celery, peaches and cream and coffee was good, not too expensive, and made interesting by the character who sat next to us. He was full of some interesting kind of philosophy, and was very witty. We wondered about his sanity, as his views on life were extremely unusual, and after a while, we began to see that he was deliberately trying to make us think just this.

After dinner we went to see "*Oliver*" and found it very enjoyable, although the seats (in the upper balcony) were most uncomfortable. Since I was already familiar with the music, I had a head start on Rick who was not as impressed. I hear that it has made quite a hit in New York though.

After the show we stopped in a bar for a drink of Scotch and afterwards returned to the hotel. There we ran into our two roommates, one from New York, the other a military man who was doing a little traveling. They were both undesirable, the fellow from New York very obnoxious, and in addition, had a most distinct and repulsive odor. I assumed that he hadn't had a bath in days, and it made me wonder rather embarrassedly whether I had ever smelled that bad. The other fellow was not much more pleasant, and Rick and I kept giving each other looks of disgust.

We all did have one bond, however—disgust with this miserable hotel. The fellow from New York told us about breakfast and an experience which he had with some of the ladies of the establishment. He had asked for coffee without cream, and the creature replied in a very cockney accent, "I'm very sorry, we have coffee without milk but not without cream." Figure that one out!

Oh, I almost forgot to mention that we stopped in to see Bill and Freddy after the show and we found their hotel to be 200% finer than ours and they were paying less than we. So we decided to find a different place to stay tomorrow. Bill, Rick and I took off from here as he had just received a great deal of slides. We went into a hotel lobby where we sat looking at the slides until about 1:00. After being kicked out of here, we found another hotel lobby, where we finished up this operation. His slides are good and they brought back a lot of memories.

So, it is again time to say, until tomorrow, good night.

Love, Tom

London, England—Wednesday, August 28, 1963

Hi–

We were awakened this morning by what I have termed in my notes "witch." This hotel is something else. It is the most degenerated place one could imagine. The first thing that happened yesterday that made me wonder just how safe the place is, I leaned back against the wall while sitting on the bed, and all of a sudden there wasn't a wall. It was an old door that wasn't very well attached, at least with my weight against it, and through I went. It wouldn't have been so bad if there hadn't been some startled gentleman in the room I so rudely interrupted who was in the process of getting dressed. We exchanged looks and smiles as I realized that he must be on a tight travel budget also. The worst thing about this flea-trap was the personnel. The maids looked like they had somehow lost their tickets to the human race—and words like ugly or repulsive would not be adequate. They were unbelievable examples of women who moved like turtles, were as cleanly as reptiles who wallow in mud all day, and had as much personality as a dead cat. But I'm wrong there. They did have personality. When we moved in yesterday, one of these creatures came into the room to clean up. She was repulsive and pathetic at the same time. But at that point we would much rather have been observing her on a screen or in the zoo than to be cavorting with her in this hotel room. The poor thing was so slow-moving that Rick and I thought that she was on dope—but that seemed unlikely. She was probably endowed with a dopey way.

Needless to say, Rick and I were glad to get out of there. Rick had made the mistake of paying two nights in advance and we had to argue with the red-haired wench for about fifteen minutes in order to get his money back. But he finally was successful.

After a horrible breakfast with coffee "without milk" we left in search of a new place to stay. Luckily the place where Bill and Freddy were staying had some vacancies, and lo an' behold, we both got single rooms for less money—and to top it off, the place was neat, clean and run by sane people, and it had no stench. We were wallowing in luxury! We were surprised to find Karl also at the hotel. He had just come in from his wild jaunt to Ireland. The three of us walked down toward the main part of the city, and passing the theater where "*Pickwick*"[4] is playing, I stopped in and bought a ticket for this afternoon. It is one of these English musicals and it will be interesting to see how it compares to ours. We also stopped in another theater and bought a ticket for tonight's performance of "*Mary, Mary*."[5] We then took a subway from Piccadilly Circus to Hyde Park.

Hyde Park is London's largest park—covering 640 acres when combined with the Kensington gardens into which Hyde Park runs. One of the most interesting things about the park is a dog cemetery located there. Some Duchess had a pet that she highly revered, and insisted on having a formal burial place for it. Till the cemetery was closed in 1915, there were buried there 300 poor unsuspecting canines. Henry VIII was really responsible for the park as he was for the St. James Park. He had it made into a deer park and royal hunting ground. It's an attractive enough place, but doesn't compare to St. James Park. Somehow it is too big, and doesn't seem to be nearly as well kept as the St. James.

I left the other two about 2:00 so that I could get to the theater by 3:00. Forgot to mention that we ate lunch in the park—nothing very exciting about that, so I won't expound.

"*Pickwick*" was good, but that's all. These English musicals don't have the spunk and sparkle that the American musicals have. The music especially was mediocre. The star, whose name slips my mind, was excellent—the only thing that saved the show! It was based on Charles Dickens's "*The Pickwick Papers*," and the lead is a roly-poly man with spectacles who is the epitome of the confirmed bachelor and extremely funny. He cavorted about the stage as if he owned it, and at the same time, sang beautifully...quite a talent!

I left the theater about 5:30 and headed back to the hotel. The hotel is about a mile and a half from the main part of London—at least the theater district—so it seems much more interesting to walk back. On the way, a fellow about my age with a very British accent stopped me and asked me how to get somewhere. I obviously didn't know, and it didn't take me long to figure out that he had an ulterior motive in starting the conversation. He is planning a trip to the United States someday and he is trying to meet as many Americans as possible so that he will have people to visit when he comes to America—smart lad! I embarrassed him by figuring him out immediately, but really couldn't have cared less, knowing how great it is to be treated with some kind of hospitality in a strange land. What did irritate me was that as soon as he got my name and address he went scooting off as if he were looking for some other American to add to his list. I told him that the other guys would probably enjoy talking to him as we knew no one here in London except John Pickton, Rick's friend, but he gave me some excuse and hurried off. I swear if he calls me ever at home, I'll probably tell him that I'm sorry that I'm too busy to give any of my time as a tourist guide of America—that's a lie, knowing me, I'll probably be more than happy to entertain him.

Back at our London home the whole group was gathered together for the first time since Edinburgh—a fact that by this time is of no great consequence. After changing clothes, we all left, heading for someplace to eat. We found this Italian restaurant (in London, no less!) and had a fairly decent meal of ravioli, roast beef, chips, peas and good old American Coke.

"*Mary, Mary*" is a very funny play. I was in stitches throughout the whole thing—and between acts as well. The star again, made the show.[6] She was a girl that had gone to Oxford to school, and had entirely mastered the Brooklyn accent, which seems to me to be quite a feat. Afterwards, we saw her dash out of the stage door and run down a dark London street. It happened so fast that even the autograph hounds had no chance to really figure out what had happened.

We crossed the street to a pub that seemed to be real active. It was the sort of pub that London pubs are supposed to be—lively, beemed [beamed], full of all kinds of funny looking and interesting characters and topped off with robustness that rounded out its rather crude perfection.

We all ordered a round of bitter beer (London's best) and sat around enjoying the pretty girls and the atmosphere. Freddy and Rick left shortly leaving Bill and I to continue an interesting discussion we had started. (Karl had gone to see *My Fair Lady*.) In no time at all, at least it seemed to us, the bartender rang the 11:00 bell. All London bars close at 11:00 and much to our disappointment, we had to head back to the hotel. Everything in London closes up at 11:00. It's a law . . . and probably a good one, even though we didn't think so at the time.

I read a while before deciding to write and retire—and so until tomorrow—good night.

Love, Tom

London, England—Thursday, August 29, 1963

Hi–

This morning breakfast was finished being served at 8:30 and I got up at 8:45—typical! But the good woman (we call her "Ma") said I could get some anyway, and complained at me the whole time she was serving. I told Bill that I would meet him at Trafalgar Square at 1:00 for lunch, and everyone went off in his own direction. I left the hotel, found a public telephone booth, and tried desperately to get hold of Kay Olson, the girl I was out with in Salzburg, if you remember. The number she gave me to call for hours was busy, and by the time it did answer, she wasn't there, they didn't know when she would be, and doubted if she ever would, even with her bags there. That did seem peculiar, but I took it for what it was worth. I was rather irritated, since Kay and I had decided to get together here in London and see some plays together, so the whole fiasco was disappointing.

I walked down to Trafalgar Square and spent the next several hours watching the fountains, pigeons, kids and kooky people who hung out there. It is a beautiful place and seems to be rightly called the center of London attractions. Surrounded by famous museums, churches and stately government buildings, to me its charm is its people. Turning in any direction from the square, old famous sights can be easily seen, including Whitehall, the old center of the Court of England, the Houses of Parliament, Westminster Abbey, Westminster Cathedral, St. James Park, Buckingham Palace and St. James Palace.

The weather today has been beautiful. I go nowhere without my trusty umbrella because there is at least one good shower a day, but we have had no consistent bad weather.

While standing there engrossed in some little girl who was swarmed with pigeons perched on her shoulders, eating out of her hands and fairly covering her in their begging's for bread or whatever she was feeding them, I heard a familiar voice call my name, and coming out of my daze, I saw Karl. I hadn't expected him as he had been gone when I got up, but he had seen Bill, and agreed to meet us for lunch.

Shortly, Bill showed up and the three of us found a pub near the square and stopped there for some lunch. These London pubs are great. They are very clean, full of atmosphere and have wonderful food for lunch. Dishes like steak and kidney pie, cottage pie (cheese, onions and potatoes) and wonderful corned beef or ham sandwiches with a glass of bitter beer make great food for lunch. The small pub was full of businessmen, most distinguished looking and wearing mustaches—the mustache is quite the thing in England in the upper circles.

Afterwards, Karl took off for some personal sightseeing and Bill and I started wandering ourselves, not knowing exactly where we were going. We passed the theater where "*How To Succeed*"[7] is playing and I couldn't resist buying a ticket—and Bill joined me. Then planning on doing some sightseeing, we passed the theater where "*Blitz!*"[8] is playing and I couldn't pass it without seeing what they had left in the way of tickets for the matinee. Incidentally, I've found that I'm spending most of my London time in the theater, and have actually done very little sightseeing, per se. I have to admit that I've had my fill of churches, cathedrals and capitals—and the theater prices here are so low—no more than 50 cents for balcony seats.

So I dragged Bill in to "*Blitz*," and even though by Lionel Bart, the author of the show "*Oliver*," it left much to be desired. This is my second disappointment in British musicals—and I've even considered the possibility of my own effectiveness here. It might be much easier to get started here than in New York.

After the show, we returned to the hotel. No one else was there and we had no idea where they were. Bill and I left at 6:30, stopping in a small snack shop for some dinner. "*How To Succeed*" was as good as I remembered it being when I saw it in New York two years ago and it simply confirmed my opinions about the excellence of American musicals.

On the way back we stopped in the Hotel President for a drink and when leaving ran into Rick and Freddy; we then took off for the London version of Whimpy's [Wimpy's] Hamburger Joint and had two hamburgers, coffee and good old American atmosphere. This London is in many ways very much like the United States. It's the first place we've been so far this summer where hamburger joints can be found in abundance if you really want to find them. Of course, we are trying to soak up as much local culture as possible and as a rule have been avoiding the American looking places, but it has been harder in London.

Upon returning, I did my laundry (I now have only one of these washable shirts since leaving my other one in Edinburgh.) And it is again time to say, until tomorrow, good night.

Love, Tom

London, England—Friday, August 30, 1963

Hi–

Got up this morning at 8:30, had the usual breakfast, and afterwards took a "free" bath which is quite the innovation since arriving in England. I really feel for the poor tourist who travels the Continent with too little money to buy a bath—they must leave odors everywhere they go.

I left the hotel at 10:00 and walked down toward the main part of London, stopping on the way to drop off some film to be developed.

Heading down toward Trafalgar Square, I went through the Admiralty Arch, which is the entrance to the Mall, the great processional entrance to Buckingham Palace. I decided that I couldn't leave London without seeing the changing of the guard at the Palace so I headed in that direction. The throngs of people who were gathered in this area were proof that the great "guard change" was near at hand.

The impressive changing of the guard at Buckingham Palace

The Palace itself is, to put it bluntly, one of the dullest buildings we've seen. It is large, dreary looking, and is saved only by the grounds and parks surrounding it. The changing of the guard is impressive with the stately English guards on horses pushing back the crowds before the regiments come marching in, the uniforms of a beautiful bright red topped with those big black furry hats, and the complete regimentation of the whole thing, the rhythmic exactness of the movement and the serious tone that goes along with it.

One of the Queen's foot guards keeping watch

There were so many people there that I had to cram and strain and jump to see up and around all the people when the procession went into the courtyard of the Palace and I soon began to wonder if it were all worth it. Since it is such a "small" world I ran into Karl and Bill who were there to see the sight also—and afterwards, we all walked back toward Trafalgar Square together. We had lunch in the same pub we ate in yesterday and I ate the same thing, the cottage pie and ham sandwich with a glass of bitter beer. These pubs are great!

After lunch Bill and Karl took off and I headed toward Grosvenor Square where the American Embassy is located. You know that Gene Thraillkill[9] works there and I thought I would surprise him since he doesn't know I'm here I'm sure. But on the way I ran into Steph Borloff, one of the girls we had been with in Berlin, which was quite a surprise. She had just arrived in London with the other Alpha Chi's.[10] Before long, the other girls came running up—and they had an addition to their party—Jan St. Clair from Champaign who had spent a year in school in Munich. I immediately decided to forget the

The iconic Big Ben in the heart of London

American Embassy and Gene—and Steph, Jan and I took off for some coffee. We had a great conversation—mostly about the differences between Europe and the United States, the good and bad, of which there is plenty of both.

About three, they had to leave so I then headed toward the Embassy and once there found that Gene worked in an office in some other building—and upon arriving there, found that it was his day off, so I got his phone number, intending on calling him later.

When I left, it was pouring rain and I was glad to have my umbrella. I walked back to Piccadilly Circus, and by this time was pooped out, so headed back to the hotel.

Karl was the only one there and soon we went out to get something to eat. We had a mediocre dinner somewhere near Leicester Square and afterwards I went to the theater where the English musical *"Half a Sixpence"* is playing. I secured a ticket for tonight's performance and Karl then took off—as he wanted to see something else.

All I could get was a standing room ticket and the show was not really worth standing through. It was again in the style of most of these shows, very old fashioned and lacking in the real stuff that the American shows have.

After the show I was feeling in a slightly daring mood and I decided that I couldn't leave London without finding out what kind of opportunities were around for Americans interested in writing for the theater. So I went to the stage door. I stood there for a while not knowing who to stop or who to talk to, feeling pretty stupid, while all these painted actors and actresses were filing out one at a time, most of them in little groups that looked as if they didn't want intrusion.

Presently a young man came out who looked like he might at least tell me who to talk to, so I very awkwardly said "Pardon me, I'm an American, I write musicals, who do I talk to" in about two seconds. He must have thought that I was really a kook! He said, "Go inside the door and talk to someone else, I'm busy." Feeling even more stupid than ever, and regretting my ridiculous exposition, I waited there a few more minutes when another fellow came out. I said, "Pardon me, I'm interested in writing for the musical theater, and I wonder if you could give me any information on London's opportunities for an American." For some unknown reason, this time it all came out sounding like I was really "human," and he smiled and said that he had a few minutes before he met his fiancée and to come across the street and have an ale with him. This I did, and we talked about the English theater in general for a while and then Brian agreed to listen to some of my music before the performance Monday. He seemed like a nice enough fellow, but only a member of the chorus and obviously not someone who could be a great deal of help. We both took a subway to Trafalgar Square where I got off and headed home, at the time elated about this "break."

When I got back, Bill was still up and I told him about what happened and we ended up talking for hours about the theater, futures, life in general and the summer, which now is so nearly over.

And so—until tomorrow—goodnight.

Love, Tom

London, England—Saturday, August 31, 1963

Hi–

Only four more days left of a trip that has been more than an education—it has been an insight, a grand unveiling of what a small part of the world is like and how little so many people know about any of it. The trip has opened my mind's doors to an interest in history, politics, deepened my interest in people and travel, and confirmed my convictions concerning basic human nature. Just traveling with a group of five people for two and a half months whom you thought you knew and then finding out gradually what they are really like has been education enough.

Today I made it to breakfast on time and "Ma" (our landlady) I'm sure was as surprised to see me there as I was surprised to be up. Another American chap about our age joined us for the meal and after talking with him for a while found out that he has quite an interesting background in the theater. He spent last year in Japan on a theater scholarship and has been fascinated by Japanese theater forms all of his life. This summer he has done some German theater in East Berlin, but is now heading back to school in the U.S. which is in Pittsburgh (Pittsburgh University, I believe). Anyway, I told him of my interest in musical theater and he agreed to listen to some of my stuff if I would meet him back here at 12:30.

I took off shortly for Westminster Abbey where I was to meet Rick. I arrived about a half-hour late and didn't see him anywhere. It didn't take me long to find out just why he didn't seem to be anywhere around. I approached a dignified elderly Englishman standing near one of the doors and asked him when the next tour of the Abbey would be leaving. Replying in a rather grave tone that was spiced by the accent plus a hint of sarcasm, he said, "Well sir, why don't you step over to the Abbey and inquire there. These are the Houses of Parliament!" As he pointed his finger to the large ominous cathedral across the street I was struggling to keep my wits as well as to keep from losing my tongue. I smiled, thanked him for the information, and sheepishly walked away. It then became evident to me that my interest in London was certainly more directed toward the theater than toward the historical sites. And so ends my sojorn [sojourn] on finding Westminster Abbey.

The thing that impressed me most about the Abbey is that everybody is buried there—from Shakespeare to Newton, I swear I've never seen so many graves concentrated in such a small area. Actually, the church isn't small, but rather than a church it seemed like one big glorious tomb. They have bodies in the pillars, in the floor, in the wall, stacked so as to conserve space, and even special chapels built that house even more bodies. Other than that special feature it was simply another cathedral to join the now seemingly endless list of others I've seen.

Tower Bridge—world famous symbol of London

After wandering around there for a while, knowing that finding Rick was a lost cause now anyway, I headed back to what I originally thought was the Abbey, the Houses of Parliament. I didn't wait for the next tour of place, instead wandered around at my own pace, catching bits and snatches of the tours as I went. It is a beautiful building, much of it new since the war, but looking as old as it probably always has. It's amazing how old they have been able to make some of these places look that were destroyed by the war, as if they were refusing to acknowledge that the war ever happened at all and rather—taking up where they left off immediately before.

The architecture of the building on the outside is an ornate Gothic style and a comment I find amazing in the guide book states that the face of the building is elaborately decorated; "there are over three hundred statues of kings, queens, saints and worthies." I wonder what crowning distinction puts one in the category of a "worthy"? I'll tell you this much. If it were my statue on the Parliament, I might even consider it an insult to be referred to as almost a footnote: "worthy."

Perhaps the most enlightening thing was seeing the chair where Churchill sits when he graces the House of Lords with his presence. This will be his last year they say. And this reminds me of how reminiscent and sentimental people can get over mere objects they encounter on trips such as this. To get weepy over a chair that Churchill sits in is pretty assenine [asinine], agreed? But human weaknesses such as this sometimes make life more enjoyable—as long as you don't let such things take control. How much fun do cynics have?

After touring these two famous places I headed back to the hotel to meet Ken and arrived fifteen minutes late only to be greeted by a note saying that he wouldn't be back until one. That was fine with me as I had plenty of things to do—personal things that one easily neglects with lack of time.

When Ken did show up, we took off to find something to eat, ending up in a local pub with roast beef sandwiches and a couple of stines [steins] of red barrel beer. During lunch Ken challenged me to a game of English pool, a favorite game in such places. Actually it is a miniature pool table and the rules are similar to standard pool but somewhat altered. Having never played much pool anyway, I was reluctant, but figured I really had nothing to lose, and ended up beating him. After lunch we walked over to the University of London in search for a piano, but never did find one, and we looked everywhere.

In fact, we hunted until about three so finally gave up and headed back to the hotel, stopping on the way back for a beer. From what I could tell of the way Ken talked about himself, he was quite a talented fellow, was most serious about becoming an actor, but had no definite plans for the future. He is an only child, comes originally from California and both his parents are artists, his mother one who has made quite a sum on doing art work in brass and copper murals. I forget now what his Dad does, but I think he is some kind of painter. We had a good conversation, but I had to leave at 4:00 as I had planned on meeting Karl and Rick at the theater at 4:30. We had tickets for the "*Mousetrap*," the play by Agatha Christie that has been running for eleven years, the longest running play in modern English theater history.

Rick didn't show up at the theater so we finally went in without him, leaving Rick's ticket at the window, hoping that they could sell it. The play was good, true to Christie style of suspense in not revealing the actual murderer until the end, and a fitting change from all the musicals I'd seen. After the show, the funniest thing happened outside the theater. I ran into a girl that I'd met in American Express in Florence over a month ago. She was heading for New York in the morning and seemed to be having her last final fling in the big city. Karl and I asked her to join us this evening but she said that she already had plans, so we could do nothing but put our tails between our legs and shuffle off for home.

When we got back, Bill and Freddy were already there both twiddling their thumbs and presently Rick showed up with John Pickton, his friend who lives here in London. We then spent the rest of the evening in the corner pub singing all of the American songs we could think of and drinking quite a lot of beer. Even "Ma" with her red-headed grandson was there in all of their Irish glory, and we had, so to speak, a "jolly good time."

When the pub closed at 11:00 as all English pubs do, we walked over a couple of streets where Steph Borloff and some of the other Illinois girls were staying, to see if they would care to join is in a small private party. Unfortunately, they weren't around, so we goofed around for a while, eventually saw Rick and John off on the subway, and headed back to the hotel for bed.

It's been a long day—so until tomorrow, good night.

Love, Tom

London, England—Sunday, September 1, 1963

Hi–

Today has been a change of pace. Friday you remember I tried to look up Gene Thraillkill from home and he was off. Well I've spent the whole day out at his place meeting his friends here and it has been interesting.

I got up this morning about 9:30, was fed as usual by our old Irish "Ma," horsed around for a while, and left the hotel about 11:00. I called Gene and he seemed almost overjoyed to talk to someone from home. I don't think that Gene is exactly the world traveler type although he seems to be enjoying his stay in London well enough. He insisted that I come out to his place, that he would meet me at the subway if I would call upon my arrival. I told him that I was headed to Madame Tussaud's Wax Museum and would be out as soon as I had been there. So I took the "tube" from Russell Square to Baker Street and proceeded to the museum.

This world-famous place is not shy on living up to its name. There are 351 exhibits or wax figures of famous people from American presidents to every monarch of England since the beginning. They are amazingly lifelike, almost uncannily so. One exhibit was entitled "Sleeping Beauty" and consisted of a beautiful young girl lying in a casket. Nothing seemed unusual about this until I looked closer and I couldn't help but do a double take. The girl was breathing. At least her chest was moving up and down as most chests do of living people. And there was no doubt that she was. This I suppose is a trick they use in wax museums to liven things up. For the moment, believe me, this beautiful young breathing creature did liven things up! I was there about two hours and just as I left I ran into Freddy who had been here all along. I forgot to mention that in the basement is the "Chamber of Horrors" where are located most of the famous English murderers preserved in wax. While I was taking this in, there was a small girl, hysterical because she had obviously lost her parents. What a place to get lost! And I thought department stores were bad! But to get lost in a chamber where everywhere you turn are evil faces of murderers that look like they need very little coaxing to recreate their crimes would be worse than a nightmare to a small child. But she was soon found, much to my relief and the relief of some others who were wondering where her lost parents were.

I explained to Freddy that I was going to see this friend of mine from High School who is stationed here in London and we consequently took off in our own directions.

Gene lives quite a ways out of London, in a suburb called Harrow. I arrived at the station, called him, and he picked me up shortly. For two fellows who have so little in common except for a home town, we certainly found a lot to talk about. He lives in Harrow with three other American Army fellows and Sunday is their big day for food, rest, etc. When we arrived Gene introduced me to the group that was gathered there. First the three other fellows, Jim, Bob and Dick. Then there was the English girl Monica, the couple—an English girl, Caroline and her husband Art Brown and another couple, Hank and Kay. We had what I thought was a good old-fashioned American meal of ham, mashed potatoes, green beans, etc. and right after eating I went with Gene and Caroline to get her two children Mandy and Robbie. Caroline is a fiery type of woman, very emotional. She and Gene were obviously very close friends (or something.) She is divorced and just recently married Art. Such an unlikely couple I've seldom seen. Caroline, a bright, good looking girl seemed so much farther above her husband Art, a rather quiet, homely and uninteresting guy. He obviously adored her, and she took him very much for granted, ordering him about, treating him almost like a nuisance. But they say that love acts in strange ways—and if this is love, I believe it!

The other couple, Hank and Kay, were both very handsome people, but such non-entities! Neither of them said a word throughout the meal and the whole time we were there, they merely sat there and ate. They had no expression, no sign of compassion or feeling for anyone or anything except each other, and even that was hard to detect. I feel sorry for people like that. You'd like to shake them, scream at them: "Wake up, wake up, will you. It's a real, big, wide, wonderful world out there with thousands of interesting things to do, full of interesting people." But mentally, you sit there realizing that they would only look at you dumbfounded and wonder what kind of nut you are, if even that much.

The rest of the afternoon was spent with Gene's tape recorder. He has begun making tapes and sending them back and forth rather than letters. So I listened to his most recent tape from home which sounded like a rehearsal for "This is Your Life" and even added my two cents worth on the end of the tape he was making to send next. I'm sure his family was overjoyed to hear from me. I hardly know them!

Most of the group by this time had taken off for the movies so I spent the rest of the evening playing my "repertoire" for Gene and Caroline. A piano had been part of the furnishings that came along with the house. About 10:30 we stopped for some coffee and pie, Monica and Rick joining. The others showed up about 11:15. Monica is quite an attractive girl—very lively and even more interesting because of her British accent. Dick, Gene's friend who goes with her, impressed me at first as a nice enough fellow, but the more I got to know him, the less I liked him.

They decided to give me a ride back as Dick had to take Monica home, so we left shortly. Gene was feeling tired so didn't join us. So I bade goodbye to Gene and promised him that I would look up his parents when I got back to Murphysboro.

Bob, Dick and Monica gave me a ride home and on the way an incident occurred that confirmed my ill feelings for Dick. We pulled into a gas station to have the tires checked and just as we did an Englishman with his family was just pulling out—and it was obvious that one of the other of us had to back up to let the other one out. Well, it was Dick's place to do so as there was no place for the Englishman to back. Well, Dick for some reason just sat there, refusing to move, and the Englishman did the same. Before long there were words and it looked like there might even be a fight. This whole thing outraged me so much because Dick made such an ass out of himself about the whole thing. I couldn't believe that people enjoyed making trouble so much. It proves that one can be surrounded too much by one particular type of person and miss a great deal of life—at least from an observation point of view. I did check my irritance [irritation] enough to realize that there must be something in him which causes such behavior—either trying to impress Monica or me—or a cause of transference from something more deep-rooted in his past. Finding reasons for human behavior is certainly not my goal here but I did want to qualify my feelings at the time.

They dropped me at Russell Square, and after handshaking and goodbyes, I walked back to the hotel where I now find bed very inviting.

And so, until tomorrow, good night.

Love Tom

London, England—Monday, September 2, 1963

Hi–

Today was in some ways depressing—being the last day of our trip, and anticlimactical. The summer has gone by so fast that it seems unjustified that this can be the last day. It makes me want to plan now to have another trip like this soon. Am I dreaming?

I was late again this morning for breakfast, and "Ma" was unusually nice (for the second time in a row) and I appreciated that. She must think that all Americans are lazy. I've never made it down to breakfast on time. The problem, of course, is the late hours. Bill and Karl left early to look up some girls whom they had met—they were arranging some dates or something. I left shortly to call Kay, whom I've tried to call since I've been in London, but again no luck. When I got back to the hotel, Rick still wasn't around and I wasn't about to sit twiddling my thumbs waiting for him today! After taking a sponge bath I left for American Express about 11:00 to check on mail. I thought there might be some last minute instructions from you or Dad, but I received nothing. While I was there I ran into one of the girls from school who was on the plane and she didn't even recognize me, with long hair, etc. By this time, I look like either a native Britisher or a beatnick [beatnik] (by American standards) and I think that she was shocked.

Around noon I left Amer. Express and headed to the office building where John Pickton works, hoping to catch him for lunch. We went to the usual pub for lunch where I had a chicken and corned beef sandwich and some red barrel bitter beer. These English pubs should be lifted and placed in America—what an institution! John and I had an interesting conversation about the English, the Queen and Princess Margaret and all of her loves, etc. while playing an English penny game. John was much more skilled than I, so we didn't play long, as my American pride was slowly losing ground. After about two hours of this I bade John goodbye and headed back to American Express to get some money cashed. I then forced myself for most of the remainder of the afternoon to do more London sightseeing—even though by this time I was about "touristed" out.

First I headed toward St. Paul's cathedral, which is the famous one designed by Christopher Wren. I spent no more than ten minutes gazing at the dreary interior of this place—I began to see these cathedrals as nothing more than places to go to bolster a bad morale—sarcastic, but true. More than any other countries, England seems to be full of cathedrals where people cried rather than prayed. Perhaps they regard religion as a healer rather than a preventer. After a short pause on the steps of St. Paul's to gaze at the pigeons, I left and headed for the Tower of London, which had more intrigue for me than other sights, as it is the home of many gory beheadings and imprisonments famous in British history. I found it quite interesting, but was disappointed that the beefeaters were no longer on duty. I did observe a few of them talking to some interested tourists—their red and black striped uniforms decorating the dismal area surrounding the tower—an interesting paradox. I gazed at the spot where Mary, Queen of Scots,[11] was beheaded, and seemed to get no real inspiration from this sight other than a tug at the nerves in my neck which seemed to be moaning to themselves that this was indeed a very hideous way to die—especially for someone who probably had so much to live for. There was a line about a "mile" long waiting to see the crown jewels, and I had not the patience nor the desire to wait.

I left the Tower about 5:25, heading for the Cambridge theater, where I was to meet Brian[12] at 5:45. We went into the basement of the theater and finally found an old piano that was in miserable tune, and a rather sad instrument on which to attempt to impress one with my talent. Nevertheless, he listened to "Now is the Time" and "The Creation" and seemed duly impressed, but certainly not overwhelmed. The fact was that he really was in no position to be able to offer me any real opportunity in any way—so probably felt as helpless as I. Afterwards we went to a small restaurant and had a couple of sandwiches. There I met a few more people in the cast of the show, and they seemed a great deal like some theater people I've met at home—totally affected and not at all impressive. I look on the whole fiasco as rather uninspiring and unproductive—even though I did get a small glance inside the British musical theater.

On the way back to the hotel I picked up some post cards as sort of a last gesture in tourism before leaving England. When I got back I could find no one. I waited around for a while and then went down to the corner pub for a drink. I even went over to see if Betsy and the girls were around, but couldn't find them.

Feeling lonely and depressed, I returned to the hotel to write. Anything I do now seems extremely anticlimactical—the trip soon to become a memory.

Before long, the other guys began returning, and we decided to celebrate our last night with a bottle of Scotch, which we promptly purchased and consumed till about 4:00 AM. Reminiscing over the trip was the topic of conversation—and our thoughts seemed to get more jumbled and contradictory as the night progressed.

And so, until tomorrow, when I'll again be saying goodnight in the real American way on true American soil, "cheerio."

Love, Tom

Saturn Airways awaits the five guys for their return trip to Chicago

EPILOGUE

What a gift this opportunity was to spend a whole summer traveling around Europe—with hardly a care in the world, and a lifetime ahead. At age twenty-one I was already interested in art and music but had little knowledge of history and politics. So, this trip became an important part of my education.

Although we were not close friends to start, and despite some conflicts during the trip, the five of us ended up being friends by the end. In fact, we have stayed in touch in these ensuing years. We started formal ten-year reunions in 1993 (thirty years!) and have repeated them ever since.

I point with pride to the accomplishments of my traveling pals. Two became distinguished attorneys—one a leader of all things Lincoln in Springfield, Illinois and the other a legal counsel for the EPA in Washington, DC. Another became a successful business executive in the insurance industry, and one an esteemed sociology professor after getting a PhD from the University of Chicago. As for me, I have had the pleasure of becoming a songwriter for musicals and corporate events. You can see the hints of that in my constant search for a piano to play during the trip.

And yes, the trip changed my life—gave me a real interest in food and wine, inspired me to continue to travel, and showed me that compromise is sometimes the only way to achieve a shared goal. In the tradition of the "grand tour," this one must indeed qualify as the grandest!

—T. Tierney—July 8, 2020

NOTES

Chapter 1

1. My father Jack Tierney, stepmother Mary and half-sister Mary Louise.
2. Randy Richmond, good friend from high school.
3. Sorority houses at the University of Illinois.
4. A composition I was working on for the University of Illinois Men's Glee Club.
5. Another fraternity brother, President of the U. of I. chapter of Alpha Kappa Lambda.
6. My sister Ann Tierney.
7. Jeff Wides, high school friend.
8. My stepmother.
9. Murphysboro, Illinois, my hometown in Southern Illinois.
10. A small town near Murphysboro.
11. Shortcut for Murphysboro.
12. Broadway musical by Irving Berlin starring Ethel Merman.
13. A college revue I was writing music for.

Chapter 2

1. A small family restaurant in Murphysboro.
2. Queen of Bohemia, daughter of James I of England (the Winter Queen).
3. Small town in Southern Illinois (named after my maternal Grandmother).
4. Our trusty Volkswagen Beetle.

5. Sung on the Broadway cast album by Mary Sue Berry, later to become a good friend in New York City.
6. Another fraternity friend and his wife.

Chapter 3

1. Fraternity friend

Chapter 4

1. Ann Bruzilius, an exchange student from Malmo that attended Freddy's high school in the U.S.
2. Famous French film actor and singer, known for his great charm.
3. Good friend and neighbor from Murphysboro, about to be married.
4. High end jewelry store in Chicago where I worked several college summers.

Chapter 5

1. Deutsche Marks, the German currency from 1948 to 2002.
2. University of Illinois.
3. Walter Ulbricht, East German General Secretary of the Central Committee.
4. Nikita Khrushchev, Premier of the Soviet Union.
5. Friedrich Dibelius, German bishop, a conservative anti-Semite who later became a staunch opponent of Nazism and communism.
6. John F. Kennedy, U.S. President.
7. Ethnological Museum in Berlin.
8. Hit American musical based on George Bernard Shaw's *Pygmalion*.

Chapter 6

1. Rest place on expressway.
2. Restricted area.

Chapter 7

1. College friend, a talented voice major in the School of Music (later to appear on Broadway).
2. College production of the Broadway musical.
3. Former U.S. Vice President.
4. My half-sister Mary Louise Tierney.

Chapter 8

1. College friend.

Chapter 9

1. Collaborator for the upcoming college Stunt Show for which I was writing songs.
2. Marie-Gabriel-Florent-Auguste, comte de Choiseul-Gouffier (1752–1817), an antiquities collector and France's ambassador to the Ottoman government.
3. Titus Flavius Vespasian, Roman emperor from 69 to 79 AD.

Chapter 11

1. College friend, another fraternity brother.
2. President George Washington.
3. Patrick Bouvier Kennedy, infant son of President John F. Kennedy and First Lady Jacqueline Kennedy, who died in infancy.
4. On August 8, 1963, the armed robbery of £2,600,000 from the Glasgow–London Royal Mail Train.
5. Decatur, Illinois—population approximately 68,000 in 1950.

Chapter 12

1. A compact 16-millimeter camera.
2. My mother's maiden name (Jane Rollo Tierney).
3. *Agrostis* (bent or bent grass), type of grass popular for golf greens.
4. College revue I had written spoofing newspapers.

Chapter 13

1. High end shopping street in Chicago.
2. Another fraternity friend.
3. Family name (Rollo).
4. Town near Edinburgh where my great-grandfather came from (James Rollo).
5. My mother's paternal grandmother's maiden name (Lang).
6. History on my own surname (Tierney).
7. Estuary (firth) of several Scottish rivers including the River Forth. It meets the North Sea with Fife on the north coast and Lothian on the south.

Chapter 14

1. British Secretary of War John *Profumo* resigned June 5, 1963, following revelations that he had lied to the House of Commons about a sexual affair.
2. Hit musical on London's West End and Broadway based on novel *Oliver Twist* by Charles Dickens.
3. Singing group soon to become an international sensation.
4. Stage musical based on the 1837 novel *The Pickwick Papers* by Charles Dickens.
5. Play by Jean Kerr.
6. It was Maggie Smith, later to become a big star in film.
7. The Broadway musical *How to Succeed in Business Without Really Trying* by Abe Burrows and Frank Loesser.
8. London stage musical.
9. High School friend from Murphysboro working in London.
10. Sorority at University of Illinois.
11. This would have been Queen Anne Boleyn, second wife of Henry VIII.
12. Actor from musical *Half a Sixpence*.

ACKNOWLEDGMENTS

First to my mother Jane Rollo Tierney who generously provided the funds to make the trip possible, and for saving each letter and postcard. And to my father Jack Tierney and stepmother Mary who supported the idea and happily got me to and from Chicago's O'Hare Airport. Also, to my sister Ann Tierney Puttman who at age sixteen got to experience this trip via the letters and postcards.

I'm grateful to my fraternity friends who encouraged and participated in the idea: Richard Carlson, Dennis Felty, Richard Hart (and his wife Ann), Mark Juergensmeyer, Donnell Nantkes, Richard Razgaitis, John Rice (and his wife Ginny), Doug Scudamore, Bob Stauffer, Joel Suffield and John Winings.

And to our friend James Clois Smith, Jr. and Carl Condit at Sunstone Press in Santa Fe, who were supportive of this idea from the beginning and have provided invaluable advice and assistance through the process of assembling the letters, photos and other documents. Also, many thanks to Sheila Sullivan who painstakingly transcribed the original letters (and postcards) into a printable document, thus saving us the many hours that task would have required.

Maureen would like to thank her parents, Mary and David Ahearn, who enthusiastically encouraged all her endeavors.

Special thanks to half-sisters Mary Louise Tierney and Julie Tierney Battaglia who are true cheerleaders for whatever venture we undertake.

Most important, I'd like to thank my wonderful wife Maureen Ahearn Tierney who not only provided the chapter contexts but patiently advised on many of the details as the memoir was being assembled.

—T. & M. Tierney, September 1, 2020

Tom and Maureen Tierney

ABOUT THE AUTHORS

Thomas Tierney is a composer-lyricist. He wrote the music for *ELEANOR—An American Love Story* at Ford's Theatre in Washington and many other U.S. theatres—and *NARNIA*, based on *The Lion, the Witch and the Wardrobe* (London and New York—and more than 1000 productions worldwide). His musical *The Year of Living Dangerously* was produced in concert by Manhattan's popular nightclub Feinstein's/54 Below and in 2020 it was broadcast in their live-streamed series. Other shows: *Jungle Queen Debutante* (New York's NAMT Festival and Seattle's Village Theatre in Issaquah); Off-Broadway's *Pets!*; *The Dream Team* at Goodspeed Opera; Tommy Tune's one-man musical *Ichabod*; *Diamond and the North Wind*; and *ZACK HILL and the Rocket Blaster Man Adventure*. He composed six shows for TheatreWorks/USA and AT&T's theme song for Disney's EPCOT Center. For TV he composed the music for two episodes of NBC's Emmy Award winning *Unicorn Tales* and he has written many corporate shows. Tom has performed his own music at Lincoln Center and at the White House and has won numerous ASCAP awards. (www.ThomasTierney.com)

Maureen A. Tierney began life in New York's Greenwich Village and remains true to her New York roots. She started her business career as an Editor at AT&T for an employee magazine. Maureen graduated from Pace University and went on to become a District Manager at AT&T, a Dean at Fordham University Graduate School of Business and headed her own management consulting company for fifteen years. She met Tom considerably after his travels abroad. They have been married for some forty plus years. It has been a joy for her to help bring this travel journal to life.

www.ingramcontent.com/pod-product-compliance
Lightning Source LLC
Chambersburg PA
CBHW081329230426
43667CB00018B/2877